Prelude to

Algebra

Steven R. Lay
Professor of Mathematics
Lee University

L. Clark Lay
the late Professor of Mathematics Education
California State University, Fullerton

Contributing Artist: Izumi Shimizu

Cover Photo: Ruins of the Temple of Posiedon in Sounion, Greece
by John Simmons

Copyright © 2007 Steven R. Lay

Published by:
The Mathematics Division of
Cross Product Publications
Cleveland, TN

ISBN-13: 978-0-9793087-0-3
ISBN-10: 0-9793087-0-4

Printed in the United States of America.

10 9 8 7 6 5 4 3 2
11 10 09 08

Contents

Chapter 8 – Proportion and Percent   219

Chapter 9 – Signed Numbers   255

Chapter 10 – Real Numbers   287

Selected Answers   A – 1

Index   A – 13

Preface

For Students (and Parents of Students)

How does one best prepare for learning algebra? Most pre-algebra texts review what has been covered before in arithmetic and introduce a few "simple" topics from algebra. This approach is successful for some students. Indeed, some students would succeed in algebra without taking any "pre-algebra" at all. For them, arithmetic is a skill already mastered; mathematics makes sense. When introduced to a new idea, they have a solid foundation on which to build. Unfortunately, these "gifted" students are more the exception than the rule.

To answer the question of how best to prepare for learning algebra, we need to look at a related question: Why is it that algebra is difficult for so many students? Is it because they think they "can't do math" and so they don't try? Is it because they "don't like math" and never will? Is it because they are lazy and don't want to work? These reasons may apply to a few students, but not to most.

In our more than 50 years of combined experience teaching algebra, we have found the single most common reason that students struggle in algebra is that mathematics no longer makes sense to them. Somewhere along the way they stopped trying to understand math and they began to rely on memorizing rules. The reasons for this vary. It may have been a poor teacher. It may have been a poor textbook. It may have been a temporary distraction that kept them from concentrating on their class. When they were able to tune in again, they had missed too much to catch up. The reasons vary, but the result is the same. Memorizing rules may be effective in the short run, but after a while the rules get mixed up and the wrong rule is applied in the wrong place at the wrong time.

The remedy for this is to return to the simplest possible setting—the positive whole numbers and zero—and build a solid foundation based on understanding rather than rote memorization. Instead of reviewing arithmetic in the same way that failed to make sense to students the first time, this text teaches the student to think about arithmetic in a different way that emphasizes the way numbers change and anticipates the operations used in algebra.

- Conceptually, it makes better sense because it represents a dynamic model that corresponds more closely to the way people think about numbers.[1]
- Practically, it illustrates the way that arithmetic and algebra are applied in the real world.[2]
- Mathematically, it is more accurate than the traditional approach.[3]
- Historically, it has been remarkably helpful in decreasing students' fear of mathematics and increasing their success in algebra.[4]

While the text teaches new patterns of thinking about arithmetic, it does not significantly change what is written down on paper. This enables the students to return readily to a traditional algebra curriculum the next year without being penalized for writing strange things on their papers or "doing it differently." The difference is in their way of thinking and in their success in subsequent classes.

For the first six chapters (more than half of the book) we will work entirely with positive whole numbers and zero—no fractions and no negative numbers. This will enable the students with a weaker background to regain their self-confidence in doing math. In this simple setting we will ask significant questions, many of which will be new to all the students—even the most advanced.

By thinking carefully about the basic properties of arithmetic, we develop patterns that anticipate the procedures of algebra. For example, a clear understanding of how the arithmetic equation $5 - 2 = 3$ relates to the equation $2 = 5 - 3$ enables one to solve the algebraic equation $a - x = b$ for x in one step. Similarly, if one can change the equation $5(3 + 4) = 35$ into the equation $4 = \frac{35}{5} - 3$, then solving the equation $a(b + x) = c$ for x is not so intimidating.

Learning mathematics is not a spectator sport. Each lesson introduces a concept, carefully explains its usage, and gives several examples. But the real learning takes place when the students do the exercises. This is where they see for themselves how math works and begin to train their minds to think in logical ways. In the "Develop Your Skill" section of the Exercises, the students are given ample opportunity to gain confidence in the new material from the lesson. Then in the "Maintain Your Skill" section, they practice using key concepts from earlier lessons. This spiral approach to learning has been found to be very effective in increasing understanding and retention of important skills.

Steven R. Lay

slay@leeuniversity.edu

A Special Note to Parents:

If you are used to helping your child with his/her homework, that's great. But be careful. Many of the problems may look familiar to you, but we are teaching the students to think about them in a special way. Before you jump in with the "usual" explanation, you are strongly encouraged to read the lesson to see what we are doing. If you do this on a regular basis, you may even learn a few new things yourself!

---

[1] Before children encounter −1 as a mysterious negative number, they are already comfortable with the concept of decreasing by 1 if they have ever ridden on an elevator or had to share a toy with a friend.

[2] Many applications of algebra involve quantities that are changing. By emphasizing the changes involved in arithmetic computations, we develop a pattern that is easily followed when solving algebraic equations.

[3] For example, traditional texts are consistently inaccurate or unintuitive when defining exponents and frequently misleading when talking about canceling.

[4] This approach has been used for more than 20 years in remedial classes in college. Long-term studies have found that 94% of the students who completed a course using this approach were able to be successful in algebra and other courses that used algebraic skills. Hearing those students make comments such as "Why didn't they explain it this way in middle school?" has prompted the writing of this text.

About the authors:

Dr. L. Clark Lay began his teaching career in a one-room schoolhouse in southern Iowa during the Great Depression. To better identify with the children in his classes, he often walked to school barefoot. During the summers he traveled to California and earned a master's degree in mathematics from the University of Southern California. This lead to his moving to California and teaching high school in El Centro and then junior college in Pasadena. It was at Pasadena City College that he first became interested in helping World War II veterans re-enter an academic world and become successful in algebra, calculus and higher math. These returning veterans were highly motivated, but their math skills were largely undeveloped. This caused a high failure rate in remedial courses in beginning algebra.

The math department surveyed existing arithmetic textbooks, but could find none whose goals specifically included preparing students for algebra. Convinced that such an approach was needed, Lay began a study of the kinds of mistakes that students commonly make in algebra. Then he looked for ways to develop thought patterns in arithmetic that would reduce those algebraic errors. His research led to a doctor's degree in mathematics education from the University of California at Los Angeles and the course he developed at Pasadena City College greatly increased the students' chances for success in mathematics.

In 1960 he became the chairman of the department of mathematics education at California State University at Fullerton, where he trained elementary and middle school math teachers until his retirement in 1975. Over the years, he gained additional insights, made further refinements in the basic approach, and authored several books.

Dr. Lay has two sons, both mathematicians. His older son David is a Professor of Mathematics at the University of Maryland. His younger son Steven has a similar position at Lee University in Tennessee. Both are accomplished authors like their father.

Other books by L. Clark Lay include *Arithmetic, an Introduction to Mathematics* (Macmillan, 1960), *The Study of Arithmetic* (Macmillan, 1966), *From Arithmetic to Algebra* (Macmillan, 1970), *Principles of Elementary Mathematics* (1973), and *Principles of Algebra* (1980, 1985, 1988, 1990).

Dr. Steven R. Lay began teaching at Aurora University (Illinois) in 1971, after earning a Ph.D. in mathematics from the University of California at Los Angeles. He, too, wrestled with the question of how best to teach remedial algebra to under-prepared college students. When his father retired in 1975 and moved to Illinois, they began a joint project of reworking and rewriting the material that had proved so successful in California. This resulted in a new text, *Principles of Algebra*, which they continued to revise and improve for a number of years.

Steven Lay's career in mathematics was interrupted for 8 years while serving as a Christian missionary in Japan. Upon his return to the States in 1998, he joined the mathematics faculty at Lee University in Cleveland, Tennessee. Once again the need for a better remedial algebra curriculum prompted him to adapt the text he and his father had developed in Illinois. This new version concentrated more on the transition between arithmetic and algebra and less on algebra itself.

Over the years as college students have used the material in the Lays' books, they have often made comments such as: "For the first time in my life, math makes sense to me." "Why didn't they explain it this way in middle school?" or "You ought to write an 8th grade pre-algebra book so that students can learn it right the first time." This text is a response to those suggestions.

Steven and his wife Ann have two children. Their daughter BethAnn taught 8th grade math for several years and now teaches part-time at Lee University. Their son Tim is pursuing a Ph.D. in history.

Other books by Steven R. Lay include *Convex Sets and their Applications* (John Wiley and Sons, 1982; Dover Publications, 2007), *Analysis with an Introduction to Proof* (Prentice Hall, 1986, 1990, 2001, 2005), *Japanese Language and Culture* (2003, 2004, 2006), and *Principles of Algebra* (1980, 1985, 1988, 1990, 2003, 2006).

Prelude to

Algebra

Chapter 1 – Sums and Differences

1.1 – SYMBOLS AND SUMS

OBJECTIVE

1. Identify sums and even numbers.

We begin our preparation for algebra by looking at the ways numerical quantities can change. The most common numbers, often called the **natural numbers**, are those represented as 1, 2, 3, 4, 5, … . [The three dots mean that we continue on in the same manner.] When describing a set we often list the members of the set inside braces. Throughout this book the capital letter $\mathbb{N}$ will be used as a name for the set of natural numbers. That is,

$$\mathbb{N} = \{1, 2, 3, 4, \ldots\}.$$

These natural numbers serve well as counters when objects are being counted. But when changes are recorded, it is also useful to have the number *zero*. Zero can then be used to identify the beginning or original state, that is, the situation before any changes have taken place. The capital letter $\mathbb{C}$ will be used to denote the set of **counting numbers**:

$$\mathbb{C} = \{0, 1, 2, 3, 4, \ldots\}.$$

Yeah!
No fractions!

For the first part of this course, we are going to work entirely with numbers from $\mathbb{N}$ and $\mathbb{C}$. This means that we will not be using any fractions or negative numbers. This will enable us to prepare for algebra in a simple setting. Later when we introduce fractions and signed numbers (in Chapters 5 and 6), the rules for computing with them will seem more reasonable.

The letters $\mathbb{N}$ and $\mathbb{C}$ are used here as **constants**. They are abbreviations for particular sets. Letters can also be used to great advantage without giving them a single fixed meaning. For example, we may write

Let x be a counting number.

In this case the letter x is used as a **variable**, or placeholder. It holds in reserve a place in the sentence. It is not required that a particular number be chosen. But if the letter x is replaced by a constant, this constant should be a counting number.

1

Suppose two counting numbers are chosen, a first and a second. If there is a rule that determines a third counting number to correspond to the chosen pair, we speak of an **operation** on the first two numbers to produce the third number. For example, the familiar rule for the **addition** of two numbers is an operation on the set $\mathbb{C}$ of counting numbers.

Definition of a Sum

> If x and y are counting numbers, then addition assigns to x and y a unique third counting number $x + y$, called the **sum** of x and y.

Example 1   **Find a Sum**

Find the sum of each pair of counting numbers.

   (a) m and n (b) 4 and t (c) 5 and 3

Using the definition above, we obtain the following:

   (a) $m + n$ (b) $4 + t$ (c) $5 + 3$

A symbol (mark) or a collection of symbols that stands for a single number is called a **numeral**. Thus 5, 3, and $5 + 3$ are all called numerals when referring to the marks themselves. Since these symbols represent numbers, they are also commonly called numbers when no confusion results.

While the definition states that $5 + 3$ is the sum of 5 and 3, it is also true that 8 is the sum of 5 and 3. The numerals $5 + 3$ and 8 both represent the number eight. Of the many possible numerals for the number eight, the numeral 8 has been chosen as the simplest form for the recognition of this number. Hence 8 is called the **basic numeral** for the number eight. We can state that $5 + 3$ and 8 are names (numerals) for the same number by writing the equation

$$5 + 3 = 8.$$

The equation $5 + 3 = 8$ allows two different meanings for the word "sum." The practice in arithmetic has been to think of $5 + 3$ as a problem yet to be done.

This is sometimes suggested by writing "5 + 3 = ?". In this case the + sign is read as a command to do something to 5 and 3. The answer to this problem (the number 8) is then called the sum. But note that the replacement of 5 + 3 by 8 is a change of form only and *not* a change in the number represented. Replacing 5 + 3 by 8 is an example of an addition computation.

Key Point

> A **computation** is a change of form where the basic numeral replaces any other numeral for a number.

Example 2   **Compute a Sum**

Compute the basic numeral for each sum.

  (a) $2 + 7$ (b) $26 + 47$ (c) $x + 4$

(a) $2 + 7 = 9$ (b) $26 + 47 = 73$

(c) Since the value of x is not known, it is not possible to compute.

In Example 2(c) it was not possible to compute the basic numeral for the sum $x + 4$. This is because x is just a symbol for a blank space. Unless x is replaced by a particular number, no computation is possible.

Thus we see that in algebra the word "sum" is the *name of a form*. That is, "sum" describes the appearance of $x + 4$, even though no computation is possible. Similarly, we say that 5 + 3 is a sum because of its form.

When a number is added to itself, the result is called an even number. We make this more precise in the following definition.

Definition of

Even and Odd

> If for a counting number x there is a counting number n such that $n + n = x$, then x is an **even** number. If there is no counting number n that meets this condition, then x is an **odd** number.

When a variable is used in more than one place in an equation, it must be understood that the same number is to be substituted for the variable wherever it occurs. Thus in the equation $n + n = x$, if one of the n's is replaced by a number, then the other n must be replaced by the same number. Since x is a different letter from n, this allows x and n to be replaced by different numbers. However, the same number can replace both x and n, if that is desired.

Example 3   **Show a Number is Even**

Show that 0, 2, *and* 4 *are each even numbers by writing the equations required by the definition of an even number.*

0 is even since $0 + 0 = 0$.

2 is even since $1 + 1 = 2$.

4 is even since $2 + 2 = 4$.

EXERCISE 1.1

DEVELOP YOUR SKILL

Indicate whether each statement in Exercises 1 – 4 is True or False.

1. 2 is a natural number.

2. 5 is a counting number.

3. 1 is a counting number.

4. 0 is a natural number.

5. What, by definition, is the sum of r and s?

6. What, by definition, is the sum of t and t?

7. What, by definition, is the sum of 4 and 5?

8. What, by definition, is the sum of 7 and 8?

Compute the basic numeral for each sum. If no computation is possible, write "not possible."

9. $23 + 12$

10. $45 + 19$

11. $24 + x$

12. $72 + 16$

13. $48 + 33$

14. $76 + 39$

15. $17 + 42$

16. $y + 13$

17. $71 + 45$

18. $13 + x$

19. $27 + 34$

20. $23 + 28$

21. $55 + y$

22. $62 + 48$

23. $147 + 35$

24. $29 + 175$

Show that each statement is true by writing the equation required by its definition.

25. 10 is an even number.

26. 6 is an even number.

27. 0 is an even number.

28. 84 is an even number.

29. 632 is an even number.

30. 164 is an even number.

EXTEND YOUR SKILL

31. What is the difference between the natural numbers and the counting numbers?

32. Explain why 6 is an even number.

33. If $x + y = z$ and $z = x$, what number is y?

1.2 – INEQUALITIES

OBJECTIVE

1. Explain inequalities.

For any two counting numbers it is always possible to say that the first number is equal to the second, or the first is less than the second, or the first is greater than the second. This basic principle is restated below, together with the definitions of less than and greater than.

Definitions of

Less Than

and

Greater Than

If x and y are counting numbers, then exactly one of these statements is true:

1. $x = y$ Read, "x equals y."
    This is true if x and y are the same number.

2. $x < y$ Read, "x is **less than** y."
    Definition: $x < y$ if there is a natural number n such that $x + n = y$.

3. $x > y$ Read, "x is **greater than** y."
    Definition: $x > y$ if there is a natural number n such that $x = y + n$.

Example 1   **Justify a "Less Than" Inequality**

Show that 5 < 9 by writing the equation required by the definition.

Since 5 is smaller than 9, something must be added to 5, namely 4, to make it equal to 9. Keep the two numbers, 5 and 9, in the same order and add the 4 to the smaller side. The desired equation is $5 + 4 = 9$.

Notice the order of the numbers on the left side of the equation in the solution to Example 1. We have to be very precise in using a definition. While it is true that $4 + 5 = 9$, this equation is not the equation required by the definition of "less than." The required definition adds the natural number n (in this case 4) to the right side of 5. Thus we must write $5 + 4 = 9$ and not $4 + 5 = 9$. We shall see later that $x + n$ and $n + x$ always represent the same number, but in terms of their form, they are different.

Study Tip:

Note that the answer to Example 2 is
$7 = 4 + 3$
and not
$7 = 3 + 4$
or $4 + 3 = 7$.
The form of the definition must be followed exactly.

Example 2   **Justify a "Greater Than" Inequality**

Show that 7 > 4 by writing the equation required by the definition.

Since 7 is larger than 4, something must be added to 4, namely 3, to make it equal to 7. Keep the two numbers, 7 and 4, in the same order and add the 3 to the smaller side. The desired equation is $7 = 4 + 3$.

An equation, such as $5 + 3 = 8$, is also called an **equality**. The relation $5 < 8$, which can also be written as $8 > 5$, is an example of an **inequality**. The relation of "less than or equal to" is also called an inequality. The notation $x \le y$ means that $x < y$ or $x = y$.

Similarly, for the relation "greater than or equal to" we have the inequality $x \ge y$, which holds if $x > y$ or $x = y$.

EXERCISE 1.2

DEVELOP YOUR SKILL

Show that each statement is true by writing the equation required by its definition.

1. $7 < 10$

2. $8 > 2$

3. $12 > 5$

4. $3 < 8$

5. $11 > 9$

6. $1 > 0$

7. $0 < 3$

8. $4 < 21$

9. $15 < 23$

10. $25 < 30$

11. $40 > 21$

12. $32 > 28$

MAINTAIN YOUR SKILL

13. What, by definition, is the sum of 5 and 5? [1.1]

14. What, by definition, is the sum of m and 5? [1.1]

Compute the basic numeral for each sum. If no computation is possible, write "not possible." [1.1]

15. $45 + 15$

16. $38 + 26$

17. $12 + x$

18. $32 + 14$

19. $57 + 35$

20. $m + 44$

21. $48 + 13$

22. $73 + 65$

23. $154 + 37$

24. $54 + 238$

25. $361 + y$

26. $466 + 235$

Show that each statement is true by writing the equation required by its definition. [1.1]

27. 12 is an even number.

28. 26 is an even number.

29. 38 is an even number.

30. 52 is an even number.

EXTEND YOUR SKILL

31. Explain why 5 is less than 9.

32. Explain why 10 is greater than 7.

33. If $x + y = z$ and y is a natural number, how is x related to z?

1.3 – Differences

OBJECTIVE

1. Identify the relationship between sums and differences.

The operation of subtraction assigns a unique third number to a chosen pair of first and second numbers. However, subtraction of a second number y from a first number x is only a **partial operation** on the counting numbers, since $x - y$ is not a counting number for some choices of x and y. The following definition describes subtraction by showing its relationship to addition.

Definition of Subtraction

> Let x and y be counting numbers. Then y can be subtracted from x, and we write $x - y = z$, if there is a counting number z such that $y + z = x$.

Study Tip:

The difference $x - y$ is defined only when $x \geq y$.

If $y + z = x$ and $z > 0$, then $x > y$. If $y + z = x$ and $z = 0$, then $x = y$. Hence *we can subtract y from x only when $x \geq y$*. If x and y are counting numbers and $x \geq y$, then subtraction assigns to x and y a unique third number $x - y$, called their **difference**.

The definition of subtraction establishes a dual relationship between a subtraction equation $x - y = z$ and an addition equation $y + z = x$. It asserts that one equation is true if and only if the other equation is also true. For example, we can say that $10 - 7 = 3$ because $7 + 3 = 10$. Likewise, the subtraction equation that is paired with $4 + 8 = 12$ is $12 - 4 = 8$.

Notice that the order of the terms is important here. If $4 + 8 = 12$ corresponds to $y + z = x$, then $y = 4$, $z = 8$, and $x = 12$. The subtraction equation therefore is $x - y = z$, or $12 - 4 = 8$. While it is also true that $12 - 8 = 4$, this would not be the subtraction equation that is paired with $4 + 8 = 12$. [$12 - 8 = 4$ is paired with $8 + 4 = 12$.]

Example 1   **Relate Subtraction to Addition**

Use the definition of subtraction to change each subtraction equation into the corresponding addition equation.

   (a) $65 - 13 = 52$ (b) $a - b = c$

(a) The 13 and the 52 must be added together to get their sum 65. Keep them in the same order and put them on the left side: $13 + 52 = 65$.

(b) This time we don't have numerical values, so we just have to follow the form of the definition. If $a - b = c$, then b and c are added together to get a. Keep the b and the c in the same order as the original equation: b is to the left of c. We have $b + c = a$.

Example 2   **Relate Addition to Subtraction**

Use the definition of subtraction to change each addition equation into the corresponding subtraction equation.

   (a) $17 + 29 = 46$ (b) $m + n = p$

(a) 46 is the sum of 17 and 29, so when we subtract 17 from 46 we get 29. Note that 17 is to the left of 29 in both equations: $46 - 17 = 29$.

(b) Since $m + n = p$, if we subtract m from p we will get n: $p - m = n$. Note that m is to the left of n in both equations.

Study Tip:

The expression $x - y$ is a difference, because of its form. Just like $x + y$ is a sum.

In Lesson 1.1 we saw that the word "sum" can have two meanings. It may refer to the answer to an addition problem (the arithmetic point of view), or it may refer to the form of an expression (the algebra point of view). The same is true for the word "difference." In the equation $x - y = z$ we may refer to z as the difference that results from the subtraction computation x minus y. (This is the arithmetic point of view.) But we may also refer to $x - y$ as a difference because of its form. (This is the algebra point of view.)

The number zero has distinctive properties for addition and subtraction. When zero is added to any given number, the sum is always the same as the given number. Similarly, when any given number is added to zero, the sum is again the given number. No number other than zero satisfies both conditions. This is known as the **identity property for addition**:

$$x + 0 = x \quad \text{and} \quad 0 + x = x.$$

If we look at the corresponding subtraction equations, we have

$$x - x = 0 \quad \text{and} \quad x - 0 = x.$$

> **Example 3**   **Use the Definition of Subtraction**
>
> *When the tax T is added to the cost C, their sum is the purchase price P. We may represent this by C + T = P. Use the definition of subtraction to write an equation that tells how to compute T when P and C are known.*
>
> The addition equation $C + T = P$ corresponds to the subtraction equation $P - C = T$. This shows how to find the tax T when the purchase price P and the cost C are given: subtract C from P.

EXERCISE 1.3

DEVELOP YOUR SKILL

Compute the basic numeral.

1. $12 - 5$ **2.** $18 - 4$ **3.** $16 - 7$

4. $25 - 19$ **5.** $39 - 15$

Use the definition of subtraction to change each subtraction equation to the corresponding addition equation, and each addition equation to the corresponding subtraction equation.

6. $10 - 7 = 3$ **7.** $8 + 4 = 12$ **8.** $5 + 9 = 14$

9. $11 - 5 = 6$ **10.** $23 - 15 = 8$ **11.** $27 + 16 = 43$

12. $9 + m = 22$ **13.** $n - 56 = 24$ **14.** $a - k = 19$

15. $43 - b = n$ **16.** $x + a = h$ **17.** $h - m = x$

18. If the interest i is added to the principle P, this sum is the amount A to pay at the close of a loan. We may represent this by $P + i = A$. Use the definition of subtraction to write an equation that tells how to compute i when A and P are known.

MAINTAIN YOUR SKILL

Show that each statement is true by writing the equation required by its definition.   [1.1 and 1.2]

19. 34 is an even number.   **20.** 24 is an even number.

21. $5 < 12$ **22.** $7 < 15$

23. $30 > 22$ **24.** $21 > 16$

Compute the basic numeral for each sum. If no computation is possible, write "not possible." [1.1]

25. $27 + 34$ **26.** $52 + n$ **27.** $42 + 45$

28. $73 + 56$ **29.** $164 + 265$ **30.** $307 + 88$

EXTEND YOUR SKILL

Use the definition of subtraction to change the addition equation to the corresponding subtraction equation, and the subtraction equation to the corresponding addition equation.

31. $x + a = h$ **32.** $n - m = y$

33. If u and v are counting numbers, and $u - v$ is also a counting number, how are u and v related?

1.4 – DIFFERENCES AND THE ORDER OF OPERATIONS

OBJECTIVE

1. Use the order of operations.

Up to this point we have only considered expressions that contain one operation. If we have an expression involving more than one operation, then there must be an agreement about the order in which the operations are to be performed. Sentences in English are read from left to right. When computing a mathematical expression we also work from left to right, unless we are told to do otherwise. If we want to alter this natural left to right order of operations, we use parentheses. Whenever parentheses are used, we always do the operation inside the parentheses first. This is summarized in the following:

Order of Operations for Sums and Differences

When computing with sums and differences, work from left to right, unless told to do otherwise by parentheses. When parentheses are used, do the operation inside the parentheses first.

For example, $10 - 7 + 2$ is computed as $10 - 7 = 3$ and then as $3 + 2 = 5$. This would be the same as if it were written as

$$
\begin{aligned}
10 - 7 + 2 &= (10 - 7) + 2 \\
&= \quad 3 + 2 \\
&= \quad\quad 5
\end{aligned}
$$

In the expression $10 - (7 + 2)$, the $7 + 2$ is computed first because it is inside the parentheses:

$$
\begin{aligned}
10 - (7 + 2) &= 10 - (7 + 2) \\
&= 10 - \quad 9 \\
&= \quad\quad 1
\end{aligned}
$$

Notice that $10 - 7 + 2 \neq 10 - (7 + 2)$.

Example 1   **Use the Order of Operations**

Compute the basic numeral.

    (a) $13 - 5 + 4$ (b) $13 - (5 + 4)$

    (c) $12 + 4 - 1$ (d) $12 + (4 - 1)$

(a) $13 - 5 + 4 = (13 - 5) + 4 = 8 + 4 = 12$

(b) $13 - (5 + 4) = 13 - 9 = 4$

(c) $12 + 4 - 1 = (12 + 4) - 1 = 16 - 1 = 15$

(d) $12 + (4 - 1) = 12 + 3 = 15$

Notice in Example 1 that (a) and (b) are not equal, but (c) and (d) are. Thus, sometimes a change in the order changes the value and sometimes it does not. We shall look at this more carefully in the next two sections.

At this time we are limiting ourselves to using only counting numbers. This has several advantages: it is a very simple setting, and we don't need to be concerned with fractions and negative numbers. (We will define them later.) It also has one slight disadvantage: some differences are not defined. For example, $5 - 7$ cannot be computed as a counting number. That is, there is no counting number z such that $7 + z = 5$. Thus, we say that $5 - 7$ is undefined. Remember that for $x - y$ to be defined, x must be greater than or equal to y: $x \geq y$.

Remember:

The difference
$$x - y$$
is defined only
when $x \geq y$.

Example 2   **Compute a Basic Numeral**

Compute the basic numeral for each expression that is defined as a counting number. Otherwise, write "not defined."

    (a) $7-4+5$ (b) $7-(4+5)$ (c) $3-5+7$

(a) $7-4+5 = (7-4)+5 = 3+5 = 8$

(b) $7-(4+5) = 7-9$, but this is not defined.

(c) Since we work from left to right, we must begin with $3-5$. This first step is not defined, so the whole expression is not defined.

EXERCISE 1.4

DEVELOP YOUR SKILL

Compute the basic numeral for each expression that is defined as a counting number. Otherwise, write "not defined."

1. $12-3+2$ **2.** $10-(2+4)$ **3.** $15-(4+3)$

4. $14-3-6$ **5.** $7-8+4$ **6.** $18-4-5$

7. $3+5-7$ **8.** $8-16+10$ **9.** $5-7+3$

10. $16+8-10$ **11.** $7-5+3$ **12.** $16-10-8$

MAINTAIN YOUR SKILL

Show that each statement is true by writing the equation required by its definition. [1.1 and 1.2]

13. 42 is an even number.   **14.** 38 is an even number.

15. $25<31$ **16.** $27>15$ **17.** $64>33$

18. $45>26$ **19.** $23<52$ **20.** $18<35$

21. $43>16$ **22.** $55<74$

Use the definition of subtraction to change each subtraction equation to the corresponding addition equation, and each addition equation to the corresponding subtraction equation. [1.3]

23. $32-7=25$ **24.** $15+27=42$ **25.** $45+22=67$

26. $82-38=44$ **27.** $x-15=37$ **28.** $34+m=55$

29. $18+y=31$ **30.** $n-22=46$

Extend Your Skill

31. Explain why $5 - 8$ is not defined as a counting number.

32. Explain why $3 - 5 + 7$ is not defined as a counting number.

33. Explain why $5 < 9$. [1.2]

34. Explain why $17 > 15$. [1.2]

1.5 – Properties of Sums

OBJECTIVE

1. Identify and use the commutative and associative principles.

When we write an expression like $x + y$ or $x - y$, the x and y are called **terms**. What happens if we interchange the two terms? If we interchange the terms in a sum we get an equivalent expression. For example, both $3 + 7$ and $7 + 3$ are numerals for the number 10. This illustrates the **commutative principle for addition**:

Key Concept

> If x and y are counting numbers, then $x + y = y + x$.

If we interchange the order in a difference, then the result is usually not equivalent. For example, we have $7 - 3 = 4$, but $3 - 7$ is not even defined. Thus, subtraction is *not* commutative.

Example 1   **Use the Commutative Principle**

Use the commutative principle to replace each expression by one or more equivalent expressions. Do not compute.

     (a) $3 + 12$ (b) $15 + (7 - 4)$

(a) $12 + 3$

(b) This time we treat $(7 - 4)$ as a term and interchange it with 15. The only possibility is $(7 - 4) + 15$.

> ### Example 2   **Use the Commutative Principle**
>
> *Use the commutative principle to replace each expression by one or more equivalent expressions, if possible.*
>
>   (a) $m - (y + 5)$ (b) $s - t$ (c) $r + (s + t)$
>
> (a) We can only commute the y and the 5: $m - (5 + y)$
>
> (b) Since subtraction is not commutative, it is not possible to make any changes using the commutative principle.
>
> (c) This time there are several possibilities:
>
>   We may commute the s and t within the last term: $r + (t + s)$.
>
>   We may commute the r and the term $(s + t)$: $(s + t) + r$.
>
>   We may make both changes: $(t + s) + r$.

There is another way to change the expression $r + (s + t)$ in Example 2(c). We may leave the r, s, and t written in the same order, but change the order of the addition operations. Instead of adding s and t and then adding r, we can add r and s, and then add t. This new expression, $(r + s) + t$, cannot be obtained from $r + (s + t)$ by using the commutative principle. But is it equivalent to the original? Yes, it is. For example,

$$5 + (3 + 7) = 5 + 10 = 15, \quad \text{and}$$

$$(5 + 3) + 7 = 8 + 7 = 15.$$

This illustrates the **associative principle for addition**:

Key Concept

> If x, y, and z are counting numbers, then $x + (y + z) = (x + y) + z$.

Reading from left to right, the expression

$$a + b + c + d$$

is computed as $\big((a + b) + c\big) + d$. In such "nested" parentheses, we begin on the inside and work out. First add a and b, then add c, then add d. Sometimes the

Study Tip:

In using the associative principle, the terms stay in the same order, they are just grouped (associated) differently.

outside pair of parentheses is replaced by brackets, [ ], for easier reading:

$$[(a + b) + c] + d.$$

If the associative principle is used only within the brackets, then we have

$$[a + (b + c)] + d.$$

But if $(a + b)$ is thought of as a single term, then using the associative principle with the three numbers $(a + b)$, c, and d, we have

$$(a + b) + [c + d] \quad \text{or} \quad (a + b) + (c + d).$$

Example 3   Identify the Commutative and Associative Principles

State whether the commutative principle or the associative principle is used in making each change of form.

(a) $(5 + 6) + 9 \rightarrow 5 + (6 + 9)$ (b) $(5 + 6) + 9 \rightarrow (6 + 5) + 9$

(c) $(5 + 6) + 9 \rightarrow 9 + (5 + 6)$

(a) The numbers stay in the same order, but they are grouped (associated) differently. The associative principle is used.

(b) The terms 5 and 6 have been commuted.

(c) The terms $(5 + 6)$ and 9 have been commuted.

EXERCISE 1.5
DEVELOP YOUR SKILL

Write all other possible equivalent forms that result from using only the commutative principle for addition. If there are none, write "none."

1. $a + (b + c)$ 2. $m - (n + p)$

3. $m + (4 - n)$ 4. $(r + s) - t$

5. $(x - y) + z$ 6. $r - (s - t)$

State whether the commutative or associative principle is used in making each change of form: (a) to (b), (b) to (c), etc.

7. (a) $(2 + 3) + 6$

   (b) $(3 + 2) + 6$

   (c) $3 + (2 + 6)$

   (d) $(2 + 6) + 3$

   (e) $(6 + 2) + 3$

   (f) $6 + (2 + 3)$

8. (a) $z + (y + x)$

   (b) $(z + y) + x$

   (c) $x + (z + y)$

   (d) $x + (y + z)$

   (e) $(y + z) + x$

   (f) $y + (z + x)$

MAINTAIN YOUR SKILL

Use the definition of subtraction to change each subtraction equation to the corresponding addition equation, and each addition equation to the corresponding subtraction equation. [1.3]

9. $52 - 25 = 27$

10. $n + 26 = 82$

11. $79 - m = 55$

12. $a - 31 = k$

13. $83 + n = w$

14. $y + 14 = r$

Compute the basic numeral for each expression that is defined as a counting number. Otherwise, write "not defined." [1.4]

15. $4 + 8 - 10$

16. $5 + 7 - 6$

17. $3 - 7 + 11$

18. $7 - 8 + 9$

19. $12 - 3 - 4$

20. $15 - 2 - 6$

21. $8 - 10 + 5$

22. $6 + 7 - 8$

23. $5 + 2 - 10$

24. $11 - 8 - 5$

25. $13 + 7 - 4$

26. $25 - 10 - 7$

27. $10 - 3 + 5$

28. $21 - 18 + 5$

29. $4 - 8 + 7$

30. $15 + 7 - 2$

EXTEND YOUR SKILL

31. Explain what "moves" when applying the commutative principle.

32. Explain what "moves" when applying the associative principle.

33. Explain why $12 - 7 - 8$ is not defined as a counting number. [1.4]

34. Explain why $7 - (6 + 5)$ is not defined as a counting number. [1.4]

1.6 – INVARIANT PRINCIPLES FOR SUMS AND DIFFERENCES

OBJECTIVE

1. Use the invariant principles for sums and differences.

Suppose we have two bags of marbles. The first bag contains 7 marbles and the second bag contains 3 marbles, for a total of 10 marbles in all. If we take 2 marbles out of the bag of 7 and put them in the bag of 3, then we still have 10 marbles in all—now with 5 marbles in the first bag and 5 in the second. (See Figure 1.)

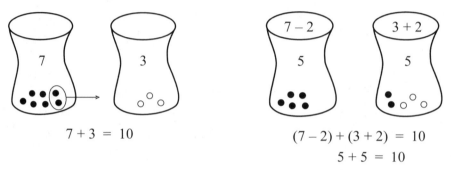

$$7 + 3 = 10$$

$$(7 - 2) + (3 + 2) = 10$$
$$5 + 5 = 10$$

Figure 1. Invariant Principle for Sums

This illustrates that the sum of two numbers is not changed by subtracting something from one number and then adding the same amount to the other number. We call this the **invariant principle for sums**:

Key Concept

Let x, y and z be counting numbers.

If $x \geq z$, then $x + y = (x - z) + (y + z)$.

If $y \geq z$, then $x + y = (x + z) + (y - z)$.

Suppose we decide to sort the books in our library. In the history pile we have 9 books and in the science pile we have 6. We see that we have 3 more history books than science books and observe that $9 - 6 = 3$. If we remove 2 books from each pile, then we will have 7 history books and 4 science books. But we will still have 3 more history books than science books, since $7 - 4 = 3$. (See Figure 2.)

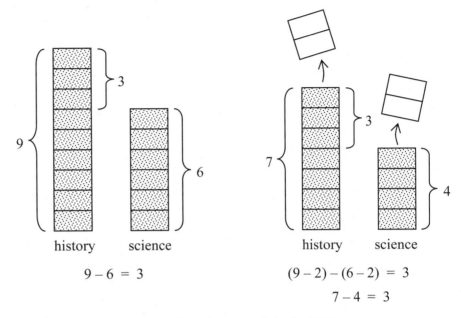

Figure 2. Invariant Principle for Differences

The same thing would happen if we added 5 books to the original piles. We would then have 14 history books and 11 science books, but the difference $14 - 11$ would still equal 3.

This illustrates that the difference between two numbers is not changed if both numbers are either increased or decreased by the same amount. We call this the **invariant principle for differences**:

Key Concept

> Let x, y and z be counting numbers.
>
> If $x \geq y$, then $x - y = (x + z) - (y + z)$.
>
> If $x \geq y$ and $y \geq z$, then $x - y = (x - z) - (y - z)$.

One use of the invariant principles for sums and differences is to change a given problem into an easier one. For example, it may be difficult to compute

5486 + 198 in your head without using a notepad or a calculator. But from the invariant principle for sums we have

$$5486 + 198 = (5486 - 2) + (198 + 2)$$
$$= 5484 + 200,$$

and this last sum is easily seen to be 5684. The idea here is to change the "difficult" number 198 into the "easy" number 200. By making the opposite change in the other term, the sum remains the same.

This makes adding and subtracting easier!

Example 1   Use the Invariant Principles

Use the invariant principles for sums or differences to simplify each expression. Then compute the basic numeral.

   (a) 295 + 637   (b) 632 + 280   (c) 453 − 298

(a) 295 is only 5 less than 300, so add 5 to 295 and subtract 5 from 637:
$$295 + 637 = (295 + 5) + (637 - 5) = 300 + 632 = 932.$$

(b) 280 is 20 less than 300, so add 20 to 280 and subtract 20 from 632:
$$632 + 280 = (632 - 20) + (280 + 20) = 612 + 300 = 912.$$

   Or, we could subtract 32 from 632 and add 32 to 280:
$$632 + 280 = (632 - 32) + (280 + 32) = 600 + 312 = 912.$$

(c) This expression is a difference, so we must make the same change in both terms. Since 298 is 2 less than 300 we write
$$453 - 298 = (453 + 2) - (298 + 2) = 455 - 300 = 155.$$

Example 2   Use the Invariant Principle for Sums

If 8452 + 3719 = 8442 + x, what is x?

   Rather than doing a lot of arithmetic, look carefully at the equation to see what is different between the two sides.

$$-10$$

$$8452 + 3719 = 8442 + x$$

$$?$$

The term 8452 in the sum on the left has decreased by 10 to become 8442 in the sum on the right. In order for the sums to remain the same, the other term on the left (3719) must be increased by 10. That is,

$$x = 3719 + 10 = 3729.$$

Example 3   **Use the Invariant Principle for Differences**

If $5713 - 1429 = 5813 - y$, *what is y?*

Compare the two sides of the equation:

$$+100$$

$$5713 - 1429 = 5813 - y$$

$$?$$

This time we want the difference to remain the same, so both terms in the difference must change in the same way. Since 5713 has increased by 100 (to get 5813), we must also increase 1429 by 100 to get y. That is,

$$y = 1429 + 100 = 1529.$$

Example 4   **Use the Invariant Principle for Sums**

If $3875 + x = 3855 + 4759$, *what is x?*

The variable x is on the left side, so we find the change from right to left.

$$+20$$

$$3875 + x = 3855 + 4759$$

$$?$$

To keep the sum the same, 4759 must be decreased by 20 to get x. That is,

$$x = 4759 - 20 = 4739.$$

EXERCISE 1.6

DEVELOP YOUR SKILL

Use the invariant principles to write equivalent sums or differences that are easier to compute.

1. $236 + 97$ **2.** $395 + 47$ **3.** $189 + 315$

4. $405 - 89$ **5.** $236 - 97$ **6.** $395 - 47$

Solve each equation by using an invariant principle.

7. What is x, if $8703 + 5964 = 8705 + x$?

8. What is x, if $x - 4093 = 7362 - 4097$?

9. What is x, if $8703 - x = 8705 - 5964$?

10. What is x, if $4906 + 5187 = x + 5190$?

11. Use an invariant principle to solve the following: The enrollment figures at Midland College at the close of registration last year were 613 men and 749 women. This year the total enrollment was the same, but there were 625 men. How many women were registered?

MAINTAIN YOUR SKILL

12. What, by definition, is the sum of 7 and 8? [1.1]

13. Show that $17 < 23$ by writing the equation required by its definition. [1.2]

14. If the discount d is subtracted from the marked price M, this difference is the selling price S. Let $M - d = S$. Use the definition of subtraction to write an equation that tells how to compute the marked price M for a desired discount d and selling price S. [1.3]

Use the definition of subtraction to change each subtraction equation to the corresponding addition equation, and each addition equation to the corresponding subtraction equation. [1.3]

15. $14 + x = m$ **16.** $w + d = p$

17. $h - r = a$ **18.** $b - 17 = k$

Compute the basic numeral for each expression that is defined as a counting number. Otherwise, write "not defined." [1.4]

19. $5 - 8 + 4$ **20.** $10 - 8 - 3$ **21.** $7 - 5 + 3$

22. $10 - 6 + 7$ **23.** $14 - 7 + 5$ **24.** $8 + 5 - 10$

25. $34 - 19 + 6$ **26.** $23 - 15 - 10$

Write all other possible equivalent forms that result from using only the commutative principle for addition. [1.5]

27. $a - (b + c)$

28. $r + (s - t)$

29. $(x - y) + z$

30. $(d + e) - f$

EXTEND YOUR SKILL

31. When using the invariant principle for sums, explain why the changes must be opposite of each other.

32. When using the invariant principle for differences, explain why the changes must be the same.

CHAPTER 1 REVIEW

1. What, by definition, is the sum of 5 and 7? [1.1]

2. What, by definition, is the sum of x and 4? [1.1]

What equation, by definition, supports the truth of each statement? [1.1 and 1.2]

3. 36 is an even number.

4. 14 is an even number.

5. $5 < 8$

6. $10 < 14$

7. $15 > 3$

8. $21 > 6$

Use the definition of subtraction to change each subtraction equation to the corresponding addition equation and each addition equation to the corresponding subtraction equation. [1.3]

9. $22 - 15 = 7$

10. $14 + x = 25$

11. $31 + m = 50$

12. $27 - n = x$

Compute the basic numeral for each expression that is defined as a counting number. Otherwise, write "not defined." [1.4]

13. $16 - 3 + 5$

14. $(12 - 5) - (13 - 8)$

15. $13 - 3 + 4$

16. $5 - 7 + 10$

17. $8 - 6 - 4$

18. $5 + 8 - 3$

19. $25 - 8 - 5$

20. $18 - 5 + 2$

21. $(10 - 2) + 5$

22. $10 - (2 + 5)$

Write all other possible equivalent forms that result from using only the commutative principle for addition. If there are none, write "none." [1.5]

23. $(x + 5) - y$

24. $x + (5 - y)$

25. $10 - (x + y)$

26. $15 - (x - y)$

Solve each equation by using an invariant principle. [1.6]

27. What is x if, $2545 + 7777 = 2540 + x$?

28. What is x if, $x - 4788 = 3243 - 1788$?

29. What is x if, $5322 - x = 5122 - 784$?

30. What is x if, $4825 + x = 5825 + 7106$?

Chapter 2 – Increases and Decreases

2.1 – ADDITION AND SUBTRACTION OPERATORS

There are two ways of thinking about the sum of two numbers. The first way sees *two* numbers combined to produce a third number. This is the way we viewed addition in Lesson 1.1. For example, the sum 5 + 3 is thought of as two numbers, namely, 5 and 3, being added together to get their sum 5 + 3. We can imagine 5 and 3 as input to an "Adding Machine" that has 5 + 3 as the output.

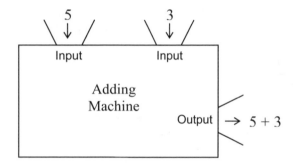

The second way of thinking about the sum 5 + 3 is to see the first number, 5, changing into the sum 5 + 3 by joining an increase of 3. We can imagine the number 5 as input to an "Increase of 3 Machine" that has 5 + 3 as the output.

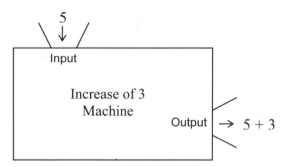

This second approach sees one number being changed into a second number. It emphasizes the *change* involved in forming a sum, and it frequently provides a better model for the process. In this case we refer to the numeral 5 as the **operand**.

It represents the beginning (initial) state. The symbol $+3$ is an **addition operator**. It represents the change: an **increase** of 3. The numeral $5 + 3$ is the **transform**. It represents the final state.

In analyzing the sum $5 + 3$, we can also think of 3 as the operand and view $5 +$ as an addition operator applied to the left side of 3. Thus we see that increases can be represented by **right operators** of the form $+ n$ and **left operators** of the form $n +$.

Since subtraction is not commutative, an expression such as $5 - 3$ must be computed by starting with 5 and subtracting 3 from it. Thus **decreases** are only represented by right operators of the form $- n$.

Study Tip:

Addition operators can be applied on the right or on the left. Subtraction operators can only be applied on the right.

Example 1   **Name the Operand and Operator**

List all the ways to name the operand and the operator in each expression.

   (a) $8 + 5$ (b) $7 - x$ (c) $(k + 3) - 5$

 (a) The operand is 8 and the operator $+ 5$, or the operand is 5 and the operator is $8 +$.

(b) The operand is 7 and the operator is $- x$.

(c) Because of the parentheses around $k + 3$, we group it together as one term. Thus the operand is $k + 3$ and the operator is $- 5$.

EXERCISE 2.1

DEVELOP YOUR SKILL

Each expression is to be viewed as consisting of one operand and one operator. List all the ways to name the operand and the operator.

1. $x + 23$	**2.** $x - 17$	**3.** $x - 8$
4. $12 + x$	**5.** $34 - x$	**6.** $21 - x$
7. $(a + 4) - x$	**8.** $x + (a - 5)$	**9.** $(k - 7) + x$
10. $x - (3 + b)$	**11.** $(m + 3) + x$	**12.** $x - (7 - b)$

MAINTAIN YOUR SKILL

Use the definition of subtraction to change each subtraction equation to the corresponding addition equation, and each addition equation to the corresponding subtraction equation. [1.3]

13. $46 - 13 = d$

14. $c - 22 = 15$

15. $a + 5 = b$

16. $x + y = 14$

Compute the basic numeral for each expression that is defined as a counting number. Otherwise, write "not defined." [1.4]

17. $14 + 3 - 8$

18. $11 - 5 + 9$

19. $20 - 5 - 3$

20. $3 + 7 - 8 + 2$

21. $6 - 3 - 4 + 8$

22. $12 - 7 - 2 + 1$

23. $10 - 5 + 3 - 6$

Write all other possible equivalent forms that result from using only the commutative principle for addition. [1.5]

24. $a - (b - c)$

25. $r + (s + t)$

26. $x + (y - z)$

27. $d - (e + f)$

Solve each equation by using an invariant principle. [1.6]

28. What is x, if $7328 + 5751 = 7348 + x$?

29. What is x, if $7328 - 5751 = 7348 - x$?

30. Use an invariant principle to solve the following: Last year the sticker price for one car model was $15,710 and the dealer's invoice was $15,438. This year's invoice for the same model will be $15,498. What should be the new sticker price to keep the same margin? [1.6]

EXTEND YOUR SKILL

31. Explain why $7 + 4$ has two possible operands, but $7 - 4$ only has one.

2.2 – COMPOSITION OF TWO INCREASES OR TWO DECREASES

OBJECTIVE

1. Combine two increases or two decreases and display them as vectors.

The combining of two operators is called the **composition** of operators. This composition is accomplished by writing the operators in succession. For example, the operator $+5+3$ is the composite of $+5$ and $+3$. When $+5+3$ is applied to the operand 4, the transform is the same as when the operator $+8$ is applied to 4:

$$4 + 5 + 3 \ = \ 12 \quad \text{and} \quad 4 + 8 \ = \ 12$$

We say that two operators are **equivalent** if they give the same transform when joined to an operand. Thus $+5+3$ is equivalent to the operator $+8$. The form $+8$ is called the **basic** operator for this combined change.

Example 1   **Find a Combined Change**

Suppose the temperature is 70° at 8 a.m., 75° at 10 a.m., and 78° at noon. Describe the temperate changes from 8 a.m. to 10 a.m., from 10 a.m. to noon, and the combined change from 8 a.m. to noon.

Here are the three temperatures: $70° \ \rightarrow \ 75° \ \rightarrow \ 78°$

The change from 8 a.m. to 10 a.m. is an increase of 5, or $+5$.
The change from 10 a.m. to noon is an increase of 3, or $+3$.
The combined change from 8 a.m. to noon is an increase of 8, or $+8$.

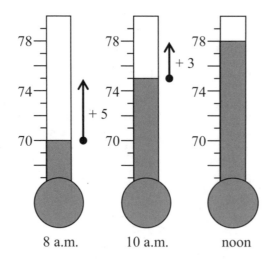

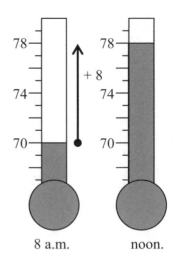

Definition:

A **vector** is a line segment that has direction and length.

In the diagram above, we have labeled the increases with arrows (or vectors) that show the amount of the change. We can simplify the drawings by omitting the thermometers and drawing the vectors horizontally. It is customary to let a vector pointing to the right represent an increase.

First we represent $+5$ by a vector of length 5 pointing to the right.

$+5$

The change $+3$ must start where $+5$ ends.

$+5$

$+3$

The composite $+5+3$ (or $+8$) begins at the point where $+5$ begins and ends at the point where $+3$ ends. We obtain the following vector model for the composition of the two operators, where we have separated the two individual increases from the composite by a broken line.

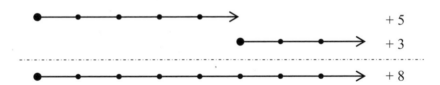

$+5$

$+3$

$+8$

If we focus our attention on the operators involved, we obtain the operator equation

$$+5+3 \ = \ +(5+3) \ = \ +8.$$

Since it is also true that $+3+5 \ = \ +8$, we have the following general rule for the composition of two increases:

The operator equation

$+5+3 = +8$

is read as

"An increase of 5 followed by an increase of 3 is equivalent to an increase of 8."

Case 1 An increase of a and an increase of b.

The composite of an increase of a and an increase of b is equivalent to an increase whose magnitude is $a+b$ (or $b+a$). The operator equations are

$$+a+b \ = \ +(a+b) \ = \ +(b+a)$$

$$+b+a \ = \ +(b+a) \ = \ +(a+b)$$

Example 2   **Find a Combined Change**

Suppose the temperature is 79° at 4 p.m., 74° at 6 p.m., and 71° at 8 p.m. Describe the temperate changes from 4 p.m. to 6 p.m., from 6 p.m. to 8 p.m., and the combined change from 4 p.m. to 8 p.m.

Here are the three temperatures: 79° → 74° → 71°

The change from 4 p.m. to 6 p.m. is a decrease of 5, or -5.

The change from 6 p.m. to 8 p.m. is a decrease of 3, or -3.

The combined change from 4 p.m. to 8 p.m. is a decrease of 8, or -8.

The vector model for the changes in Example 2 is drawn with the vectors pointing to the left, since they are decreases.

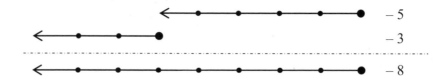

The operator equation for these changes is given by

$$-5 - 3 = -(5 + 3) = -8.$$

Since it is also true that $-3 - 5 = -8$, we have the following general rule for the composition of two decreases:

Case 2 A decrease of a and a decrease of b.

The composite of a decrease of a and a decrease of b is equivalent to a decrease whose magnitude is $a + b$ (or $b + a$). The operator equations are

$$-a - b = -(a + b) = -(b + a)$$

$$-b - a = -(b + a) = -(a + b)$$

We may summarize the composition of two increases or decreases as follows:

Key Point

> The composition of two changes of the same kind produces a larger change of the same kind. The magnitude of the composite change is the sum of the magnitudes of the individual changes.

Study Tip:

The answer to part (a) must be $+12$ and not just 12. We are composing operators, not adding numbers. Our answer must be the operator $+12$ and not the number 12.

Example 3   **Compute the Basic Form**

Compute the basic form for each composite operator.

   (a) $+5+7$ (b) $-6-9$ (c) $-3-8-2$

(a) $+5+7 = +(5+7) = +12$ (b) $-6-9 = -(6+9) = -15$

(c) This time we have three operators to combine. We can do this in either order by grouping the first two or the last two:

$$-3-8-2 = -(3+8)-2 = -11-2 = -(11+2) = -13$$
$$-3-8-2 = -3-(8+2) = -3-10 = -(3+10) = -13$$

Or we can combine all three decreases together:

$$-3-8-2 = -(3+8+2) = -13$$

EXERCISE 2.2

DEVELOP YOUR SKILL

In Exercises $1-4$, a series of three temperatures is given. In each exercise find the following: (a) the change from the first to the second temperature; (b) the change from the second to the third temperature; (c) the composite change from the first to the third temperature; and (d) draw a vector diagram to illustrate your answers to parts (a), (b) and (c).

1. 70, 76, 80   **2.** 72, 75, 81

3. 85, 80, 76   **4.** 82, 79, 73

Construct a vector model for the composition of the operators.

5. $+3+4$ **6.** $+5+1$ **7.** $-4-5$

8. $-2-3$ **9.** $+2+5+1$ **10.** $-4-1-3$

Compute the basic form for each composite operator.

11. $+4+5+7$

12. $+6+2+3$

13. $-5-7-3$

14. $-2-8-5$

Use composition of operators to write an equivalent single operator.

15. $+x+y$

16. $-x-y$

Maintain Your Skill

Show that each statement is true by writing the equation required by its definition. [1.1 and 1.2]

17. 54 is an even number.

18. $34 > 28$

19. $38 < 56$

20. $51 > 27$

Use the definition of subtraction to change each subtraction equation to the corresponding addition equation, and each addition equation to the corresponding subtraction equation. [1.3]

21. $x - 56 = 23$

22. $47 + y = 81$

23. $m - y = d$

24. $A + B = C$

Compute the basic numeral for each expression that is defined as a counting number. Otherwise, write "not defined." [1.4]

25. $27 - 5 + 9$

26. $25 - 8 + 3$

27. $17 - 12 - 8$

28. $16 - 18 - 7$

29. $15 + 13 - 7$

30. Use an invariant principle to solve the following: A grandmother and her granddaughter have the same birthday. If the grandmother was 75 when her granddaughter was 19, how old was the grandmother when her granddaughter was 15? [1.6]

Extend Your Skill

31. Frank gave $6 to Sue and $3 to Terri. Write an operator equation to show how much money Frank gave away.

32. Cassie was collecting seashells on the beach to add to her collection. On Monday she found 4 shells and Tuesday she found 2 shells. Write an operator equation to show how many shells Cassie added to her collection.

2.3 – COMPOSITION OF AN INCREASE AND A DECREASE

OBJECTIVE

1. Combine an increase with a decrease and display them as vectors.

The last lesson showed how to combine two increases or two decreases: the result is a larger change of the same kind. When combining an increase with a decrease, the two changes work against each other, so the composite will be smaller than either of the individual changes.

Example 1   **Find a Combined Change**

Suppose the temperature is 70° at noon, 78° at 4 p.m., and 73° at 8 p.m. Describe the temperate changes from noon to 4 p.m., from 4 p.m. to 8 p.m., and the combined change from noon to 8 p.m.

Here are the three temperatures: 70° → 78° → 73°

The change from noon to 4 p.m. is an increase of 8, or + 8.
The change from 4 p.m. to 8 p.m. is a decrease of 5, or − 5.
The combined change from noon to 8 p.m. is an increase of 3, or + 3.

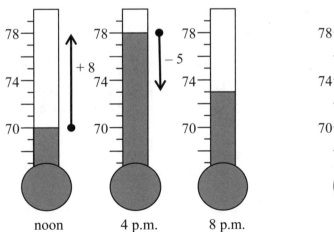

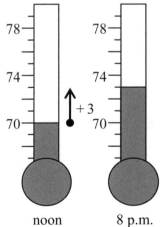

Drawing the vectors horizontally we have the following model for the composition of these changes:

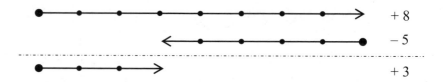

We see that the two changes are working against each other. Since the increase is larger, the composite change is an increase. The magnitude of the composite change is their difference. We would have obtained the same composite change if the decrease of 5 had come first and then the increase of 8:

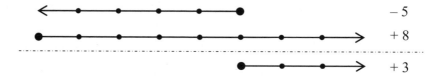

If we focus our attention on the operators involved, we obtain the operator equations

$$+8-5 = +(8-5) = +3 \quad \text{and} \quad -5+8 = +(8-5) = +3.$$

Here is the general rule for the composition of an increase and a decrease, when the increase is larger:

<u>Case 3</u> An increase of a and a decrease of b, where $a \geq b$.

If $a \geq b$, the composite of an increase of a and a decrease of b is equivalent to an increase whose magnitude is $a - b$. The operator equations are

$$+a-b = +(a-b)$$
$$-b+a = +(a-b)$$

Example 2   Find a Combined Change

Suppose the temperature is 75° at noon, 78° at 4 p.m., and 70° at 8 p.m. Describe the temperate changes from noon to 4 p.m., from 4 p.m. to 8 p.m., and the combined change from noon to 8 p.m.

Here are the three temperatures: $75° \rightarrow 78° \rightarrow 70°$

The change from noon to 4 p.m. is an increase of 3, or $+3$.

The change from 4 p.m. to 8 p.m. is a decrease of 8, or -8.

The combined change from noon to 8 p.m. is a decrease of 5, or -5.

This time the decrease is larger than the increase, so the combined change is a decrease. Here is the vector model for the composition of the operators:

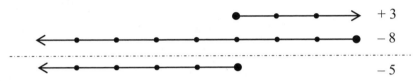

Once again, the two changes could occur in either order and produce the same result. Here is the general rule for the composition of an increase and a decrease, when the decrease is larger:

<u>Case 4</u> An increase of a and a decrease of b, where $b \geq a$.

If $b \geq a$, the composite of an increase of a and a decrease of b is equivalent to a decrease whose magnitude is $b - a$. The operator equations are

$$+a - b = -(b - a)$$
$$-b + a = -(b - a)$$

Study Tip:

The answer to (a) must be $+4$ and not just 4. We are composing operators and not adding and subtracting numbers. Our answer must be the operator $+4$ and not the number 4.

Example 3   **Compute the Basic Form**

Compute the basic form for each composite operator.

(a) $-5 + 9$ (b) $+3 - 10$

(a) Since the increase of 9 is larger than the decrease of 5, the combined change will be an increase. The size of the change is their difference, $9 - 5$. That is, $-5 + 9 = +(9 - 5) = +4$.

(b) This time the decrease of 10 is larger than the increase of 3, so the combined change will be a decrease. The size of the change is their difference, $10 - 3$. That is, $+3 - 10 = -(10 - 3) = -7$.

In summary, we have the following rules for the composition of addition and subtraction operators (increases and decreases):

Key Point

---

1. Like changes help each other to give a larger composite change of the same kind. Add their magnitudes.

2. Opposite changes work against each other. The larger change will dominate the smaller and determine the kind of composite change. Subtract the smaller magnitude from the larger.

The operators $+\,0$, $0\,+$, and $-\,0$ represent no change; they are the **identity** operators for increases and decreases. The operators $+\,3$ and $-\,3$ give changes of the same magnitude (size), but they are of opposite kind. In general, $+\,n$ and $-\,n$ are said to be **inverse** to each other.

If two inverse operators such as $+\,3$ and $-\,3$ are used in immediate succession, their changes "undo" or "cancel" each other, so that the final result is no change at all. For example, $8 + 3 - 3 = 8$, $8 - 3 + 3 = 8$, and $8 + 0 = 8$. This shows that $+\,3 - 3$, $-\,3 + 3$, and $+\,0$ are all equivalent. In general, an increase $+\,n$ followed by a decrease $-\,n$ is equivalent to no change $+\,0$.

$$+\,n - n \;=\; +\,0$$

And a decrease $-\,n$ followed by an increase $+\,n$ is equivalent to no change when the operand is large enough for the expression to be defined.

$$-\,n + n \;=\; +\,0$$

for any operand m for which $m \geq n$.

Example 4   **Find the Inverse of an Operator**

Write the inverse of each operator.

   (a) $+\,9$ (b) $-\,2$

(a) The inverse of an increase of 9 is a decrease of 9: $-\,9$.

(b) The inverse of a decrease of 2 is an increase of 2: $+\,2$.

Note to the student:

At this time you are encouraged *not* to think of addition and subtraction operators as positive and negative numbers. True, the notation is the same for both ways of thinking, and there is no conflict in the manipulations. But increases and decreases match the true meaning better for most of the uses of elementary algebra. Thus you are urged at this time to think of -5 and $+3$ as "a decrease of 5" and "an increase of 3," but not as "negative five" or "positive three."

EXERCISE 2.3

DEVELOP YOUR SKILL

In Exercises 1 – 4, a series of three temperatures is given. In each exercise find the following: (a) the change from the first to the second temperature; (b) the change from the second to the third temperature; (c) the composite change from the first to the third temperature; and (d) draw a vector diagram to illustrate your answers to parts (a), (b) and (c).

1. 70, 76, 72   **2.** 72, 77, 68   **3.** 80, 72, 76   **4.** 78, 75, 80

Construct a vector model for the composition of the operators.

5. $+2+3$ **6.** $+4-6$ **7.** $-2+7$

8. $-4-2$ **9.** $-3+2+4$ **10.** $+4+2-7$

Compute the basic form for each composite operator.

11. $+9-7$ **12.** $-11+4$ **13.** $+5+13$

14. $-12-3$ **15.** $+20-39$ **16.** $+4-5+9$

17. $-2-8+6$

Use composition of operators to write an equivalent single operator.

18. $+x-y$, where $y \geq x$ **19.** $-x+y$, where $y \geq x$

20. The temperature rose 6° in the first hour, rose 8° in the second hour, and fell 3° in the third hour. Construct an operator equation to model the changes over this three hour period. Put a sequence of operators on the left side of the equation and the basic form of the composite operator on the right side.

Write the inverse of each operator.

21. $+7$ **22.** $+3$ **23.** -8 **24.** -5

MAINTAIN YOUR SKILL

Compute the basic numeral for each expression that is defined as a counting number. Otherwise, write "not defined." [1.4]

25. $5 + 7 - 4 + 8$

26. $6 - 2 - 1 + 5$

27. $7 - 5 + 3 - 9$

Each expression is to be viewed as consisting of one operand and one operator. List all the ways to name the operand and the operator. [2.1]

28. $x + (m + 15)$

29. $x - (n - 17)$

30. $(a - 8) - x$

EXTEND YOUR SKILL

31. When an increase is followed by a decrease, explain how to determine whether the composite change is an increase or a decrease.

32. When a decrease is followed by an increase, explain how to determine the magnitude of the composite change.

2.4 – INSERTING PARENTHESES

OBJECTIVE

1. Combine two changes into a composite change.

In the last two lessons we have seen how increases and decreases interact with each other to form a combined change:

---

1.   Like changes help each other to give a larger composite change of the same kind. Add their magnitudes.

2.   Opposite changes work against each other. The larger change will dominate the smaller and determine the kind of composite change. Subtract the smaller magnitude from the larger.

It is important to gain confidence in forming these combinations. In this lesson we practice this process without doing the final computation. This will help prepare us for algebra, where the use of letters prevents us from relying on the numerical values.

Example 1   **Insert Parentheses**

Do not compute, but write an equivalent expression with parentheses around a sum or a difference. Do not change the first term. When possible, give a second alternate form.

(a) $20 - 9 - 5$ (b) $20 + 5 - 9$ (c) $20 + 9 - 5$

(d) $20 - 5 + 9$ (e) $20 + 5 + 9$

(a) The two decreases combine to give a larger decrease. We want to add their magnitudes. This can be done in either order:

$$20 - (9 + 5) \quad \text{or} \quad 20 - (5 + 9).$$

(b) The increase and the decrease are working against each other and the decrease is stronger. This means the combined change is a decrease and the size of the decrease is the difference in the magnitudes: $20 - (9 - 5)$.

(c) This time the increase is stronger, so the combined change is an increase: $20 + (9 - 5)$

(d) This is the same as (c). It doesn't matter which change comes first, only which change is stronger: $20 + (9 - 5)$

(e) The two increases combine to give a larger increase; add their magnitudes in either order:

$$20 + (9 + 5) \quad \text{or} \quad 20 + (5 + 9).$$

Example 2   **Insert Parentheses**

Write an equivalent expression with parentheses around a sum or a difference. Do not change the first term. Assume that $x \geq y$ and that all differences are defined. When possible, give a second alternate form.

(a) $15 - y + x$ (b) $15 + x - y$ (c) $15 - x - y$

(d) $15 + x + y$ (e) $15 - x + y$ (f) $15 + y - x$

(a) The changes are working against each other and the increase is stronger: Subtract the smaller magnitude from the larger: $15 + (x - y)$.

$$15 - (x + y) \quad \text{or} \quad 15 - (y + x).$$

(d) The two increases combine to give a larger increase:

$$15 + (x + y) \quad \text{or} \quad 15 + (y + x).$$

(e) The changes are working against each other and the decrease is stronger: Subtract the smaller magnitude from the larger: $15 - (x - y)$.

(f) This is the same as part (e): $15 - (x - y)$.

EXERCISE 2.4

DEVELOP YOUR SKILL

Do not compute, but write an equivalent expression with parentheses around a sum or a difference. Do not change the first term. When possible, give a second alternate form.

1. $15 - 8 - 2$ **2.** $17 + 5 + 9$ **3.** $15 - 2 + 8$

4. $17 + 9 - 5$ **5.** $15 + 2 - 8$ **6.** $17 + 5 - 9$

7. $15 + 8 + 2$ **8.** $17 - 9 - 5$

Write an equivalent expression with parentheses around a sum or a difference. Do not change the first term. Assume that $m \geq n$ and that all differences are defined. When possible, give a second alternate form.

9. $24 - m - n$ **10.** $24 - m + n$ **11.** $24 - n + m$

12. $24 + n + m$ **13.** $24 + n - m$ **14.** $24 + m - n$

MAINTAIN YOUR SKILL

Compute the basic numeral for each expression that is defined as a counting number. Otherwise, write "not defined." [1.4]

15. $4 + 7 - 3$ **16.** $15 - 3 + 5$ **17.** $11 - 5 + 4$

18. $7 - 5 - 3$ **19.** $13 + 5 - 7 + 3$ **20.** $12 - 4 - 3 + 8$

21. $15 - (7 + 2) + 3$ **22.** $21 - (12 - 2 + 7)$

Solve each equation by using an invariant principle. [1.6]

23. What is x, if $4823 + x = 4523 + 3549$?   **24.** What is x, if $5024 - x = 5324 - 2718$?

Construct a vector model for the composition of the operators. [2.3]

25. $+7-3$ **26.** $-3+7$

Compute the basic form for each composite operator. [2.3]

27. $+8-6$ **28.** $-4+10$

29. $+3-15$ **30.** $-7-2$

EXTEND YOUR SKILL

31. When taking the composition of two decreases, does it ever matter which one comes first? Explain your answer.

32. When taking the composition of an increase and a decrease, does it ever matter which one comes first? Explain your answer.

33. Explain the process of computing the composition of an increase of 4 and a decrease of 7.

2.5 – REMOVING PARENTHESES

OBJECTIVE

1. Replace a composite change by two consecutive changes.

In Lessons 2.2 and 2.3 we examined the four ways in which increases and decreases can be composed. For example, we saw that

$$+3-5 = -(5-3) = -2.$$

Now we want to reverse the process. We want to take an operator like $-(5-3)$ and write it as two consecutive operators $+3-5$ or $-5+3$. Once again there are four cases, and they correspond to the four cases in Lessons 2.2 and 2.3.

Case 1 An increase of a sum: $+(a+b)$

This comes from two increases working together to give a larger increase. The increases can occur in either order. In general,

$$+(a+b) = +a+b = +b+a.$$

<u>Case 2</u> A decrease of a sum: $-(a + b)$

This comes from two decreases working together to give a larger decrease. The decreases can occur in either order. In general,

$$-(a + b) = -a - b = -b - a.$$

<u>Case 3</u> An increase of a difference: $+(a - b)$

Having a difference inside the parentheses comes from an increase and a decrease working against each other. Since the composite change is an increase, the larger individual change must be the increase. In order for $a - b$ to be defined we must have $a \geq b$. Thus a is the magnitude of the larger change (the increase), and we have

$$+(a - b) = +a - b = -b + a.$$

Study Tip:

A difference inside the parentheses comes from opposite changes working against each other.

<u>Case 4</u> A decrease of a difference: $-(b - a)$

A decrease of a difference $-(b - a)$ is the composite of a decrease and an increase working against each other. We know that the decrease is larger since the composite change is a decrease. In order for $b - a$ to be defined, $b \geq a$. Thus b is the magnitude of the decrease, and we have

$$-(b - a) = -b + a = +a - b.$$

Example 1   **Remove Parentheses**

Do not compute, but write an equivalent expression without parentheses. Do not change the first term. When possible, give a second alternate form.

   (a) $12 + (7 + 3)$ (b) $2 + (7 - 3)$ (c) $8 - (7 - 3)$

   (d) $5 - (7 - 3)$ (e) $14 - (7 + 3)$

(a) An increase of a sum comes from two increases working together, in either order: $12 + 7 + 3$ or $12 + 3 + 7$.

(b) An increase of a difference comes from an increase and a decrease working against each other with the increase larger: $2 + 7 - 3$. [We do not include the form $2 - 3 + 7$ because it is not defined.]

(c) A decrease of a difference comes from an increase and a decrease working against each other with the decrease larger: $8 + 3 - 7$ or $8 - 7 + 3$.

(d) This is similar to (c), but the increase must come first: $5 + 3 - 7$. [The form $5 - 7 + 3$ is not defined.]

(e) A decrease of a sum comes from two decreases working together, in either order: $14 - 7 - 3$ or $14 - 3 - 7$.

Example 2   **Remove Parentheses**

Write an equivalent expression without parentheses. Do not change the first term. Assume all differences are defined. When possible, give a second alternate form.

(a) $24 + (x - y)$ (b) $35 - (n - a)$

(c) $18 - (a + b)$ (d) $27 + (x + y)$

(a) The difference inside the parentheses comes from an increase and a decrease working against each other. In order for the difference $x - y$ to be defined, the larger magnitude must be x. Since the combined change is an increase, the increase must have magnitude x. The decrease must have magnitude y. We obtain $24 + x - y$ or $24 - y + x$.

(b) Again we have an increase and a decrease working against each other to produce the difference inside the parentheses. This time the decrease must be the larger change since the composite change is a decrease. We have $35 + a - n$ or $35 - n + a$.

(c) A decrease of a sum comes from two decreases working together, in either order: $18 - a - b$ or $18 - b - a$.

(d) An increase of a sum comes from two increases working together, in either order: $27 + x + y$ or $27 + y + x$.

EXERCISE 2.5

DEVELOP YOUR SKILL

Do not compute, but write equivalent expressions without parentheses. Do not change the first term. When possible, give a second alternate form.

1. $20 - (7 + 3)$
2. $10 + (7 + 8)$
3. $5 + (10 - 7)$
4. $13 + (10 - 4)$
5. $5 + (9 + 3)$
6. $14 - (10 - 7)$
7. $5 - (10 - 8)$
8. $7 + (20 - 10)$

Write an equivalent expression without parentheses. Do not change the first term. Assume all differences are defined. When possible, give a second alternate form.

9. $34 - (a + b)$
10. $26 + (x - n)$
11. $13 + (r + t)$
12. $44 - (y - m)$

MAINTAIN YOUR SKILL

Use the definition of subtraction to change each subtraction equation to the corresponding addition equation, and each addition equation to the corresponding subtraction equation. [1.3]

13. $23 + 17 = 40$
14. $54 - 28 = 26$
15. $87 - x = 15$
16. $y + 55 = 91$

Solve each equation by using an invariant principle. [1.6]

17. What is x, if $8419 + 6523 = 8119 + x$?
18. What is x, if $8419 - 6523 = 8119 - x$?

Construct a vector model for the composition of the operators. [2.3]

19. $+ 7 - 3$
20. $+ 2 - 8$
21. $- 5 + 3$
22. $- 2 - 5$

Compute the basic form for each composite operator. [2.3]

23. $+ 10 - 16$
24. $- 15 + 3$
25. $- 18 - 15$
26. $+ 10 - (8 - 3)$
27. $+ 10 - 8 - 3$
28. $+ 10 - 8 + 3$
29. $+ 10 + 8 - 3$

30. On Monday, the value of WXY stock rose 3 cents. On Tuesday, it fell 8 cents. On Wednesday, it rose 4 cents. Construct an operator equation to model the changes in the value of WXY stock over these three days. Put a sequence of operators on the left side of the equation and the basic form of the composite operator on the right side. [2.3]

EXTEND YOUR SKILL

31. If you have a decrease of a sum, are the individual changes working together or against each other?

32. If you have a decrease of a difference, are the individual changes working together or against each other?

2.6 – SIMPLIFYING INCREASES AND DECREASES

OBJECTIVE

1. Simplify expressions involving increases and decreases.

A study of the four cases involving increases and decreases shows that the order of the operations can be interchanged when the operand is large enough. When x, a, and b are counting numbers, then

$$x + a + b = x + b + a, \qquad \text{so} \qquad + a + b = + b + a.$$

If $x \geq a + b$, then

$$x - a - b = x - b - a, \qquad \text{so} \qquad - a - b = - b - a.$$

If $x \geq b$, then

$$x + a - b = x - b + a, \qquad \text{so} \qquad + a - b = - b + a.$$

The commutative principle for addition also shows that the left operator $a +$ and the right operator $+ a$ can be exchanged. This can be useful in simplifying the composition of operators.

Example 1   **Simplify an Expression**

Simplify the expression $7 + (x - 5)$.

$$
\begin{aligned}
7 + (x - 5) &= (x - 5) + 7 & &\text{Change from } 7 + \text{ to } + 7. \\
&= x + 2 & &\text{Composition of } - 5 \text{ and } + 7.
\end{aligned}
$$

In a given problem it may be helpful to use both computation of basic forms and composition of operators; that is, sometimes adding or subtracting numbers, and sometimes using addition or subtraction operators. Remember that we always work from left to right when there are no parentheses. Thus $(x - 5) + 7$ and $x - 5 + 7$ are interchangeable in Example 1, as are $(7 - b) + 5$ and $7 - b + 5$ in Example 2.

Example 2   **Simplify an Expression**

Simplify the expression $(7 - b) + 5$.

One way is to change $+ 5$ into $5 +$, like in Example 1:

$$
\begin{aligned}
(7 - b) + 5 &= 5 + (7 - b) &&\text{Change from } + 5 \text{ to } 5 +. \\
&= 5 + 7 - b &&\text{See Case 3.} \\
&= 12 - b &&\text{Addition of 5 and 7.}
\end{aligned}
$$

We can also simplify this expression by using the commutative principle directly:

$$
\begin{aligned}
(7 - b) + 5 &= 7 + 5 - b &&\text{Commutation of } - b \text{ and } + 5. \\
&= 12 - b &&\text{Addition of 7 and 5.}
\end{aligned}
$$

EXERCISE 2.6

DEVELOP YOUR SKILL

Simplify each expression. Compute as needed.

1. $x + 7 + 4$	**2.** $y - 5 - 12$	**3.** $y - 13 + 8$
4. $11 - y + 2$	**5.** $15 + z - 7$	**6.** $z - 6 + 13$
7. $x - 5 - 9$	**8.** $z + 9 - 3$	**9.** $11 - (y + 4)$
10. $10 + (y - 2)$	**11.** $x + (12 - 3)$	**12.** $4 - (9 - x)$

MAINTAIN YOUR SKILL

Compute the basic numeral for each expression that is defined as a counting number. Otherwise, write "not defined." [1.4]

13. $3 + 12 - 7 - 2$	**14.** $3 + 5 - 10 + 4$
15. $12 - 8 + 3 - 7$	**16.** $4 + 7 - 5 - 3$

Compute the basic form for each composite operator. [2.3]

17. $- 15 + 7$	**18.** $- 4 + 9$
19. $- 5 - 9 + 3$	**20.** $+ 5 - 7 + 10$

Write the inverse of each operator. [2.3]

21. $- 12$	**22.** $+ 15$

Do not compute, but write an equivalent expression with parentheses around a sum or a difference. Do not change the first term. When possible, give a second alternate form. [2.4]

23. $48 - 3 + 5$

24. $27 - 6 - 9$

25. $13 + 4 - 12$

26. $7 + 8 - 9$

Do not compute, but write equivalent expressions without parentheses. Do not change the first term. When possible, give a second alternate form. [2.5]

27. $55 + (23 - 17)$

28. $17 + (44 - 20)$

29. $38 - (14 + 11)$

30. $15 - (23 - 10)$

EXTEND YOUR SKILL

31. Simplify $9 + (x + 3)$ by using the invariant principle for sums. Explain your reasoning.

32. Simplify $12 - (x - 5)$ by using the invariant principle for differences. Explain your reasoning.

33. Which invariant principle could be used to simplify $15 - (x + 3)$? Explain your answer.

CHAPTER 2 REVIEW

Each expression is to be viewed as consisting of one operand and one operator. List all the ways to name the operand and the operator. [2.1]

1. $x + 10$

2. $15 - (y + 3)$

Compute the basic form for each composite operator. [2.2 and 2.3]

3. $- 3 + 14$

4. $+ 3 - 8 + 6$

5. $- 3 - 4 - 5$

6. $+ 5 - 6 + 2$

Use composition of operators to write an equivalent single operator. [2.3]

7. $+ m - n$, where $n \geq m$

8. $+ m - n$, where $m \geq n$

9. The thermometer reading dropped 7 degrees from noon to 8 p.m., dropped 22 degrees from 8 p.m. to 4 a.m. the next morning, and then rose 15 degrees from 4 a.m. until noon. Compute the combined change in temperature for this 24-hour period. [2.3]

Construct a vector model for the composition of the operators. [2.3]

10. $-3+7$

11. $+2-3+4$

Write the inverse of each operator. [2.3]

12. $+23$

13. -12

14. $+6$

Do not compute, but write equivalent expressions with parentheses around a sum or a difference. Do not change the first term. When possible, give a second alternate form. [2.4]

15. $6+9-5$

16. $14+7-12$

17. $25-10-7$

18. $15-4+7$

19. $12+7+3$

20. $31+12-8$

Do not compute, but write an equivalent expression without parentheses. Do not change the first term. When possible, give a second alternate form. [2.5]

21. $23+(14-5)$

22. $45-(6+8)$

23. $67-(84-75)$

24. $20+(9+11)$

Simplify each expression. Compute as needed. [2.6]

25. $x-8+5$

26. $25-y+3$

27. $12+8-z$

28. $16+x-5$

29. $22-(y+8)$

30. $6-(8-z)$

Chapter 3 — Products and Quotients

3.1 – MULTIPLICATION

OBJECTIVES

1. Express multiplication as repeated addition.

2. Model multiplication by comparing line segments.

When an increase is repeatedly applied to 0, this sequence of increases can be abbreviated by multiplication.

> If x and y are counting numbers, then multiplication assigns to x and y a unique third counting number $x \cdot y$, called the **product** of x and y.

In the product $x \cdot y$, we may think of x as counting the number of times that the increase $+y$ is applied to 0.

Example 1　　　　**An Operator Model for Multiplication**

Product Form	Number of Increases	Operator Model	Basic Numeral
$0 \cdot 5$	none	0	0
$1 \cdot 5$	one	$0 + 5$	5
$2 \cdot 5$	two	$0 + 5 + 5$	10
$3 \cdot 5$	three	$0 + 5 + 5 + 5$	15

Study Tip:

3 and 5 are **factors** of 15, because $3 \cdot 5 = 15$.

The word "product," like "sum" and "difference," is used with two meanings. The product of 3 and 5 is 15, since a multiplication computation gives the basic numeral of 15. But $x \cdot y$ and $3 \cdot 5$ are also called products because of their form. The numbers 3 and 5 are **factors** of the product $3 \cdot 5$, and hence are factors of 15.

A variety of notations are used for products:

$$3 \times 5 \qquad (3)(5) \qquad (3)5 \qquad x(y) \qquad xy \qquad 3x$$

$$3 \cdot 5 \qquad (x)(y) \qquad 3(5) \qquad (x)y \qquad x \cdot y \qquad 3 \cdot x$$

Sometimes we even use brackets when more than one product is indicated: $[(3)(5)](7)$.

Example 1 shows us the distinctive properties that the number zero has as a factor of a product. In the product $0 \cdot x$, there is no increase applied to 0. Thus for each counting number x we have $0 \cdot x = 0$. On the other hand, in the product $x \cdot 0$, the result will be zero no matter how many times the operator $+ 0$ is joined to zero. Thus for each counting number x we have $x \cdot 0 = 0$. Thus,

$$0 \cdot x = 0 \quad \text{and} \quad x \cdot 0 = 0.$$

Furthermore, if $x \cdot y = 0$, then either x or y or both must be zero. Otherwise, when x and y are both not zero, there would be at least one nonzero increase so that the final result could not be zero. This is called the Zero-Factor Property.

Zero-Factor Property

> If $x \cdot y = 0$, then either $x = 0$ or $y = 0$,

Example 1 also shows us that $1 \cdot x = 0 + x = x$, and it can be used to check that $x \cdot 1 = x$, for all x. Thus the number 1 is the **identity** for multiplication:

$$1 \cdot x = x \quad \text{and} \quad x \cdot 1 = x.$$

A product such as $3 \cdot 5$ or $3(5)$ can also be viewed as the result when the multiplication operator $3 \cdot$ or $3(\ )$ is applied to the operand 5. Such operators make changes to the initial state that may be called **expansion,** stretching or magnification. If $n > 1$ and $x > 0$, then the operator $n(\ )$ yields a transform that is larger than the operand x. It is this property that justifies the name multiplier (many thicknesses) as well as expander, stretcher, or magnifier.

Both $3 \cdot$ and $3(\ )$ are left operators. We can also view the product $3 \cdot 5$ or $(3)5$ as the result when the right operator $\cdot 5$ or $(\ )5$ is applied to the operand 3.

To obtain a graphical model for expansions, we compare the length of line segments, where the length of the second line segment results from the expansion applied to the first line segment. For example, to visualize the action of the operator $3(\ )$, we start with a line segment such as ●———● and copy it 3 times below. The length of the lower line is then the length of the upper line times 3.

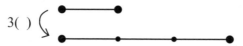

$3(\ )$

It may be helpful to think of the line segment as a rubber band that can be stretched to 3 times its length.

Study Tip:

When writing an expansion of 5 by itself, it is preferable to use $(\ )5$ or $5(\ )$ since the raised dot in $\cdot 5$ is easily missed.

EXERCISE 3.1

DEVELOP YOUR SKILL

1. What, by definition, is the product of 6 and 8?

2. What, by definition, is the product of 5 and *m*?

Compute the basic numeral for each product. If no computation is possible, write "not possible."

3. $5 \cdot 8$

4. $3 \cdot 7$

5. $4 \cdot 9$

6. $6 \cdot 4$

7. $8 \cdot 8$

8. $x \cdot 12$

9. $7 \cdot 7$

10. $11 \cdot 5$

11. $8 \cdot 6$

12. $12 \cdot 3$

13. $14 \cdot y$

14. $10 \cdot 7$

15. Give two operator models for $2 \cdot 6$, one with increases of 2 and one with increases of 6, as in Example 1. Construct a graphical model for each expansion operator.

16. 4( )

17. 2( )

18. 6( )

MAINTAIN YOUR SKILL

Show that each statement is true by writing the equation required by its definition. [1.1 and 1.2]

19. 38 is an even number.

20. $47 < 66$

Each expression is to be viewed as consisting of one operand and one operator. List all the ways to name the operand and the operator. [2.1]

21. $x - (4 + m)$

22. $(y - 3) + x$

Use the composition of operators to write an equivalent single operator. [2.3]

23. $+ r - s$, where $r \geq s$

24. $- s + r$, where $s \geq r$

Do not compute, but write an equivalent expression without parentheses. Do not change the first term. When possible, give a second alternate form. [2.5]

25. $24 - (15 + 6)$

26. $31 + (17 - 2)$

27. $43 - (21 - 14)$

Simplify each expression. Compute as needed. [2.6]

28. $17 - z - 6$

29. $x - 13 + 6$

30. $5 + 11 + x$

EXTEND YOUR SKILL

31. Use the definition of multiplication to explain why $0 \cdot 7 = 0$.

32. Use the definition of multiplication to explain why $7 \cdot 0 = 0$.

33. Use the definition of multiplication to explain why $1 \cdot 7 = 7$.

3.2 – DIVISION

OBJECTIVE

1. Identify the relationship between products and quotients.

Division is a rule for assigning a unique third number to chosen first and second numbers. But division, like subtraction, is only a *partial* operation on the counting numbers. The division of a first number x by a second number y fails for many choices of counting numbers x and y. Just as subtraction was defined in terms of addition, division is defined in terms of multiplication.

Definition of

Division

> Let x and y be counting numbers with $y \neq 0$. Then x can be divided by y, and we write $x \div y = z$ or $\frac{x}{y} = z$, if and only if there is a unique counting number z such that $y \cdot z = x$.

Example 1   **Use the Definition of Division**

Use the definition of division to change each division equation to the corresponding multiplication equation.

(a) $\dfrac{27}{9} = 3$ (b) $\dfrac{p}{q} = r$

(a) $9 \cdot 3 = 27$ (b) $q \cdot r = p$

Note that the order of the terms is important. The definition only justifies *one* answer. For example, in (a) it is also true that $3 \cdot 9 = 27$, but this does not follow directly from the definition.

Example 2   **Use the Definition of Division**

Use the definition of division to change the multiplication equation to the corresponding division equation.

(a) $7 \cdot 13 = 91$ (b) $r \cdot s = t$

(a) $\dfrac{91}{7} = 13$ (b) $\dfrac{t}{r} = s$

Once again, the order of the terms is important. The definition only justifies *one* answer. For example, in (a) it is also true that $\dfrac{91}{13} = 7$, but this does not follow directly from the definition.

If a first number x can be divided by a second number y, then we say that y **divides** x, and x is a **multiple** of y.

Example 3   **Find Divisors and Multiples**

For what counting numbers x are each of the following true? When possible, list the five smallest values for x.

  (a) x divides 5   (b) 5 divides x (c) x divides 6

(a) Since 5 can only be factored as $1 \cdot 5$, we see that 1 and 5 are the only counting numbers that divide 5.

(b) We have $0 \cdot 5 = 0$, $1 \cdot 5 = 5$, $2 \cdot 5 = 10$, $3 \cdot 5 = 15$, and $4 \cdot 5 = 20$. We could keep going, but the five smallest multiples of 5 are 0, 5, 10, 15, and 20.

(c) Since 6 can only be factored as $1 \cdot 6$ or $2 \cdot 3$, we see that 1, 2, 3 and 6 are the only counting numbers that divide 6

If y divides x, then division assigns to x and y a third number $\dfrac{x}{y}$ called the **quotient** of x and y. In this form, x is the **dividend** and y is the **divisor**. As we would expect, the word "quotient" has two meanings. A division computation for $\dfrac{15}{3}$ gives the basic numeral 5 as the quotient. But $\dfrac{x}{y}$ and $\dfrac{15}{3}$ are also called quotients as a name for their form.

Example 4   **Find Divisors and Multiples**

For what counting numbers x are each of the following quotients defined? When possible, list the five smallest values for x.

(a) $\dfrac{6}{x}$ (b) $\dfrac{x}{6}$ (c) $\dfrac{5}{x}$

(a) 1, 2, 3, 6   (b) 0, 6, 12, 18, 24   (c) 1, 5

In Lesson 3.1 we saw that 1 is the identity for multiplication:

$$1 \cdot x = x \quad \text{and} \quad x \cdot 1 = x.$$

When this is combined with the definition of division, we obtain two more useful results:

$$\frac{x}{1} = x \quad \text{and if } x \neq 0, \text{ then } \frac{x}{x} = 1.$$

The definition of division requires that every quotient be related to a certain product. Since zero dominates every product, this causes difficulties when zero is used in a quotient. Our next example illustrates the three possible types of quotients involving a zero.

Example 5   **Quotients Involving Zero**

(a) $\dfrac{0}{3} = 0$, since $3 \cdot 0 = 0$. The definition requires that $\dfrac{0}{y} = z$ if and only if $y \cdot z = 0$. If $y \neq 0$, then *z* must be zero. Hence, $\dfrac{0}{y} = 0$ for all $y \neq 0$.

(b) $\dfrac{3}{0}$ is undefined since $\dfrac{x}{0} = z$ if and only if $0 \cdot z = x$. If $x \neq 0$, then there is no *z* such that $0 \cdot z = x$. Hence, $\dfrac{x}{0}$ cannot represent a number.

(c) $\dfrac{0}{0}$ is undetermined. For $\dfrac{0}{0} = z$, the definition requires that $0 \cdot z = 0$. Since for *every z* we have $0 \cdot z = 0$, then a unique number cannot be decided for *z*. Hence, $\dfrac{0}{0}$ cannot be used.

From (b) and (c) we conclude that *zero must never be a divisor.*

A quotient such as $\frac{12}{3}$ can also be viewed as the result when the division operator $\frac{(\ )}{3}$ is applied to the operand 12. We see that the result, namely 4, is smaller than the operand 12. Thus a division operator makes a change that is a **contraction** or a compression. Since $\frac{x}{1} = x$ for all x, the **identity** operator $\frac{(\ )}{1}$ causes no change at all.

Division operators are quite restricted in use for us now because only the counting numbers are available. For the quotient $\frac{x}{n}$ to be defined, it is required that $n \mid x$. The parentheses are part of the operator $(\ ) \div 3$ when used in $(7 + 5) \div 3$. Parentheses are not needed for $\frac{7+5}{3}$, but when written without an operand, the form $\frac{(\ )}{3}$ is less likely to be misread.

Example 6   **A Graphical Model for Division**

To visualize the action of the operator $\frac{(\ )}{3}$, we start with a line segment such as ●————————● . Copy the length of this segment below it, divide the length into 3 equal parts, and select the first part. The length of the lower line is then the length of the upper line divided by 3. In the lower line, we show the rest of the original length before the contraction by a dotted line ●···········● to make the comparison easier.

It may be helpful to think of the original line segment as a stretched rubber band that has its length contracted by a factor of 3.

EXERCISE 3.2

DEVELOP YOUR SKILL

For each equation, write the corresponding equation that is matched to it by the definition of division.

1. $\dfrac{52}{4} = 13$ **2.** $\dfrac{x}{12} = 7$ **3.** $3y = 6$

4. $mn = p$ **5.** $\dfrac{a}{b} = c + d$ **6.** $a(b + c) = d$

Indicate for what counting numbers each statement is true. When possible, list the four smallest values of x.

7. 0 divides x **8.** x divides 0   **9.** 1 divides x

10. x divides 1   **11.** 2 divides x **12.** x divides 2

Indicate for what counting numbers each quotient is defined. When possible, list the four smallest values.

13. $\dfrac{9}{x}$ **14.** $\dfrac{7}{x}$ **15.** $\dfrac{x}{9}$ **16.** $\dfrac{x}{7}$

17. Use line segments to model the contraction operator $\dfrac{(\ )}{4}$.

18. Tom was 1 year old on the day his mother was 21. At that time his age divided his mother's age. At what other ages will Tom's age divide his mother's?

MAINTAIN YOUR SKILL

For each equation, write the corresponding equation that is matched to it by the definition of subtraction. [1.3]

19. $41 + 27 = 68$ **20.** $51 - 32 = 19$

Write all other possible equivalent forms that result from using only the commutative principle for addition. [1.5]

21. $(a + b) - c$ **22.** $x - (w + y)$ **23.** $(q - p) + r$

24. In January, Robert deposited $300 in his savings account. In February, he deposited $400. In March, he withdrew $200. Construct an operator equation to model the changes in Robert's account. Put a sequence of operators on the left side of the equation and the basic form of the composite operator on the right side. [2.3]

Simplify each expression. Compute as needed. [2.6]

25. $9 + x - 4$ **26.** $5 + x - 8$ **27.** $11 - x - 5$

28. $x - 15 + 3$ **29.** $y + 5 - 12$

30. What, by definition, is the product of 5 and 7? [3.1]

EXTEND YOUR SKILL

31. Explain why $\dfrac{5}{0}$ is undefined.   **32.** Explain why $\dfrac{0}{0}$ is undetermined.

33. Write 16 as many ways as possible in for form $a + b$, with $b \mid a$.

3.3 – RULES OF DIVISIBILITY

OBJECTIVE

Use simple rules for divisibility.

For several numbers, there is a simple test to check if it is a divisor of another number. The most commonly used rules check for divisibility by 2, 3, 5, and 10.

Divisibility

Rules

Divisible By	Test	Example
2	The last digit is divisible by 2.	138 is divisible by 2 because the last digit is 8, and 8 is divisible by 2.
3	The sum of the digits is divisible by 3.	84 is divisible by 3 because the sum of the digits is $8 + 4 = 12$, and 12 is divisible by 3.
5	The last digit is 0 or 5.	1,285 is divisible by 5 because the last digit is 5.
10	The last digit is 0.	43,210 is divisible by 10 because the last digit is 0.

Example 1   **Test for Divisibility**

Determine whether 165 *is divisible by* 2, 3, 5, *or* 10.

Number	Divisible?	Reason
2	no	The last digit is 5, and 5 is not divisible by 2.
3	yes	The sum of the digits is $1 + 6 + 5 = 12$, and 12 is divisible by 3.
5	yes	The last digit is 5.
10	no	The last digit is not 0.

The rules for divisibility are also useful in finding the factors of a number. When we find one factor, we can divide it into the number to obtain another factor.

Example 2   Find Factors

Find all the factors of 36.

We can make a chart that lists the potential factors and use division to find the other factor paired with it.

Factors of 36

Possible Divisors	Does it divide 36?	Factor Pairs
1	yes	$1 \cdot 36$
2	yes	$2 \cdot 18$
3	yes	$3 \cdot 12$
4	yes	$4 \cdot 9$
5	no	none
6	yes	$6 \cdot 6$

We don't have to check divisors greater than 6 in this case. For any factor greater than 6, the factor paired with it must be less than 6, and it would already appear in the list of factor pairs. Thus the factors of 36 are 1, 2, 3, 4, 6, 9, 12, 18, and 36.

EXERCISE 3.3
DEVELOP YOUR SKILL

Determine whether each number is divisible by 2, 3, 5 or 10.

1. 34   **2.** 35   **3.** 156

4. 270   **5.** 1403   **6.** 32,421

List all the factors of each number.

7. 50   **8.** 32

9. 84   **10.** 135

Maintain Your Skill

Solve each equation by using an invariant principle. [1.6]

11. What is x, if $7538 + 6159 = 7588 + x$?

12. What is x, if $8314 - 2756 = 8344 - x$?

Compute the basic form for each composite operator. [2.3]

13. $-12 + 7$	**14.** $+3 + 8$	**15.** $+10 - 17$	**16.** $-8 - 12$
17. $-2 + 5 - 3$	**18.** $+6 - 8 + 10$	**19.** $+4 - 7 + 8$	**20.** $-3 - 5 + 2$

Find the inverse of each operator. [2.3]

21. $+23$ **22.** -41

Do not compute, but write equivalent expressions without parentheses. Do not change the first term. When possible, give a second alternate form. [2.4]

23. $86 - (23 + 42)$ **24.** $47 + (25 - 18)$

25. $54 + (17 + 39)$ **26.** $22 - (35 - 26)$

For each equation, write the corresponding equation that is matched to it by the definition of division. [3.2]

27. $\dfrac{98}{7} = 14$ **28.** $xy = m + n$

29. $(b - s)d = x$ **30.** $\dfrac{a - b}{c} = d$

Extend Your Skill

31. Explain how to determine whether or not a number is divisible by 6.

32. Explain how to determine whether or not a number is divisible by 15.

3.4 – Order of Operations

OBJECTIVE

1. Use the order of operations.

Algebraic expressions often have a mixture of addition, subtraction, multiplication, and division operations. Special attention must be given to the order in which they are computed. Parentheses may be used, as in Lesson 1.4, to specify what is done first, what is next, and so on. Thus $3 + (4 \cdot 5)$ is computed by first multiplying 4 times 5, and then adding 3. But it is possible to use fewer parentheses, and thus simplify the notation, by adopting the following rule:

Order of Operations	Multiplication and division are computed before addition and subtraction, unless there are instructions otherwise.

Using this rule we see that $3 + 4 \cdot 5$ is computed as $3 + (4 \cdot 5)$ by first multiplying $4 \cdot 5$ even though this does not follow the left-to-right reading order. If it is required that adding or subtracting are to be done before multiplying or dividing, then parentheses must be used to establish this priority.

Example 1   **The Order of Operations**

$$3 + 4 \cdot 5 \ = \ 3 + 20 \ = \ 23 \qquad\qquad \text{Multiply, then add.}$$

$$(3 + 4) \cdot 5 \ = \ 7 \cdot 5 \ = \ 35 \qquad\qquad \text{Add, then multiply.}$$

$$3 \cdot (4 + 5) \ = \ 3 \cdot 9 \ = \ 27 \qquad\qquad \text{Add, then multiply.}$$

Note that the bar notation for quotients has the same effect as parentheses. The bar requires that division be done last. Thus $\frac{12+6}{2} = \frac{18}{2} = 9$. If the division sign $\div$ were to be used, then parentheses would be needed for the same order:

$$(12 + 6) \div 2 \ = \ 18 \div 2 \ = \ 9, \quad \text{but} \quad 12 + 6 \div 2 \ = \ 12 + 3 \ = \ 15.$$

When computing with products and quotients, work left to right. Thus

$$12 \div 3 \times 2 \ = \ (12 \div 3) \times 2$$
$$= \ 4 \times 2 \ = \ 8$$

But $12 \div (3 \times 2) \ = \ 12 \div 6 \ = \ 2.$

When more than one operation is used in an expression, the name given to the whole expression comes from the *last* operation used. Thus, $3 + 4 \cdot 5$ is a sum and $(3 + 4) \cdot 5$ is a product.

Example 2   **Name the Form and Compute**

Name each form and then compute the basic numeral.

(a) $3 + \dfrac{4 \cdot 6}{8}$ (b) $\dfrac{3+7}{3+2}$ (c) $25 - 4 \cdot 3$

(a) The last operation is addition, so this is a sum. We have
$$3 + \frac{4 \cdot 6}{8} = 3 + \frac{24}{8} = 3 + 3 = 6.$$

(b) This is a quotient. We have $\dfrac{3+7}{3+2} = \dfrac{10}{5} = 2.$

(c) This is a difference. We have $25 - 4 \cdot 3 = 25 - 12 = 13.$

EXERCISE 3.4

DEVELOP YOUR SKILL

Name each form (sum, difference, product, or quotient) and then compute the basic numeral.

1. $2 + 3 \cdot 5$

2. $4 \cdot 2 - 1$

3. $18 - 4 \cdot 2$

4. $3(4 + 5)$

5. $\dfrac{4 \cdot 8}{2}$

6. $4\left(\dfrac{8}{2}\right)$

7. $2 \cdot 3 + 4 \cdot 5$

8. $3 \cdot 5 + \dfrac{14}{7}$

9. $\left(\dfrac{5+7}{2}\right)5$

10. $\dfrac{6 + 4 \cdot 4}{2}$

MAINTAIN YOUR SKILL

Compute the basic form for the composite operator. [2.3]

11. $+ 12 - 15$

12. $+ 5 + 18$

13. $- 7 - 21$

14. $- 26 + 5$

Do not compute, but write an equivalent expression with parentheses around a sum or a difference. Do not change the first term. When possible, give a second alternate form. [2.4]

15. $18 - 2 - 10$

16. $5 + 13 - 17$

17. $9 + 22 - 6$

18. $15 - 9 + 3$

Construct a graphical model for each operator. [2.2, 3.1, 3.2]

19. $+5$ **20.** -6

21. $5(\ )$ **22.** $\dfrac{(\ )}{6}$

Indicate for what counting numbers each statement is true. When possible, list the four smallest values of x. [3.2]

23. 3 divides x **24.** x divides 3   **25.** x divides 6   **26.** 6 divides x

List all the factors of each number. [3.3]

27. 30   **28.** 38   **29.** 75   **30.** 98

EXTEND YOUR SKILL

31. What is there besides parentheses that can change the order of operations?

32. Explain how to determine the name of the form of an expression.

33. What counting number divides *every* counting number?

34. What counting number does *not* divide *any* counting numbers?

3.5 – PROPERTIES OF PRODUCTS AND QUOTIENTS

OBJECTIVE

1. Identify and use the commutative and associative principles for multiplication, and the distributive principle.

Multiplication, like addition, is **commutative**. But division, like subtraction, is not commutative. If x and y are counting numbers, then

$$x \cdot y = y \cdot x \ \text{ and}$$

$$x \div y \neq y \div x, \quad \text{unless } x = y.$$

Similarly, we find that multiplication is **associative** but division is not:

$$x \cdot (y \cdot z) = (x \cdot y) \cdot z, \ \text{ but}$$

$$x \div (y \div z) \neq (x \div y) \div z, \quad \text{unless } z = 1.$$

Our first example illustrates that division is not associative. When using compound quotients, the quotient with the shorter bar is computed first. This use of the division bar reduces the need for parentheses.

Example 1   **Division is Not Associative**

$8 \div (4 \div 2) = 8 \div 2 = 4$, but $(8 \div 4) \div 2 = 2 \div 2 = 1$. Using the vertical notation and the division bar we have

$$\cfrac{8}{\cfrac{4}{2}} = \frac{8}{2} = 4, \quad \text{but} \quad \cfrac{\cfrac{8}{4}}{2} = \frac{2}{2} = 1.$$

Since $4 \neq 1$, the division fails to be associative.

The interactions between multiplication/division and addition/subtraction are given by the **distributive principles**. We illustrate them with examples and then state the general rules.

Example 2   **The Distributive Principle**

(a) $2 \cdot (3 + 5) = 2 \cdot 8 = 16$

$(2 \cdot 3) + (2 \cdot 5) = 6 + 10 = 16$

Thus the *sum* $(2 \cdot 3) + (2 \cdot 5)$ is equal to the *product* $2 \cdot (3 + 5)$.

(b) $(9 - 2) \cdot 4 = 7 \cdot 4 = 28$

$(9 \cdot 4) - (2 \cdot 4) = 36 - 8 = 28$

Thus the *product* $(9 - 2) \cdot 4$ is equal to the *difference* $(9 \cdot 4) - (2 \cdot 4)$.

We can model the product in Example 2(a) by using two rows of markers, with 3 white markers and 5 black markers in each row. If we add the 3 and the 5 to get 8 and then double the 8 we have a total of $2(3 + 5) = 2 \cdot 8 = 16$ markers. If we double the number of white markers to get 6, and double the number of black markers to get 10, then the total is still $2 \cdot 3 + 2 \cdot 5 = 6 + 10 = 16$.

$$2(3 + 5) \qquad\qquad = 2(8) = 16$$

8 markers →

$$2 \cdot 3 \quad + \quad 2 \cdot 5 \qquad = 6 + 10 = 16$$

In Example 2(a), the multiplication by 2 in the product form is distributed (broken apart) and used twice in the sum form. We say that *multiplication distributes over addition*. In Example 2(b), the multiplication by 4 in the product form is distributed over the difference $9 - 2$ to give $9 \cdot 4 - 2 \cdot 4$. We say that *multiplication distributes over subtraction*.

Distributive Principles for Multiplication

If x, y and z are counting numbers, then

$$x(y + z) = xy + xz \quad \text{and} \quad (y + z)x = yx + zx.$$

Furthermore, if $y \geq z$, then

$$x(y - z) = xy - xz \quad \text{and} \quad (y - z)x = yx - zx.$$

In Examples 3 and 4, we see that division also distributes over addition and subtraction.

Example 3   **The Distributive Principle**

$$\frac{20 + 12}{4} = \frac{32}{4} = 8 \quad \text{and} \quad \frac{20}{4} + \frac{12}{4} = 5 + 3 = 8.$$

The *quotient* $\dfrac{20 + 12}{4}$ is equal to the *sum* $\dfrac{20}{4} + \dfrac{12}{4}$.

Example 4   **The Distributive Principle**

$$\frac{20 - 12}{4} = \frac{8}{4} = 2 \text{ and } \frac{20}{4} - \frac{12}{4} = 5 - 3 = 2$$

The *quotient* $\dfrac{20 - 12}{4}$ is equal to the *difference* $\dfrac{20}{4} - \dfrac{12}{4}$.

Distributive Principles for Division

If x, y and z are counting numbers with z dividing both x and y, then

$$\frac{x + y}{z} = \frac{x}{z} + \frac{y}{z}.$$

Furthermore, if $x \geq y$, then

$$\frac{x - y}{z} = \frac{x}{z} - \frac{y}{z}.$$

EXERCISE 3.5

DEVELOP YOUR SKILL

In Exercises 1 and 2, state whether the commutative or the associative principle is used to make the consecutive changes of form: (a) to (b), (b) to (c), etc.

1. (a) $2 \cdot [3 \cdot (4 \cdot 5)]$

    (b) $2 \cdot [(4 \cdot 5) \cdot 3]$

    (c) $[2 \cdot (4 \cdot 5)] \cdot 3$

    (d) $[2 \cdot (5 \cdot 4)] \cdot 3$

    (e) $[(2 \cdot 5) \cdot 4] \cdot 3$

    (f) $(2 \cdot 5)(4 \cdot 3)$

2. (a) $(w \cdot z)(y \cdot x)$

    (b) $(y \cdot x)(w \cdot z)$

    (c) $y \cdot [x \cdot (w \cdot z)]$

    (d) $[x \cdot (w \cdot z)] \cdot y$

    (e) $[(x \cdot w) \cdot z] \cdot y$

    (f) $[z \cdot (x \cdot w)] \cdot y$

Use distributive principles to replace each product or quotient by an equivalent sum or difference. Do not compute and do not use the commutative principle.

3. $6(5 + 3)$

4. $(100 - 4)3$

5. $\dfrac{24 - 16}{4}$

6. $8(x + y)$

7. $\dfrac{18 + 15}{3}$

8. $\dfrac{18 - 12}{m}$

Use distributive principles to replace each sum or difference by an equivalent product or quotient. Do not compute and do not use the commutative principle.

9. $(8)(5) - (8)(4)$

10. $\dfrac{8}{2} + \dfrac{6}{2}$

11. $7y - 3y$

12. $3x + 3y$

13. $\dfrac{x}{y} - \dfrac{z}{y}$

14. $ab - ac$

15. $4a - 4b$

16. $5a + 6a$

MAINTAIN YOUR SKILL

Compute the basic numeral for each expression that is defined as a counting number. Otherwise, write "not defined." [1.4]

17. $16 - 8 - 2$

18. $4 - 6 + 10$

19. $5 + 7 - 9$

20. $15 - 3 + 2$

Solve each equation using an invariant principle. [1.6]

21. $2574 + x = 2674 + 3829$

22. $x - 4203 = 8652 - 4223$

Construct a vector model for the composite operators. [2.3]

23. $-2 + 3 + 2$

24. $+3 - 1 - 3$

Do not compute, but write an equivalent expression with parentheses around a sum or a difference. Do not change the first term. When possible, give a second alternate form. [2.4]

25. $17 - 5 - 3$

26. $25 - 3 + 10$

27. $14 + 7 - 11$

28. $31 - 10 + 4$

29. $35 + 17 - 13$

30. $28 + 12 + 33$

EXTEND YOUR SKILL

31. Give an example of a quotient in which the dividend itself is a quotient. Then compute the basic numeral.

32. Give an example of a quotient in which the divisor itself is a quotient. Then compute the basic numeral.

3.6 – INVARIANT PRINCIPLES FOR PRODUCTS AND QUOTIENTS

OBJECTIVE

1. Use the invariant principles for products and quotients.

One way to model the product $4 \cdot 5$ is to display a rectangular array of markers arranged in 4 rows and 5 columns. We readily see that there are $4 \cdot 5 = 20$ markers in all.

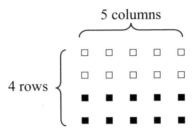

5 columns

4 rows

If the top 2 rows are moved to the right and down, then the number of rows is divided by 2 and the number of columns is multiplied by 2. The total number of markers, however, remains the same.

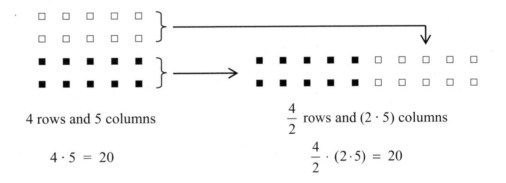

4 rows and 5 columns

$4 \cdot 5 = 20$

$\dfrac{4}{2}$ rows and $(2 \cdot 5)$ columns

$\dfrac{4}{2} \cdot (2 \cdot 5) = 20$

This illustrates the invariant principle for products: if one factor in a product is divided by a number and the other factor is multiplied by the same number, then the product remains the same.

Invariant Principle for Products

Let x, y and z be counting numbers.

If z divides x, then $xy = \left(\dfrac{x}{z}\right)(yz)$. If z divides y, then $xy = (xz)\left(\dfrac{y}{z}\right)$.

A similar property applies to quotients, but this time both the dividend and the divisor change in the same way. For example, when 12 is divided into 6 parts, each part contains 2:

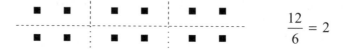

$$\frac{12}{6} = 2$$

If we just consider the top half of the diagram we see that when $\frac{12}{2}$ is divided by $\frac{6}{2}$, each part still contains 2:

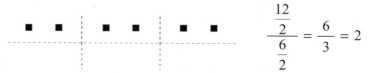

$$\frac{\dfrac{12}{2}}{\dfrac{6}{2}} = \frac{6}{3} = 2$$

Similarly, if we start with 6 and divide it into 3 parts, each part will contain 2:

$$\frac{6}{3} = 2$$

If we double this diagram we see that when $2 \cdot 6$ is divided by $2 \cdot 3$, each part still contains 2:

$$\frac{2 \cdot 6}{2 \cdot 3} = \frac{12}{6} = 2$$

This illustrates the invariant principle for quotients: if both the dividend and the divisor in a quotient are divided by the same number, the quotient remains the same. Likewise, both the dividend and the divisor may be multiplied by the same number and the quotient remains the same.

Let x, y and z be counting numbers. If y divides x and z divides both x and y,

then $\dfrac{x}{y} = \dfrac{\dfrac{x}{z}}{\dfrac{y}{z}}$. If y divides x, then $\dfrac{x}{y} = \dfrac{x \cdot z}{y \cdot z}$.

Example 1   **Use an Invariant Principle**

(a) If $35 \cdot 30 = x \cdot 150$, what is x?   (b) If $\dfrac{x}{24} = \dfrac{120}{8}$, what is x?

Let us approach this problem like we did Example 2 in Section 1.6. We want to see what is different between the two sides of each equation. In (a), we note that 30 can be multiplied by 5 to get 150. Thus, 35 must be divided by 5 in order to preserve the same product. That is, $x = 35 \div 5 = 7$.

In (b), we need to look from right to left since the variable x is on the left. In moving from 8 to 24 in the divisors, we have multiplied by 3. To keep the same value for both quotients, in moving from 120 to x we must also multiply by 3. That is, $x = 120 \cdot 3 = 360$.

Study Tip:

Products behave like sums: if one term gets larger, the other term must get smaller to maintain the same product.

Quotients behave like differences: both terms change in the same way.

EXERCISE 3.6

DEVELOP YOUR SKILL

Solve each equation by using an invariant principle.

1. $5 \cdot 28 = 10 \cdot x$

2. $55 \cdot 20 = x \cdot 100$

3. $100 \cdot x = 25 \cdot 48$

4. $\dfrac{115}{5} = \dfrac{x}{10}$

5. $\dfrac{x}{100} = \dfrac{1200}{25}$

6. $\dfrac{x}{14} = \dfrac{140}{28}$

MAINTAIN YOUR SKILL

Use the composition of operators to write an equivalent single operator. [2.3]

7. $+ m - n$, where $n \geq m$

8. $- n + m$, where $m \geq n$

Do not compute, but write equivalent expressions without parentheses. Do not change the first term. When possible, give a second alternate form. [2.5]

9. $36 + (14 - 6)$

10. $62 - (21 + 13)$

11. $29 - (34 - 20)$

12. $15 + (43 - 27)$

13. List all x such that x divides 30 and 5 divides x. [3.2]

14. (a) What is the smallest x such that x divides both 9 and 12? [3.2]

(b) What is the largest x such that x divides both 9 and 12?

(c) What is the smallest nonzero x such that 9 and 12 both divide x?

Determine whether each number is divisible by 2, 3, 5 or 10. [3.3]

15. 135   **16.** 1160

Name each form (sum, difference, product, or quotient) and then compute the basic numeral. [3.4]

17. $15 - 3 \cdot 4$ **18.** $\dfrac{6 \cdot 2}{3}$ **19.** $5\left(\dfrac{9+3}{4}\right)$ **20.** $(5-2)(7)$

Use distributive principles to replace each product or quotient by an equivalent sum or difference and to replace each sum or difference by an equivalent product or quotient. Do not compute and do not use the commutative principle. [3.5]

21. $7(12 + 15)$ **22.** $(7)(3) - (4)(3)$ **23.** $\dfrac{45}{5} - \dfrac{20}{5}$

24. $\dfrac{18+12}{3}$ **25.** $2x + 2y$ **26.** $5x + 7x$

27. $\dfrac{ab+c}{d}$ **28.** $\dfrac{a}{3x} - \dfrac{by}{3x}$ **29.** $yw + 3xw$

30. $(ab)(x - y)$

EXTEND YOUR SKILL

31. If the length of a rectangle is divided by 3 and the area of the rectangle is to remain the same, what must be done to the width? What mathematical principle have you used in your answer?

32. The ideal gas law states that the pressure (P), the temperature (T), and the volume (V) of an ideal gas are related by the formula $kP = \dfrac{T}{V}$, where k is a constant. If the temperature of an ideal gas is multiplied by 2, what must happen to the volume in order to keep the same pressure? What mathematical principle have you used in your answer?

CHAPTER 3 REVIEW

1. Construct a graphical model for the expansion operator $7(\ )$. [3.1]

2. Construct a graphical model for the contraction operator $\dfrac{(\ )}{6}$. [3.2]

For each equation, write the corresponding equation that is matched to it by the definition of division. [3.2]

3. $\dfrac{56}{7} = 8$ **4.** $5x = y$ **5.** $\dfrac{m}{s} = 24$

Indicate for what counting numbers each statement is true. When possible, list the four smallest values of x. [3.2]

6. 6 divides x **7.** x divides 10   **8.** 0 divides x **9.** x divides 0

Indicate for what counting numbers each quotient is defined. When possible, list the four smallest values of x. [3.2]

10. $\dfrac{30}{x}$ **11.** $\dfrac{x}{30}$

Determine whether each number is divisible by 2, 3, 5, or 10. [3.3]

12. 1350   **13.** 2781   **14.** 8735

Name each form and then compute the basic numeral. [3.4]

15. $4(8 - 3)$ **16.** $5 \cdot 7 + \dfrac{8}{2}$

17. $2 + 3 \cdot 5$ **18.** $4 \cdot 5 - 2$

19. $3\left(\dfrac{12}{4}\right)$ **20.** $\dfrac{3 \cdot 12}{4}$

21. $\dfrac{21}{3} - \dfrac{20}{5}$ **22.** $15 - (3 + 4)$

Use distributive principles to replace each product or quotient by an equivalent sum or difference, and to replace each sum or difference by an equivalent product or quotient. Do <u>not</u> compute and do not use the commutative principle. [3.5]

23. $4x + 4y$ **24.** $\dfrac{12}{2} - \dfrac{m}{2}$

25. $m(ax - b)$ **26.** $\dfrac{a + b}{xy}$

27. $(x + 5)y$ **28.** $7a - 5a$

Solve each equation by using an invariant principle. [3.6]

29. $x \cdot 4 = 424 \cdot 8$ **30.** $\dfrac{x}{240} = \dfrac{72}{24}$

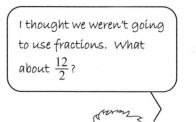

Chapter 4 – Expansions and Contractions

4.1 – COMPOSITION OF TWO EXPANSIONS OR TWO CONTRACTIONS

OBJECTIVE

1. Combine two expansions or two contractions and model their actions by comparing line segments.

The compositions of expansions and contractions follow a set of rules that are very similar to the rules for increases and decreases. (See Lessons 2.2 and 2.3.) In this lesson we look at the composition of two expansions or two contractions. In Lesson 4.2 we consider how they interact with each other.

<u>Case 1</u> The composition of two expansions.

For example, consider the effect of multiplying by 4 and then multiplying by 3.

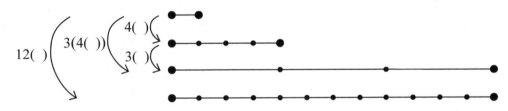

We see that multiplying by 4 and then multiplying by 3 is the same as multiplying by their product 12.

$$3(4(\ )) = (3 \cdot 4)(\ )$$

Furthermore, if we multiply first by 3 and then by 4, we obtain the same result.

Thus,

$$3(4(\ )) = (3 \cdot 4)(\ ) = (4 \cdot 3)(\ ) = 4(3(\ )).$$

Here is the general rule:

<u>Case 1</u>   An expansion by a and an expansion by b.

The composite of two expansions (multiplying by a and multiplying by b) is equivalent to the expansion resulting from multiplying by the product ab (or multiplying by ba). The successive expansions can be in either order.

$$b(a(\ )) = ab(\ ) = ba(\ ) = a(b(\ ))$$

<u>Case 2</u>   The composition of two contractions.

For example, consider the effect of dividing by 3 and then dividing by 2.

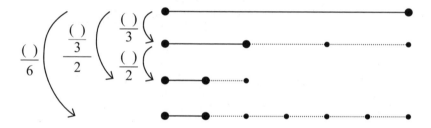

We see that dividing by 3 and then dividing by 2 is the same as dividing by their product 6.

$$\frac{\frac{(\ )}{3}}{2} = \frac{(\ )}{3 \cdot 2}$$

Furthermore, if we divide first by 2 and then by 3, the result is the same.

Thus,

$$\frac{\frac{(\ )}{3}}{2} = \frac{(\ )}{3\cdot 2} = \frac{(\ )}{2\cdot 3} = \frac{\frac{(\ )}{2}}{3}$$

Here is the general rule:

Case 2   A contraction by a and a contraction by b.

The composite of two contractions (dividing by a and dividing by b) is equivalent to the contraction resulting from dividing by the product ab (or dividing by ba). The successive contractions can be in either order.

$$\frac{\frac{(\ )}{a}}{b} = \frac{(\ )}{ab} = \frac{(\ )}{ba} = \frac{\frac{(\ )}{b}}{a}$$

Example 1   **The Composition of Operators**

Write an equivalent operator in basic form.

(a) $5(3(\ ))$ (b) $\dfrac{\frac{(\ )}{4}}{2}$

(a) The two expansions work together to give a larger expansion:

$$5(3(\ )) = (5\cdot 3)(\ ) = 15(\ )$$

(b) The two contractions work together to give a larger contraction:

$$\frac{\frac{(\ )}{4}}{2} = \frac{(\ )}{4\cdot 2} = \frac{(\ )}{8}$$

In Case 1 we saw that the order of two expansions can be interchanged. Likewise in Case 2, the order of two contractions can be interchanged. This is another example of the commutative principle: two successive expansions (or contractions) commute with each other.

Example 2   **The Commutative Principle**

Use commutativity to interchange the order of the two operators.

(a) 6(4( ))   (b) $\dfrac{\dfrac{(\ )}{3}}{7}$

(a) The expression 6(4( )) tells us to multiply by 4 and then multiply by 6. If we interchange the order, we multiply first by 6 and then by 4. The operator looks like this: 4(6( )).

(b) This expression says to divide by 3 and then divide by 7. If we divide first by 7 and then by 3 the operator looks like this:

$$\dfrac{\dfrac{(\ )}{7}}{3}$$

Study Tip:

When using parentheses, we start on the inside and work out. That's why 6(4( )) means multiply first by 4 and then by 6.

We may summarize the composition of two expansions or two contractions as follows:

Composition of Two Expansions or Two Contractions

The composition of two expansions or two contractions work together to give a stronger composite change of the same kind. Multiply their magnitudes. The order of the two operators can be commuted and yield the same result.

EXERCISE 4.1

DEVELOP YOUR SKILL

Construct a graphical model for the composition of the operators.

1. 4(2( ))

2. $\dfrac{\dfrac{(\ )}{2}}{4}$

Write an equivalent operator in basic form.

3. $5(6(\ ))$
4. $m(n(\ ))$
5. $\dfrac{\dfrac{(\ )}{3}}{4}$
6. $\dfrac{\dfrac{(\ )}{m}}{n}$

Use commutativity to interchange the order of the two operators.

7. $5(6(\ ))$
8. $m(n(\ ))$
9. $\dfrac{\dfrac{(\ )}{3}}{4}$
10. $\dfrac{\dfrac{(\ )}{m}}{n}$

MAINTAIN YOUR SKILL

For each equation, write the corresponding equation that is matched to it by the definition of subtraction or the definition of division. [1.3, 3.2]

11. $64 - 16 = 48$

12. $10 + 15 = 25$

13. $\dfrac{64}{16} = 4$

14. $(10)(15) = 150$

Do not compute, but write equivalent expressions without parentheses. Do not change the first term. When possible, give a second alternate form. [2.5]

15. $42 - (14 + 15)$

16. $23 - (35 - 24)$

17. $15 + (28 - 26)$

18. $18 + (12 + 35)$

Simplify each expression. Compute as needed. [2.6]

19. $12 + x - 5$

20. $7 + x - 10$

21. $x - 17 + 4$

22. $14 - y - 6$

23. $y + 3 - 9$

24. $8 - y + 7$

Name each form (sum, difference, product, or quotient) and then compute the basic numeral. [3.4]

25. $4 \cdot 6 - 5$

26. $10 + 3 \cdot 7$

27. $5(12 - 7)$

28. $4 \cdot 5 + 3 \cdot 5$

29. $3\left(\dfrac{12 - 4}{4}\right)$

30. $\dfrac{6 + 3 \cdot 4}{3}$

EXTEND YOUR SKILL

31. Explain how to find the magnitude of the combined change when you take the composition of two contractions.

32. Illustrate the commutative principle by applying the operators $\dfrac{(\ )}{2}$ and $\dfrac{(\ )}{3}$ to the operand 18.

4.2 – COMPOSITION OF AN EXPANSION AND A CONTRACTION

OBJECTIVE

1. Combine expansions and contractions and model their actions by comparing line segments.

The last lesson showed how to combine two expansions or two contractions: the result is a larger change of the same kind. When combining an expansion with a contraction, the two changes work against each other, so the composite will be smaller than either of the individual changes.

<u>Case 3</u>   The composition of an expansion and a contraction, where the expansion is larger.

For example, consider the effect of multiplying by 6 and then dividing by 2. Since the expansion is stronger than the contraction, we expect the combined change to be an expansion.

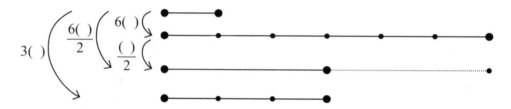

We see that multiplying by 6 and then dividing by 2 is the same as multiplying by 3. Where does this 3 come from? It is the larger magnitude 6 divided by the smaller magnitude 2.

$$\frac{6(\ )}{2} = \frac{6}{2}(\ )$$

Furthermore, if we first divide by 2 and then multiply by 6, the result is the same.

$$6\left(\frac{(\ )}{2}\right)\left(\begin{array}{c}\frac{(\ )}{2}\\6(\ )\end{array}\right.$$

Thus,

$$\frac{6(\ )}{2} = \frac{6}{2}(\ ) = 6\left(\frac{(\ )}{2}\right)$$

Here is the general rule:

<u>Case 3</u> An expansion by a and a contraction by b, where b divides a.

The composite of an expansion (multiplying by a) and a contraction (dividing by b), where b divides a, is equivalent to the expansion resulting from multiplying by $\frac{a}{b}$. The successive changes can be in either order.

$$\frac{a(\ )}{b} = \frac{a}{b}(\ ) = a\left(\frac{(\ )}{b}\right)$$

<u>Case 4</u> The composition of an expansion and a contraction, where the contraction is larger.

For example, consider the effect of multiplying by 3 and then dividing by 6. Since the contraction is stronger than the expansion, we expect the combined change to be a contraction.

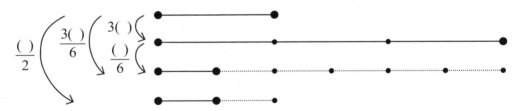

We see that multiplying by 3 and then dividing by 6 is the same as dividing by 2. The magnitude 2 of the composition comes from taking the larger magnitude 6 and dividing by the smaller magnitude 3.

$$\frac{3(\ )}{6} = \frac{(\ )}{\frac{6}{3}}$$

Furthermore, if we first divide by 6 and then multiply by 3, the result is the same.

$$3\left(\frac{(\ )}{6}\right)\left(\begin{matrix} \frac{(\ )}{6} \\ 3(\ ) \end{matrix}\right.$$

Thus,

$$\frac{3(\ )}{6} = \frac{(\ )}{\frac{6}{3}} = 3\left(\frac{(\ )}{6}\right).$$

Here is the general rule:

<u>Case 4</u> An expansion by a and a contraction by b, where a divides b.

The composite of an expansion (multiplying by a) and a contraction (dividing by b), where a divides b, is equivalent to the contraction resulting from dividing by $\frac{b}{a}$. The successive changes can be in either order.

$$\frac{a(\ )}{b} = \frac{(\ )}{\frac{b}{a}} = a\left(\frac{(\ )}{b}\right)$$

We may summarize the results from the last two lessons as follows:

Composition of Expansions and Contractions

1. Like changes help each other to give a stronger composite change of the same kind. Multiply their magnitudes.

2. Expansions and contractions work against each other. The stronger change will dominate the weaker change and determine the kind of composite change. Divide the larger magnitude by the smaller.

3. Expansions and contractions commute with each other and with themselves. If two successive changes are made in either order, the resultant change is the same.

Example 1   **Find a Composite Operator**

Compute the basic form for each composite operator, when possible. If the basic form is not yet defined, write "not defined."

(a) $4\left(\dfrac{(\ )}{20}\right)$ (b) $\dfrac{\frac{(\ )}{8}}{4}$ (c) $\dfrac{20(\ )}{5}$ (d) $\dfrac{4(\ )}{3}$

(a) The contraction $\dfrac{(\ )}{20}$ and the expansion $4(\ )$ are working against each other. The contraction is stronger: $4\left(\dfrac{(\ )}{20}\right) = \dfrac{(\ )}{\frac{20}{4}} = \dfrac{(\ )}{5}$.

(b) The two contractions $\dfrac{(\ )}{8}$ and $\dfrac{(\ )}{4}$ work together to give a larger contraction: $\dfrac{\frac{(\ )}{8}}{4} = \dfrac{(\ )}{8 \cdot 4} = \dfrac{(\ )}{32}$.

(c) The expansion $20(\ )$ and the contraction $\dfrac{(\ )}{5}$ are working against each other. The expansion is stronger: $\dfrac{20(\ )}{5} = \dfrac{20}{5}(\ ) = 4(\ )$.

(d) $\dfrac{4(\ )}{3}$ is not defined yet, since 3 does not divide 4 and 4 does not divide 3.

Caution:

The answer to part (c) is an expansion 4( ), not just the number 4.

Example 2   **The Commutative Principle**

Use commutativity to interchange the order of the two operators.

(a) $4\left(\dfrac{(\ )}{20}\right)$ (b) $\dfrac{\frac{(\ )}{8}}{4}$ (c) $\dfrac{30(\ )}{10}$

(a) The expression $4\left(\dfrac{(\ )}{20}\right)$ tells us to divide by 20 and then multiply by 4. If we interchange the order, we multiply first by 4 and then divide by 20. The operator looks like this: $\dfrac{4(\ )}{20}$.

(b) The expression $\dfrac{\frac{(\ )}{8}}{4}$ tells us to divide by 8 and then divide by 4. If we interchange the order, we divide first by 4 and then by 8. The operator looks like this: $\dfrac{\frac{(\ )}{4}}{8}$.

(c) The expression $\dfrac{30(\ )}{10}$ tells us to multiply by 30 and then divide by 10. If we interchange the order, we first divide by 10 and then multiply by 30. We obtain $30\left(\dfrac{(\ )}{10}\right)$.

Study Tip:

The inverse of

$n(\ )$ is $\dfrac{(\ )}{n}$

and the inverse of

$\dfrac{(\ )}{n}$ is $n(\ )$.

The operators $n(\ )$ and $\dfrac{(\ )}{n}$ are **inverses**: each will undo the change made by the other. Their composite is an identity operator in one of the three forms: $1(\ )$, $(\ )1$, or $\dfrac{(\ )}{1}$. Thus if $n \neq 0$, then $\dfrac{nx}{n} = x$. Furthermore, if $n\,|\,x$, then $n\left(\dfrac{x}{n}\right) = x$.

Example 3   **Find an Inverse Operator**

Write the inverse of each operator.

(a) $5(\ )$ (b) $\dfrac{(\ )}{7}$ (c) $+6$ (d) -8

(a) The inverse of multiplying by 5 is dividing by 5: $\dfrac{(\ )}{5}$.

(b) The inverse of dividing by 7 is multiplying by 7: $7(\ )$.

(c) The inverse of adding 6 is subtracting 6: -6.

(d) The inverse of subtracting 8 is adding 8: $+8$.

The set of all possible multiplication and division operators will be called the multiplication-division **family** of operators. Likewise, the set of all possible addition and subtraction operators will be called the addition-subtraction family. Note that the composition of operators has been limited to combinations within a family. Indeed, two operators from different families will *not* have a composite that is a member of either family.

For example, the operator $3(\ ) + 4$ represents an expansion (multiplying by 3) followed by an increase (adding 4). But there is no single expansion or increase that makes the same change. We will look more carefully at this kind of combination in the next lesson.

EXERCISE 4.2

DEVELOP YOUR SKILL

Construct a graphical model for the composition of the operators.

1. $4\left(\dfrac{(\ )}{2}\right)$

2. $\dfrac{2(\ )}{4}$

Write an equivalent operator in basic form, when this is defined. If this basic form is not yet defined, write "not defined."

3. $\dfrac{20(\ )}{10}$

4. $3(7(\ ))$

5. $\dfrac{3(\ )}{7}$

6. $2\left(\dfrac{(\ )}{8}\right)$

7. $\dfrac{\dfrac{(\ )}{7}}{3}$

8. $18\left(\dfrac{(\ )}{9}\right)$

9. $\dfrac{3(\ )}{12}$

10. $5\left(\dfrac{(\ )}{4}\right)$

Use commutativity to interchange the order of the two operators.

11. $\dfrac{3(\ )}{15}$

12. $\dfrac{\dfrac{(\ )}{7}}{9}$

13. $6\left(\dfrac{(\ )}{18}\right)$

14. $3(5(\ ))$

15. $r\left(\dfrac{(\ )}{s}\right)$

16. $\dfrac{m(\ )}{n}$

Write the inverse of each operator.

17. $2(\ )$

18. $\dfrac{(\ )}{6}$

19. -14

20. $+32$

MAINTAIN YOUR SKILL

21. As the storm was approaching, the tide rose 2 feet. Then it rose 5 feet more, and then an additional 4 feet. After the storm passed, it initially fell 6 feet. Construct an operator equation to model the changes in the tide over this period of time. [2.3]

22. (a) What is the smallest x such that x divides both 18 and 24? [3.2]

(b) What is the largest x such that x divides both 18 and 24?

(c) What is the smallest nonzero x such that 18 and 24 both divide x?

Determine whether each number is divisible by 2, 3, 5 or 10. [3.3]

23. 12,345

24. 24,680

25. 35,241

26. 173,452

Solve each equation by using an invariant principle. [3.6]

27. $24 \cdot 25 = 12 \cdot x$

28. $33 \cdot x = 11 \cdot 30$

29. $\dfrac{75}{x} = \dfrac{25}{5}$

30. $\dfrac{80}{16} = \dfrac{x}{4}$

EXTEND YOUR SKILL

31. Explain how to find the magnitude of the combined change when you take the composition of an expansion and a contraction.

32. Illustrate the commutative principle by applying the operators $6(\ )$ and $\dfrac{(\ )}{2}$ to the operand 12.

4.3 – BUILDING COMPOUND EXPRESSIONS

OBJECTIVE

1. Build compound expressions one step at a time.

Sometimes algebraic expressions contain several different operations. In analyzing the compound expression it is helpful to think of it as having been built up one step at a time by a sequence of operators. The operators we have seen so far are

$$+n, \quad n+, \quad -n, \quad n(\ ), \quad (\ )n, \quad \text{and} \quad \dfrac{(\ )}{n} \quad \text{when } n \neq 0.$$

We begin by applying a sequence of operators to an operand to see how a compound expression may be constructed.

Example 1   **Construct an Expression**

Construct the form that results when the operand 12 is operated on by the operators -4, $\frac{()}{2}$, $+5$, *and* $3(\ )$, *in that order. Do not compute.*

Start with 12. Then write $12 - 4$, then $\frac{12 - 4}{2}$, then $\frac{12 - 4}{2} + 5$, and finally $3\left(\frac{12 - 4}{2} + 5\right)$.

In practice, we often want to work backwards from what we did in Example 1. That is, we are given a compound expression and we wish to develop it by applying a sequence of operators to a single operand. To do this, we begin at the inside and work out, remembering the order of operations.

Remember the order of operations:

Multiplication and division are computed before addition and subtraction, unless directed otherwise by parentheses.

Example 2   **Analyze an Expression**

Analyze each expression by stating an operand and then listing a sequence of basic operators that can be joined one at a time to produce it.

  (a) $5 \cdot 7 - 4$ (b) $m + \dfrac{x}{y}$ (c) $u\left(\frac{w}{x} - y\right) + z$

(a) We do multiplication before subtraction, so we start with $5 \cdot 7$. There are two choices: use 5 as the operand and apply the operators $\cdot\, 7$ and -4, or use 7 as the operand and apply the operators $5 \cdot$ and -4.

(b) Division is done before addition, so we must start with the operand x and apply the operators $\dfrac{()}{y}$ and $m+$, in that order.

(c) The initial operand must have been w. The operators are $\dfrac{()}{x}$, $-y$, $u(\ )$, and $+z$, in that order.

EXERCISE 4.3

DEVELOP YOUR SKILL

In Exercises 1 – 4, an operand number is given, followed by operators to be used in succession in the order stated. Construct this form. If the form defines a counting number, then compute this number. If it does not, write "not defined."

1. $5; +3, \dfrac{(\ )}{2}, -1$

2. $7; (\ )2, +1, \dfrac{(\ )}{3}$

3. $6; +3, 2(\ ), \dfrac{(\ )}{3}$

4. $12; \dfrac{(\ )}{2}, -7, +3$

Analyze each expression by stating an operand and then listing a sequence of basic operators that can be joined one at a time to produce the given expression. If more than one operand and sequence of operators can be used, give the alternate possibilities.

5. $13 - 5$

6. $13 + 5$

7. $4 + 3 \cdot 5$

8. $\dfrac{12 - 3}{3} + 3$

9. $\dfrac{32}{8}$

10. $\dfrac{x + y}{m}$

11. $w(a - b)$

12. $mx + b$

13. $a + \dfrac{b}{c}$

MAINTAIN YOUR SKILL

Use an invariant principle to write an equivalent sum or difference that is easier to compute. Then compute. [1.6]

14. $294 + 147$

15. $421 - 395$

Construct a vector model for the composition of the operators. [2.3]

16. $+6 - 8$

17. $-4 + 7$

Write the composition of the two given operators as an equivalent single operator. [2.3 and 4.2]

18. $+x - y$, if $x \geq y$

19. $+x - y$, if $y \geq x$

20. $\dfrac{x(\ )}{y}$, if y divides x

21. $\dfrac{x(\ )}{y}$, if x divides y

Do not compute, but write equivalent expressions without parentheses. Do not change the first term. When possible, give a second alternate form. [2.5]

22. $47 - (52 - 35)$

23. $18 + (31 - 27)$

24. $56 + (23 - 15)$

25. $38 - (12 + 9)$

Use distributive principles to replace the product by an equivalent difference and to replace the sums by an equivalent quotient or product. Do not compute and do not use the commutative principle. [3.5]

26. $(12 - 7)5$

27. $\dfrac{15}{3} + \dfrac{27}{3}$

28. $8x + 3x$

Construct a graphical model for the composition of the operators. [4.2]

29. $\dfrac{3(\;)}{6}$

30. $\dfrac{6(\;)}{3}$

EXTEND YOUR SKILL

31. Explain how to find the original operand in a compound expression.

32. When taking the composition of an expansion and a contraction, what determines the kind of combined change?

4.4 – CANCELING OPERATORS

OBJECTIVE

1. Cancel operators.

In Lesson 2.2 we saw that the operators $+n$ and $-n$ are inverse to each other. That is, when one is applied immediately after the other, the combined result is no change. The operators $+n$ and $-n$ are called **additive inverses** because their composition is equivalent to the additive identity operator $+0$.

In Lesson 4.2 we saw that the operators $n(\;)$ and $\dfrac{(\;)}{n}$ are also inverses to each other. Again, when one is applied immediately after the other, the combined result is no change. The operators $n(\;)$ and $\dfrac{(\;)}{n}$ are called **multiplicative inverses** because their composition is equivalent to the multiplicative identity $1(\;)$.

It must be kept in mind that two operators can be inverse to each other, and hence undo the changes made by each other, only when both are members of the same family. In Example 1 we simplify several expressions by the removal of two inverse operators that are joined in immediate succession. This process is called **canceling** the operators.

Example 1   **Canceling Operators**

(a) $7 + 4 - 4 = 7$ In general, $x + y - y = x$.

(b) $7 - 4 + 4 = 7$ In general, if $y \leq x$, then $x - y + y = x$.

(c) $\dfrac{4 \cdot 7}{4} = 7$ In general, if $y \neq 0$, then $\dfrac{y(x)}{y} = x$.

(d) $4\left(\dfrac{12}{4}\right) = 12$ In general, if y divides x, then $y\left(\dfrac{x}{y}\right) = x$.

It is operators, but never numbers, that cancel each other. If only the 4's are removed from $\dfrac{4 \cdot 7}{4}$, the result is $\dfrac{\cdot 7}{}$, which is nonsense. It is the operators $4 \cdot$ and $\dfrac{(\,)}{4}$ that can be canceled to get 7. Dividing by 4 undoes (cancels) the multiplying by 4.

Canceling

Operators

In order to cancel two operators in an expression, the operators must:

  (1)   Be inverses of each other.

  (2)   Occur in immediate succession.

If inverse operators such as $+ n$ and $- n$ occur in an expression, but they are not used in succession, it is sometimes possible to rearrange the order of operations and then cancel them. This rearranging can be done by using the commutative and associative properties.

Example 2   **Simplify an Expression by Canceling Operators**

Simplify each expression, if possible.

  (a) $\dfrac{x \cdot 5 \cdot y}{5}$ (b) $7 + x - 7$ (c) $\dfrac{x + 5}{5} - 5.$

(a) We have $\dfrac{x \cdot 5 \cdot y}{5} = \dfrac{5 \cdot x \cdot y}{5} = \dfrac{5(x \cdot y)}{5} = xy$. Here we have used both the commutative and the associative properties.

(b) By replacing $7 + x$ with $x + 7$ we obtain $7 + x - 7 = x + 7 - 7 = x$.

(c) No cancellation is possible in $\dfrac{x+5}{5} - 5$. The operators $+ 5$ and $\dfrac{(\;)}{5}$ are not inverses. While $+ 5$ and $- 5$ are inverse operators, they are not used in succession. The operator $\dfrac{(\;)}{5}$ is used in between $+ 5$ and $- 5$, and does not commute with either of them.

EXERCISE 4.4

DEVELOP YOUR SKILL

Simplify each expression by canceling inverse operators. If no simpler form is possible, write "not possible."

1. $x + 6 - 6$

2. $\dfrac{3 \cdot (x + y)}{3}$

3. $x + r - s - x$

4. $\dfrac{8x}{x}$

5. $\dfrac{m}{3} + 3$

6. $6 + z - z$

7. $\dfrac{6(a + b)}{6}$

8. $\dfrac{r + 2}{s - 2}$

9. $\dfrac{m + 7}{7}$

10. $\dfrac{24}{y} - y$

11. $\dfrac{(m + n)(m - n)}{m + n}$

12. $6 - \dfrac{t}{6}$

MAINTAIN YOUR SKILL

Name each form (sum, difference, product, or quotient) and then compute the basic numeral. [2.5]

13. $7 + \dfrac{2 \cdot 6}{3}$

14. $50 - (3)(6 + 4)$

15. $6\left(\dfrac{5 + 10}{3} \right)$

16. $\dfrac{15 \cdot 2}{3}$

17. $5(18 - 3 \cdot 2)$

18. $\dfrac{18}{2} - \dfrac{15}{3}$

19. $4 \cdot 5 + 5 \cdot 6$

20. $20 - 3 \cdot 2$

Use commutativity to interchange the order of the two operators. [4.2]

21. $7\left(\dfrac{(\ )}{20}\right)$

22. $\dfrac{\dfrac{(\ )}{3}}{5}$

23. $\dfrac{3(\ )}{8}$

24. $4(7(\ ))$

Write an equivalent operator in basic form, when this is defined. If this basic form is not yet defined, write "not defined." [4.2]

25. $2\left(\dfrac{(\ )}{14}\right)$

26. $\dfrac{4(\ )}{5}$

27. $\dfrac{15(\ )}{3}$

28. $\dfrac{\dfrac{(\ )}{4}}{5}$

29. $10\left(\dfrac{(\ )}{2}\right)$

30. $4(5(\ ))$

EXTEND YOUR SKILL

31. Explain what it is that is canceled when simplifying $\dfrac{5x}{5}$ to x.

32. If inverse operators are not used in immediate succession, can they be canceled? Explain your answer.

4.5 – SIMPLIFYING EXPRESSIONS

OBJECTIVE

1. Simplify compound expressions.

We now have a number of tools available to us to use in simplifying an expression. When two operators from the same family are used in succession, their composition can be computed. If they are inverses of each other and of the same magnitude they can be cancelled.

The commutative principle can be useful in several ways to change the order of operations. For example, in the expression $7 + x - 5$, the sum $7 + x$ can be commuted to $x + 7$ so that the increase of 7 and the decrease of 5 can be combined:

$$7 + x - 5 = x + 7 - 5 = x + 2.$$

Alternatively, we could have commuted the $+ x$ (an increase of x) and the $- 5$ (a decrease of 5) and then computed $7 - 5$:

$$7 + x - 5 = 7 - 5 + x = 2 + x.$$

The commutativity of contractions can be used to change

$$\frac{\frac{15}{x}}{5} \quad \text{into} \quad \frac{\frac{15}{5}}{x} \quad \text{and then compute to get} \quad \frac{3}{x}.$$

Sometimes, an invariant principle is helpful in simplifying, as we see in Example 1.

Example 1   **Simplify an Expression**

Simplify each expression. Compute as needed.

   (a) $12 - (x - 3)$

   (b) $\dfrac{12}{\frac{x}{3}}$

(a) $12 - (x - 3)$ can be simplified to $15 - x$ by using the invariant principle for subtraction. The original expression is a difference of two terms, 12 and $(x - 3)$. To simplify, we add 3 to each term: $12 + 3 = 15$ and $x - 3 + 3 = x$. [The parentheses are no longer needed.]

   As an alternate approach, we could replace $-(x - 3)$ by $-x + 3$ so that
$$12 - (x - 3) \;=\; 12 - x + 3 \;=\; 12 + 3 - x \;=\; 15 - x.$$

(b) $\dfrac{12}{\frac{x}{3}}$ can be simplified to $\dfrac{36}{x}$ by using the invariant principle for division. The original expression is a quotient, 12 divided by $\frac{x}{3}$. To simplify, multiply the dividend and divisor each by 3:

$$\frac{12}{\frac{x}{3}} = \frac{12 \cdot 3}{\frac{x}{3} \cdot 3} = \frac{36}{x}.$$

Example 2   **Simplify an Expression**

Simplify each expression. Compute as needed.

   (a) $12 - (3 - x)$

   (b) $\dfrac{12}{\frac{3}{x}}$

   (c) $2\left(\dfrac{x}{8}\right)$

(a)   There are two ways to begin: We may use the invariant principle for differences to add x to both 12 and $3 - x$. In this case, 12 becomes $12 + x$ and $3 - x$ becomes $3 - x + x = 3$, so we have $(12 + x) - 3$. From this we obtain $x + 12 - 3$ and $x + 9$.

For an easier approach, we can begin by breaking up the operator $-(3 - x)$ into the two operators $-3 + x$ to obtain $12 - 3 + x = 9 + x$.

(b)   We have $\dfrac{12}{\frac{3}{x}} = \dfrac{12 \cdot x}{\frac{3}{x} \cdot x}$ Multiply dividend and divisor by x.

$\qquad\qquad = \dfrac{12x}{3}$ Cancel the multiplying and dividing by x.

$\qquad\qquad = \dfrac{4x}{1} = 4x$ Divide both $12x$ and 3 by 3 and simplify.

(c)   We have $2\left(\dfrac{x}{8}\right) = \dfrac{2x}{8}$ Commute the contraction and the expansion.

$\qquad\qquad = \dfrac{(2x) \div 2}{8 \div 2}$ Divide dividend and divisor by 2.

$\qquad\qquad = \dfrac{x}{4}$ Compute.

Example 3   **Simplify an Expression**

Simplify each expression. Compute as needed.

(a) $\dfrac{\frac{12}{x}}{3}$ (b) $12\left(\dfrac{3}{x}\right)$

Both of these expressions can be simplified by using commutativity.

(a)   Interchange the order of the two contractions, then compute:

$$\frac{\frac{12}{x}}{3} = \frac{\frac{12}{3}}{x} = \frac{4}{x}.$$

(b)   Instead of dividing by x and then multiplying by 12, do the multiplying first:

$$12\left(\frac{3}{x}\right) = \frac{12 \cdot 3}{x} = \frac{36}{x}.$$

EXERCISE 4.5

DEVELOP YOUR SKILL

Simplify each expression. Compute as needed.

1. $15 - (x - 4)$ **2.** $17 - (8 - x)$ **3.** $10 + (x - 6)$ **4.** $13 + (5 - x)$

5. $7(2x)$ **6.** $12\left(\dfrac{3}{x}\right)$ **7.** $\dfrac{\frac{30}{x}}{3}$ **8.** $\dfrac{60}{x \cdot 12}$

9. $5\left(\dfrac{x}{25}\right)$ **10.** $\dfrac{4}{\frac{x}{12}}$ **11.** $2\left(\dfrac{4}{x}\right)$ **12.** $24\left(\dfrac{x}{6}\right)$

MAINTAIN YOUR SKILL

Compute the basic form for each composite operator. [2.3]

13. $+5 - 8$ **14.** $+14 - 9$ **15.** $+17 - 8 - 13$ **16.** $-6 + 10 - 7$

Each expression is to be viewed as consisting of one operand and one operator. List all the ways to name the operand and the operator. [2.1, 3.2, 3.2]

17. $18 - x$ **18.** $a \cdot x$ **19.** $\dfrac{x}{5}$ **20.** $y + 7$

Write the inverse of each operator. [4.2]

21. $+7$ **22.** -25 **23.** $3(\ )$ **24.** $\dfrac{(\ )}{8}$

Analyze each expression by stating an operand and then listing a sequence of basic operators that can be joined one at a time to produce the given expression. If more than one operand and sequence of operators can be used, give the alternate possibilities. [4.3]

25. $27 - 13 + 2$ **26.** $\dfrac{8}{4} + 3$ **27.** $2(7 - 3)$

28. $\dfrac{a - b}{c}$ **29.** $m + 3x$ **30.** $4 + \dfrac{5 + 7}{n}$

EXTEND YOUR SKILL

31. Explain how to use commutativity to simplify the expression $\dfrac{\frac{40}{x}}{2}$.

32. Explain how to use an invariant principle to simplify the expression $\dfrac{\frac{40}{x}}{2}$.

4.6 – OPERATORS APPLIED TO OPERATORS

OBJECTIVES

1. Apply one operator to another operator.

2. Use the sign operators.

Thus far, multiplication and division operators have been used to change numbers only. But they can also change the size of increases and decreases. This provides an alternate way of thinking about the distributive properties.

Consider the equation $5(7 + 3) = 35 + 15$. Think of $5(\ )$ as a multiplication operator. 7 and 35 are numbers, and $+3$ and $+15$ are increases.

$$5(\overset{\frown}{7} \ \overset{\frown}{+3}) = \overset{\frown}{35} \ \overset{\frown}{+15} \ .$$

We have placed marks over the 7 and the $+3$ to emphasize how they are being viewed. If the number 7 is the operand, then the operator $5(\ )$ gives a transform of 35. If the operator $+3$ is the operand, then the operator $5(\ )$ gives a transform of $+15$.

Similarly, if we have the equation $5(7 - 3) = 35 - 15$, we may see it as

$$5(\overset{\frown}{7} \ \overset{\frown}{-3}) = \overset{\frown}{35} \ \overset{\frown}{-15} \ .$$

Reading Tip:

You should read $5(-3) = -15$ as "Five times a decrease of 3 is a decrease of 15."

We think, but need not write, $5(7) = 35$ and $5(-3) = -15$. That is, if the operator -3 is the operand, the operator $5(\ )$ gives a transform of -15.

We can see from these examples how multipliers distribute over sums and differences. The effect of the multiplication operator upon the increase or decrease is that of multiplying (expanding) its magnitude. Division operators also distribute over sums and differences, and the effect on an increase or a decrease is that of contracting the magnitude of the change:

$$\frac{\overset{\frown}{20} \ \overset{\frown}{+12}}{4} = \overset{\frown}{5} \ \overset{\frown}{+3} \quad \text{and} \quad \frac{\overset{\frown}{20} \ \overset{\frown}{-12}}{4} = \overset{\frown}{5} \ \overset{\frown}{-3}$$

If the number 20 is the operand, then the operator $\dfrac{(\ )}{4}$ gives a transform of 5. If the operator $+12$ is the operand, then the operator $\dfrac{(\ )}{4}$ gives a transform of $+3$.

If the operator -12 is the operand, then the operator $\dfrac{(\ )}{4}$ gives a transform of -3.

Example 1 **Distributing Expansions and Contractions**

Replace each expression by an equivalent one in which the multiplier and the divider have been distributed. Do not compute.

(a) $4(x - y)$ (b) $\dfrac{28 - 21}{7}$

(a) Multiplying by 4 changes x into $4x$ and it changes $-y$ into $-4y$:

$$4(x - y) = 4x - 4y$$

(b) Dividing by 7 changes 28 into $\dfrac{28}{7}$ and it changes -21 into $-\dfrac{21}{7}$:

$$\dfrac{28 - 21}{7} = \dfrac{28}{7} - \dfrac{21}{7}$$

The numeral 5 represents the number five, but with a plus sign at its left it becomes the operator $+5$, and then represents an increase of five. With a minus sign at its left it becomes -5, a decrease of five. These changes from a number to an operator are the work of the **sign operators**, $+(\ )$ and $-(\ )$. The sign operators can also be applied to other operators. In fact, the four cases of removing parentheses from increases and decreases (in Lesson 2.5) can be viewed in this light.

In Case 1 we saw that $+(a + b) = +a + b$. If we think of the plus operator $+(\ )$ distributing over the number a and the operator $+b$ we have

$$+(a + b) = +(a) + (+b) = +a + b, \quad \text{so that } +(+b) = +b.$$

Likewise, from Case 3 we know that $+(a - b) = +a - b$. That is,

$$+(a - b) = +(a) + (-b) = +a - b, \quad \text{so that } +(-b) = -b.$$

Combining these together, we can see that the plus sign operator $+(\ )$ has no effect on an increase or a decrease:

$$+(+b) = +b \qquad \text{and} \qquad +(-b) = -b.$$

In Case 2 of Lesson 2.5 we saw that $-(a + b) = -a - b$. If we distribute the minus sign operator $-(\ )$ over the number a and the operator $+b$ we obtain

$$-(a + b) = -(a) - (+b) = -a - b, \quad \text{so that } -(+b) = -b.$$

That is, the sign operator $-(\ )$ changes the increase $+b$ into the decrease $-b$.

Study Tip:

The plus sign is made bold to emphasize its role. It is not a new symbol.

Likewise, from Case 4 we know that $-(a - b) = -a + b$. Thus

$$-(a - b) = -(a) - (-b) = -a + b, \quad \text{so that } -(-b) = +b.$$

This time the operator $-(\ )$ changes the decrease $-b$ into the increase $+b$. This is why we refer to the sign operator $-(\ )$ as the **opposite** operator.

We may summarize this discussion as follows:

Sign

Operators

This will be important later.

$+(\ )$ changes a number into an increase: $+(b) = +b$.

$-(\ )$ changes a number into a decrease: $-(b) = -b$.

$+(\ )$ leaves an increase or a decrease the same:

$$+(+b) = +b \quad \text{and} \quad +(-b) = -b.$$

$-(\ )$ changes an increase into a decrease and a decrease into an increase:

$$-(+b) = -b \quad \text{and} \quad -(-b) = +b.$$

Example 2   **Distributing Sign Operators**

Replace each expression by an equivalent one in which sign operators have been distributed. Do not compute.

(a) $3 + (7 - 4)$ (b) $12 - (5 + 2)$

(a) The plus sign operator changes 7 into $+7$ and leaves -4 as -4:

$$3 + (7 - 4) = 3 + 7 + (-4) = 3 + 7 - 4$$

(b) The minus sign operator changes 5 into -5 and it changes $+2$ into -2:

$$12 - (5 + 2) = 12 - 5 - (+2) = 12 - 5 - 2$$

EXERCISE 4.6

DEVELOP YOUR SKILL

Replace each expression by an equivalent one in which the multipliers, dividers, and sign operators have been distributed. Do not compute.

1. $3(9 + 2)$

2. $15 - (9 + 3)$

3. $\dfrac{25 + 15}{5}$

4. $12 + (6 - y)$

5. $(10 - 4)(5)$

6. $\dfrac{35 - 14}{7}$

7. $12 - (x - 3)$

8. $15 + (7 + 4)$

MAINTAIN YOUR SKILL

Write the corresponding equation that is matched to it by the definition of subtraction or the definition of division. [1.3, 3.2]

9. $a - m = k$

10. $b + x = c$

11. $\dfrac{d}{c} = y$

12. $wx = k$

List all the factors of each number. [3.3]

13. 45

14. 48

Name each form (sum, difference, product, or quotient) and then compute the basic numeral. [3.4]

15. $3 \cdot 7 - 2 \cdot 8$

16. $20 + 3 \cdot 4$

17. $4 \cdot 5 - 2$

18. $5(7 + 13)$

19. $\dfrac{8}{2} + \dfrac{15}{3}$

20. $\dfrac{2 \cdot 14 - 3}{5}$

Write the composition of the two operators as an equivalent single operator in basic form. [4.2]

21. $3\left(\dfrac{(\ )}{12}\right)$

22. $12\left(\dfrac{(\ )}{3}\right)$

In Exercises 23 – 24, an operand number is given, followed by operators to be used in succession in the order stated. Construct this form. If the form defines a counting number, then compute this number. If it does not, write "not defined." [4.3]

23. $10;\ \dfrac{(\ )}{2},\ +5,\ \dfrac{(\ )}{3}$

24. $42;\ \dfrac{(\ )}{2},\ \dfrac{(\ )}{3},\ -4$

Analyze each expression by stating an operand and then listing a sequence of operators that can be joined one at a time to produce the given expression. If more than one operand and sequence of operators can be used, give the alternate possibilities. [4.3]

25. $12 + 5 \cdot 6$

26. $\dfrac{18 - 3}{5}$

27. $\dfrac{21}{3} - 5$

Simplify each expression. If no simpler form is possible, write "not possible." [4.3]

28. $\dfrac{(5x - y)(5)}{5}$

29. $\dfrac{x - 3}{y + 3}$

30. $\dfrac{a + bc}{a + b}$

EXTEND YOUR SKILL

31. Explain what the plus sign operator does to increases, decreases, and numbers.

32. Explain what the minus sign operator does to increases, decreases, and numbers.

4.7 – DOUBLE OPERATORS

OBJECTIVE

1. Use sign operators and double operators.

Consistent, confident, and accurate use of the sign operators $+(\ )$ and $-(\ )$ that were introduced in Lesson 4.6 are essential to success in algebra. In this lesson we describe their use in another application that involves increases and decreases. The patterns presented here illustrate four key phrases that help us remember how the sign operators interact with each other.

You're going to like this!

Key Phrase $\longrightarrow$

Pattern 1

Compare $12 + [5]$ with $12 + [5 + 3]$.

The increase of 5 on the left has been increased by 3 on the right. Since $12 + [5] = 17$ and $12 + [5 + 3] = 20$, the value of the whole expression has increased by 3. Thus, when an increase is increased, the effect is an increase. Or,

"If you receive more, you will have more."

This corresponds to the operator equation

$$+(+a) = +a.$$

Pattern 2

Compare $12 + [5]$ with $12 + [5 - 3]$.

This time the increase of 5 on the left has been decreased by 3. We have $12 + [5] = 17$ and $12 + [5 - 3] = 14$, so the overall value has decreased by 3. Thus, when an increase is decreased, the effect is a decrease. Or,

Key Phrase ⟶   "If you receive less, you will have less."

This corresponds to the operator equation

$$+ (- a) = - a.$$

Pattern 3

Compare $12 - [5]$ with $12 - [5 + 3]$.

The decrease of 5 is increased by 3. Now $12 - [5] = 7$ and $12 - [5 + 3] = 4$, so the value has decreased by 3. Thus, when a decrease is increased, the effect is a decrease. Or,

Key Phrase ⟶   "If you give more away, you will have less left."

This corresponds to the operator equation

$$- (+ a) = - a.$$

Pattern 4

Compare $12 - [5]$ with $12 - [5 - 3]$.

The decrease of 5 is decreased by 3. Since $12 - [5] = 7$ and $12 - [5 - 3] = 10$, the overall effect is an increase of 3. Thus, when a decrease is decreased, the effect is an increase. Or,

Key Phrase ⟶   "If you give less away, you will have more left."

This corresponds to the operator equation

$$- (- a) = + a.$$

Example 1   Identify the Key Phrase

State the key phrase and the operator equation that corresponds to the following situation: Becca owns stock in the ABC Company. The company was projected to pay a certain dividend to stockholders at the end of the quarter. But the company profits were down and the dividend was less than expected. How did the company's lower profits affect the amount of money Becca had after receiving the stock dividend?

The amount she expected to receive was reduced. That is, her increase was decreased. The key phrase is "If you receive less, you will have less." The operator equation is $+(-a) = -a.$

When the sign operators are applied to expansions and contractions, we get a **double operator**. That is, there are two operators acting together on the operand. Here are some examples:

First Operator	Second Operator	Double Operator	
$5(\ )$	$+(\ )$	$+5(\ )$	an increase of 5 times something
$5(\ )$	$-(\ )$	$-5(\ )$	a decrease of 5 times something
$\dfrac{(\ )}{2}$	$+(\ )$	$+\dfrac{(\ )}{2}$	an increase of something divided by 2
$\dfrac{(\ )}{2}$	$-(\ )$	$-\dfrac{(\ )}{2}$	a decrease of something divided by 2

We see that the $+(\ )$ and the $-(\ )$ determine the kind of change, while the $5(\ )$ and the $\dfrac{(\ )}{2}$ effect the size of the change. These double operators also distribute over sums and differences. To do this we first distribute the expansion or the contraction, and then we distribute the sign operator. In general we have,

$$+a(b+c) = +[a(b+c)] = +[ab+ac] = +ab+ac$$
$$-a(b+c) = -[a(b+c)] = -[ab+ac] = -ab-ac$$
$$+a(b-c) = +[a(b-c)] = +[ab-ac] = +ab-ac$$
$$-a(b-c) = -[a(b-c)] = -[ab-ac] = -ab+ac$$

Similar equations apply for $+\dfrac{(\ )}{a}$ and $-\dfrac{(\ )}{a}$.

Study Tip:

With practice,
the two operators
can be distributed
at the same time.

Example 2   **Distributing Operators**

Replace each expression by an equivalent one in which the multipliers, dividers, and sign operators have been distributed.

(a) $3 + 2(x - y)$ (b) $45 - \dfrac{m-5}{y}$

(a) $3 + 2(x - y)$ $=$ $3 + (2x - 2y)$ Distribute the expansion 2( ).
   $=$ $3 + 2x - 2y$ Distribute the sign operator + ( ).

(b) $45 - \dfrac{m-5}{y} = 45 - \left(\dfrac{m}{y} - \dfrac{5}{y} \right)$ Distribute the contraction $\dfrac{(\ )}{y}$.

   $= 45 - \dfrac{m}{y} + \dfrac{5}{y}$ Distribute the sign operator − ( ).

EXERCISE 4.7

DEVELOP YOUR SKILL

In Exercises 1 – 4, state the key phrase and the operator equation from the four patterns in the lesson that correspond to the situation described.

Key Phrase	Operator Equation
"If you receive more, you will have more."	$+ (+ a) = + a$
"If you receive less, you will have less."	$+ (- a) = - a$
"If you give more away, you will have less left."	$- (+ a) = - a$
"If you give less away, you will have more left."	$- (- a) = + a$

1. Ann went to the home center to buy pansies for her flower garden. She was planning to buy 16 plants, but when she saw how beautiful they were, she decided to buy 24. How did buying the extra plants affect the amount of money she had when she finished shopping?

2. Bruce works as a waiter at a local restaurant. He receives an hourly salary and gets to keep all his tips. How do his tips affect the amount in his bank account after he deposits his income?

3. Carol was looking forward to her first paycheck from her new job. When she got the paycheck, she was surprised to find that money had been deducted from her check for income tax and social security. How did these deductions affect the amount of her savings after she deposited the check?

4. Drew went shopping to buy a new table saw. When he got to the home center he discovered that the power tools were on sale for 10% off. How did the sale affect the amount of money he had when he finished shopping?

Replace each expression with an equivalent one in which the multipliers, dividers, and sign operators have been distributed. Do not compute.

5. $40 - 2(9 + 8)$

6. $18 - \dfrac{18 - 12}{3}$

7. $3 + \dfrac{20 - 5}{5}$

8. $16 + \dfrac{32 + 24}{8}$

9. $37 - 3(9 - 4)$

10. $p - \dfrac{r + s}{t}$

11. $a + b(c - d)$

12. $m + \dfrac{n - p}{r}$

13. $w - \dfrac{x - y}{z}$

14. $p(t - r) - s$

MAINTAIN YOUR SKILL

15. Susan went shopping on Michigan Avenue in Chicago. As she visited different stores, she walked 3 blocks north, 5 blocks south, and then 1 block north. Construct an operator equation to model her walking, where walking north is considered an increase. [2.3]

Do not compute, but write equivalent expressions with parentheses around a sum or a difference. Do not change the first term. When possible, give a second alternate form. [2.4]

16. $53 + 25 - 17$

17. $47 - 12 - 8$

18. $31 + 14 - 26$

19. $54 - 27 + 32$

20. List all x such that x is a multiple of 3 and x divides 36. [3.2]

21. Find the largest x such that x divides both 35 and 21. [3.2]

Use an invariant principle to solve each equation. [3.6]

22. $28 \cdot 32 = 14 \cdot x$

23. $42 \cdot x = 21 \cdot 18$

24. $\dfrac{1750}{50} = \dfrac{x}{100}$

25. $\dfrac{96}{6} = \dfrac{32}{x}$

Construct each expression by stating an operand and then listing a sequence of operators that can be joined one at a time to produce the given expression. If more than one operand and sequence of operators can be used, give the alternate possibilities. [4.3]

26. $4 \cdot 7 - 3$

27. $2\left(\dfrac{24 - 15}{3}\right)$

Simplify each expression. Compute as needed. [4.5]

28. $\dfrac{56}{8x}$

29. $9\left(\dfrac{3}{x}\right)$

30. $\dfrac{24}{\dfrac{3}{x}}$

EXTEND YOUR SKILL

31. Explain the operator equation $-(+a) = -a$ by using the minus sign operator.

32. Explain the operator equation $-(+a) = -a$ by using a key phrase from this lesson.

CHAPTER 4 REVIEW

Construct a graphical model for the composition of the operators. [4.1, 4.2]

1. $\dfrac{\dfrac{(\ )}{3}}{2}$

2. $\dfrac{2(\ )}{6}$.

3. $2\left(\dfrac{(\ )}{6}\right)$

Write an equivalent operator in basic form. [4.1, 4.2]

4. $\dfrac{\dfrac{(\ )}{3}}{6}$

5. $\dfrac{5(\ )}{30}$

6. $24\left(\dfrac{(\ )}{3}\right)$

7. $4(8(\ ))$

Use commutativity to interchange the order of the two operators. [4.1, 4.2]

8. $x\left(\dfrac{(\ )}{y}\right)$

9. $\dfrac{\dfrac{(\ )}{x}}{y}$

Write the inverse of each operator. [4.2]

10. $+8$

11. $\dfrac{(\ )}{7}$

12. -6

13. $5(\ )$

An operand is given below, followed by operators to be used in succession in the order stated. Construct this form and compute the basic numeral. [4.3]

14. $7;\ +5,\ 2(\ ),\ \dfrac{(\ )}{3}$

15. $9;\ +3,\ \dfrac{(\ )}{2},\ -1$

Analyze each expression by stating an operand and then listing a sequence of operators that can be joined one at a time to produce the given expression. If more than one operand and sequence of operators can be used, give the alternate possibilities. [4.3]

16. $\dfrac{27-15}{3}$

17. $3+\dfrac{24}{x}$

Simplify each expression. Compute as needed. If no simpler form is possible, write "not possible." [4.4, 4.5]

18. $15+x-3$

19. $25-(x-4)$

20. $30-(7-x)$

21. $x-\dfrac{x}{y}$

22. $\dfrac{(x+5)s}{s}$

23. $\dfrac{xy}{x-y}$

24. $\dfrac{\frac{12}{x}}{3}$

25. $\dfrac{12}{\frac{x}{3}}$

26. $3\left(\dfrac{x}{18}\right)$

27. $\dfrac{4+m-m}{m}$

28. $\dfrac{2x+6}{2x+3}$

Replace each expression with an equivalent one in which the multipliers, dividers, and sign operators have been distributed. [4.6, 4.7]

29. $a-b(c+d)$

30. $w-\dfrac{x-y}{z}$

Chapter 5 – Powers

5.1 – EXPONENTS

OBJECTIVE

1. Use counting numbers as exponents.

In Chapter 2 we studied the addition-subtraction family of operators. In Chapter 3 we developed multiplication as repeated addition, and this led in Chapter 4 to a new level of operation—the multiplication-division family of operators. In this chapter we will use repeated multiplication to introduce a third level of operation called **exponentiation**, or more commonly, raising to a power.

Definition of Power

> If b and n are counting numbers, except that b and n are not both zero, then exponentiation assigns to b and n a unique counting number b^n. For the **power** b^n, b is called the **base** and n is called the **exponent**.

To compute the power b^n, we begin with 1 and multiply by b a total of n times. Thus the exponent counts the number of times that the unit 1 is multiplied by the base. Or, in the terminology of operators, the exponent n counts the number of times that the expansion $\cdot\, b$ is joined to 1:

$$b^n = 1 \cdot \underbrace{b \cdot b \cdot b \cdot \,\cdots\, \cdot b}_{n \text{ times}}$$

Reading Tip:

The notation "$n = 0, 1, 2, 3, 4$" stands for "$n = 0$, or $n = 1$, or $n = 2$, or $n = 3$, or $n = 4$."

Example 1   **An Operator Model for Powers**

Construct an operator model for 3^n, where $n = 0, 1, 2, 3, 4$. Then compute the basic numeral.

Power Form	Number of Expansions	Operator Model	Basic Numeral
3^0	none	1	1
3^1	one	$1 \cdot 3$	3
3^2	two	$1 \cdot 3 \cdot 3$	9
3^3	three	$1 \cdot 3 \cdot 3 \cdot 3$	27
3^4	four	$1 \cdot 3 \cdot 3 \cdot 3 \cdot 3$	81

[Compare this with Example 1 in Lesson 3.1.]

Let us compute several more powers and see what patterns may develop.

$3^3 = 1 \cdot 3 \cdot 3 \cdot 3 = 27$ $3^2 = 1 \cdot 3 \cdot 3 = 9$ $3^1 = 1 \cdot 3 = 3$ $3^0 = 1$

$2^3 = 1 \cdot 2 \cdot 2 \cdot 2 = 8$ $2^2 = 1 \cdot 2 \cdot 2 = 4$ $2^1 = 1 \cdot 2 = 2$ $2^0 = 1$

$1^3 = 1 \cdot 1 \cdot 1 \cdot 1 = 1$ $1^2 = 1 \cdot 1 \cdot 1 = 1$ $1^1 = 1 \cdot 1 = 1$ $1^0 = 1$

$0^3 = 1 \cdot 0 \cdot 0 \cdot 0 = 0$ $0^2 = 1 \cdot 0 \cdot 0 = 0$ $0^1 = 1 \cdot 0 = 0$ $\boxed{}$

We have the following general rules:

Key Point

> For all b, $b^1 = b$.   For all $b \neq 0$, $b^0 = 1$.   For all $n \neq 0$, $0^n = 0$.

In the list above, the entry for 0^0 is omitted. If we were to decide that $0^0 = 1$, this would be an exception in the bottom row, since all other powers are 0 when the base is 0. But if we decide that $0^0 = 0$, this would be an exception in the right column, since all other powers are 1 when 0 is the exponent. This conflict can be avoided by not giving a meaning to 0^0.

Example 2   **Compute a Power**

Compute the following powers.

(a) 6^2 (b) 2^4 (c) 5^0

(a) By definition, $6^2 = 1 \cdot 6 \cdot 6 = 36$. When the exponent is greater than 1, the computation of a power can be shortened by dropping the $1 \cdot$ at the front. Thus we may compute 6^2 as $6 \cdot 6 = 36$. It is important, however, to retain the initial term 1 when computing a power having zero as an exponent.

(b) We may compute 2^4 as $2 \cdot 2 \cdot 2 \cdot 2 = 16$.

(c) Since the exponent is 0, we have to use the definition. Namely, we think of 1 multiplied by 5 no times to just have 1. Thus $5^0 = 1$.

When repeated factors have the same base, they can be written together as a power of that base. For example, $7 \cdot 7 \cdot 7 \cdot 7$ can be written as 7^4. When letters are used instead of numbers, we can't compute the basic numeral, but we can still combine repeated factors together as a power if they have the same base. For example, we may write $b \cdot b \cdot b$ as b^3.

Example 3   **Write Repeated Factors with Exponents**

Write each expression using exponents.

   (a) $6 \cdot 6 \cdot 6 \cdot 8 \cdot 8$ (b) $b \cdot c \cdot b \cdot c \cdot c$

(a) We group the three factors of 6 together as 6^3 and the two factors of 8 together as 8^2. Thus $6 \cdot 6 \cdot 6 \cdot 8 \cdot 8 = 6^3 \cdot 8^2$

(b) $b \cdot c \cdot b \cdot c \cdot c = b \cdot b \cdot c \cdot c \cdot c$ Commutative Property

$\qquad\qquad\qquad = (b \cdot b)(c \cdot c \cdot c)$ Associative Property

$\qquad\qquad\qquad = b^2 \cdot c^3$ Definition of exponents

EXERCISE 5.1

DEVELOP YOUR SKILL

Use the definition of a power to construct an operator model with repeated multipliers. Then compute.

1. 2^3 **2.** 3^2 **3.** 2^5 **4.** 5^2

Compute the basic numeral.

5. 7^2 **6.** 5^3 **7.** 8^2 **8.** 6^0

9. 3^4 **10.** 4^3 **11.** 5^0 **12.** 9^2

Write each expression using exponents.

13. $5 \cdot 5 \cdot 5$ **14.** $3 \cdot 7 \cdot 7 \cdot 3$ **15.** $d \cdot d \cdot d \cdot d$ **16.** $x \cdot y \cdot x \cdot y \cdot x$

MAINTAIN YOUR SKILL

Write the composition of the two given operators as an equivalent single operator. [2.3 and 4.2]

17. $-5 + 8$ **18.** $-12 + 7$ **19.** $14\left(\dfrac{(\ )}{2}\right)$ **20.** $3\left(\dfrac{(\ )}{18}\right)$

Simplify each expression. If no simpler form is possible, write "not possible." [4.5]

21. $r - 7 + 7$

22. $\left(\dfrac{t^2}{5}\right)5$

23. $\dfrac{(m-n)-2}{2}$

24. $5 - \dfrac{x}{5}$

25. $\dfrac{2 \cdot 3 \cdot m}{3}$

26. $\dfrac{x(y-2)}{x}$

Replace each expression with an equivalent one in which the multipliers, dividers, and sign operators have been distributed. Do not compute. [4.6]

27. $5(7 - 4)$

28. $23 - (15 + 2)$

29. $\dfrac{24 + 45}{3}$

30. $28 + (15 - 7)$

Expand Your Skill

31. Explain why $8^0 = 1$.

32. Can we compute 2^3 by multiplying 2 times itself 3 times? Why or why not?

5.2 – Exponents and the Order of Operations

OBJECTIVE

1. Use the order of operations with expressions involving exponents.

The diagram below is suggestive of a number of ideas about the six basic operations used in arithmetic and algebra. [For a discussion of "roots" we must wait until Chapter 10.]

Figure 5.1

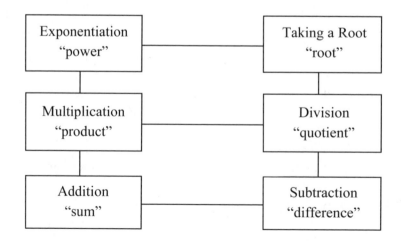

The words in quotes in Figure 5.1 are the names of the forms. The forms $x + y$, xy, and x^y are (with the single exception of 0^0) defined for every choice of two counting numbers. Addition, multiplication, and exponentiation are *direct* operations. Addition can be defined in terms of counting. Multiplication and exponentiation have been defined in terms of the next lower operation on the diagram. The remaining three operations are *indirect*: they are defined by their inverse relation to a direct operation. But they are only partial operations on the counting numbers, and this is recognized in their definitions.

The direct operations of addition and multiplication are both commutative and associative, but the indirect operations of subtraction and division have neither property. The direct operation of raising to a power is *not* commutative or associative, as shown by the counterexamples below.

Study Tip:

A "counterexample" is an example that is used to show that a possible general principle does not always hold true.

Example 1   Powers are Not Commutative or Associative

$2^3 = 2 \cdot 2 \cdot 2 = 8$, but $3^2 = 3 \cdot 3 = 9$. Thus $2^3 \neq 3^2$.

$2^{(3^2)} = 2^9 = 512$, but $(2^3)^2 = 8^2 = 64$. Thus $2^{(3^2)} \neq (2^3)^2$.

In general, $x^y \neq y^x$ and $x^{(y^z)} \neq (x^y)^z$.

We are now using five different operations, and they are at three levels of definition. [See Figure 5.1.] The following rules reduce the number of parentheses needed to control the order of use with these different operations.

Order of

Operations

Unless there are instructions otherwise,

     raising to a power is done first,

     then multiplication and division,

     and finally, addition and subtraction.

Briefly, start high on Figure 5.1 and work down. With operations from the same level, work from left to right.

Parentheses and other grouping symbols, such as the bar of division, are used to make exceptions to these rules. Remember that the name given to an entire expression comes from the *last* operation used when the specified order is followed for the computation of the basic numeral.

Study Tip:

The name of the form comes from the **last** operation used in computing the basic numeral.

Example 2   **Name the Form**

Name each form and compute the basic numeral.

   (a) $5 \cdot 2^3$ (b) $(5 \cdot 2)^3$ (c) $8 - 2 \cdot 3$

(a) Product. $5 \cdot 2^3 = 5 \cdot 8 = 40$.

(b) Power. $(5 \cdot 2)^3 = 10^3 = 1000$.

(c) Difference. $8 - 2 \cdot 3 = 8 - 6 = 2$.

When we have an expression using letters as variables, the value of the expression may change depending on the values that are assigned to each variable. In an expression like $x^2 + xy$, we can let x and y be any counting numbers. The value of $x^2 + xy$ is then obtained by substituting these values for x and y. For example, if $x = 3$ and $y = 5$, then

$$x^2 + xy = 3^2 + (3)(5) = 9 + 15 = 24.$$

Notice that in making the substitution, we replace x by 3 in both places that x appears.

Example 3   **Evaluate an Expression**

Evaluate $x^2 + xy$ when $x = 5$ and $y = 7$.

   Substitute 5 for x and 7 for y and compute:

$$x^2 + xy = 5^2 + (5)(7) = 25 + 35 = 60$$

EXERCISE 5.2

DEVELOP YOUR SKILL

Name each form and compute the basic numeral.

1. $5^2 + 3^2$ **2.** $(5 + 3)^2$ **3.** $(7 - 4)^2$

4. $7^2 - 4^2$ **5.** $3 \cdot 2^3$ **6.** $3 + 5^2$

7. $(3 \cdot 2)^3$ **8.** $(2 + 7)^2$ **9.** $11 - 3^2$

Evaluate each expression as indicated.

10. $x + yz^2$ when $x = 5, y = 1, z = 2$ **11.** $x^2 y^1 z^0$ when $x = 4, y = 2, z = 3$

12. $z^2 - (x - y)^2$ when $x = 5, y = 3, z = 4$

MAINTAIN YOUR SKILL

Find the inverse of each operator. [2.3, 2.4]

13. $+ 14$ **14.** $- 26$ **15.** $7(\ )$ **16.** $\dfrac{(\ )}{5}$

Write the composition of the two given operators as an equivalent single operator. [2.3, 2.4]

17. $- r + s$, if $s \geq r$ **18.** $- r + s$, if $r \geq s$

19. $r\left(\dfrac{(\ )}{s}\right)$, if r divides s **20.** $r\left(\dfrac{(\ )}{s}\right)$, if s divides r

Simplify each expression. If no simpler form is possible, write "not possible." [4.4]

21. $9t - \dfrac{1}{t}$ **22.** $\dfrac{5 + z}{5}$ **23.** $7 - x + x$

24. $\dfrac{5(b - 8)}{5}$ **25.** $\dfrac{a}{2} + b - 1 - \dfrac{a}{2}$ **26.** $\dfrac{(x + 3)}{3x}$

Replace each expression with an equivalent one in which the multipliers, dividers, and sign operators have been distributed. Do not compute. [4.7]

27. $52 - 3(21 + 5)$ **28.** $44 + 5(17 - 8)$

29. $47 + \dfrac{35 - 21}{7}$ **30.** $72 - \dfrac{65 - 20}{5}$

EXTEND YOUR SKILL

31. Explain how to determine the name of the form of an expression.

32. Explain why $2 \cdot 3^2$ is a product and not a power.

5.3 – PRODUCTS AND QUOTIENTS OF POWERS

OBJECTIVE

1. View powers as operators and simplify products and quotients of powers.

Raising to a power may be viewed as an operation on the base. For example, the power b^2 is the transform when the exponential operator $(\ )^2$ is joined to the operand b. This power, b^2, may be read as "the second power of b," or as "the square of b." The power b^3 is "the third power of b" or "the cube of b," so that $(\ )^3$ is the cubing operator. In general, b^n is read as "the n-th power of b," or "b to the n."

Parentheses are a necessary part of exponential operators, $(\ )^n$, when they are written without an operand. They are also needed when the operand is a sum, difference, product, quotient, or power. Without the parentheses, an exponent refers only to the single number or variable at its lower left. Thus

$$2 + 3^2 = 2 + 9 = 11 \quad \text{and} \quad (2 + 3)^2 = 5^2 = 25.$$

The operator $(\ )^0$ cannot be used with zero as an operand since 0^0 is not defined. But $(\ )^0$ dominates every nonzero operand since the transform is always 1. Also, we see that $(\ )^1$ is the **identity** operator for raising to a power. Hence b^1 is usually written more simply just as b.

$$\text{If } b \neq 0, \text{ then } b^0 = 1.$$

$$\text{For all } b, \ b^1 = 1 \cdot b = b.$$

There are five basic properties that govern the manipulation of exponents. We will cover the first two in this lesson and the last three in the next lesson.

Study Tip:

To multiply powers with the same base, add their exponents.

Example 1   **A Product of Powers**

$$7^3 \cdot 7^2 = (7 \cdot 7 \cdot 7)(7 \cdot 7) \qquad \text{by definition}$$
$$= 7 \cdot 7 \cdot 7 \cdot 7 \cdot 7 \qquad \text{by associativity}$$
$$= 7^5 \qquad \text{by definition}$$

Thus the *product of two powers* that have the same base is equivalent to a *power* of that base. The exponent for the power is the *sum* of the exponents for the powers that are factors of the product. Here is the general rule:

Product of Powers

$$x^m \cdot x^n = x^{m+n}$$

Example 2   **A Quotient of Powers**

$$\frac{7^5}{7^2} = \frac{7 \cdot 7 \cdot 7 \cdot 7 \cdot 7}{7 \cdot 7}$$ by definition

$$= \frac{(7 \cdot 7 \cdot 7)(7 \cdot 7)}{(7 \cdot 7)}$$ by associativity

$$= 7 \cdot 7 \cdot 7$$ Cancel the multiplying and dividing by ($7 \cdot 7$).

$$= 7^3$$ by definition

Study Tip:

To divide powers with the same base, subtract their exponents.

Thus a *quotient of two powers* with the same base is equivalent to a *power* of that base. Here is the general rule:

Quotient of

Powers

$$\frac{x^m}{x^n} = x^{m-n}$$

Example 3   **Change a Product or a Quotient to a Power**

Replace each product or quotient with an equivalent power. Do not compute, except as needed for exponents.

(a) $2^4 \cdot 2^3$ (b) $\frac{3^5}{3}$ (c) $9^4 \cdot 9^0$

(a)   The product $2^4 \cdot 2^3$ is equivalent to the power $2^{4+3} = 2^7$.

(b) The quotient $\dfrac{3^5}{3} = \dfrac{3^5}{3^1}$ is equivalent to the power $3^{5-1} = 3^4$.

(c) The product $9^4 \cdot 9^0$ is equivalent to the power $9^{4+0} = 9^4$. Recall that $9^0 = 1$, so multiplying by 9^0 is the same as multiplying by 1.

EXERCISE 5.3

DEVELOP YOUR SKILL

Replace each product or quotient with an equivalent power. Do not compute, except for exponents.

1. $5^2 \cdot 5^3$

2. $2^0 \cdot 2^2 \cdot 2^3$

3. $\dfrac{3^8}{3^2 \cdot 3^0}$

4. $\dfrac{7^6}{7^3}$

5. $(x+1)^3(x+1)^4$

6. $\dfrac{(y-3)^9}{y-3}$

MAINTAIN YOUR SKILL

7. List all x such that x is a multiple of 2 and x divides 42. [3.2]

8. List all x such that x is a multiple of 3 and x divides 42. [3.2]

Simplify each expression. Compute as needed. [4.5]

9. $\dfrac{\frac{3}{x}}{\frac{x}{8}}$

10. $56\left(\dfrac{x}{14}\right)$

11. $\dfrac{\frac{8}{32}}{x}$

12. $\dfrac{\frac{15}{3}}{x}$

13. $\dfrac{28}{4x}$

14. $4(5x)$

15. $5\left(\dfrac{4}{x}\right)$

16. $\dfrac{20}{2x}$

In Exercises 17 – 18, an operand number is given, followed by operators to be used in succession in the order stated. Construct this form. If the form defines a count-ing number, then compute this number. If it does not, write "not defined." [4.3]

17. $17; -5, \dfrac{(\ )}{3}, 2(\ )$

18. $5; 4(\ ), \dfrac{(\ )}{3}, +7$

Analyze each expression by stating an operand and then listing a sequence of operators that can be joined one at a time to produce the given expression. If more than one operand and sequence of operators can be used, give the alternate possibilities. [4.3]

19. $\dfrac{4 \cdot 5 - 2}{3}$

20. $2\left(\dfrac{12}{4} + 9\right)$

Name each form and compute the basic numeral. [5.2]

21. $5 + 2^3$

22. $5 \cdot 4^2$

23. $(5 + 2)^3$

24. $(5 \cdot 4)^2$

25. $(2 \cdot 5 - 3)^2$

26. $3 \cdot 5 - 3^2$

27. $(2 \cdot 5) - 3^2$

28. $3(5 - 3)^2$

29. $(3 + 5)^2$

30. $3^2 + 5^2$

EXTEND YOUR SKILL

31. Explain why $(\ \ )^1$ is the identity operator for raising to a power.

32. For what operand is the operator $(\ \ )^0$ not defined? Explain why.

In Exercises 33 – 36, write each number in the form $n^2 - 1$ where n is a natural number, then in the form $(n + 1)(n - 1)$.

33. 8

34. 15

35. 35

36. 63

5.4 – POWERS OF PRODUCTS AND QUOTIENTS

OBJECTIVES

1. Simplify a power of products or quotients.

2. Simplify a power of a power.

In the last lesson we learned how to simplify products and quotients of powers. Now let's see how to simplify powers of products and quotients.

> **Example 1** **A Power of a Product**
>
> $(5 \cdot 7)^3 = (5 \cdot 7)(5 \cdot 7)(5 \cdot 7)$ by definition
>
> $= 5 \cdot 5 \cdot 5 \cdot 7 \cdot 7 \cdot 7$ by commutativity and associativity
>
> $= 5^3 \cdot 7^3$ by definition

Thus a *power of a product* is equivalent to a *product of powers*. Here is the general rule:

Power of a Product

$$(x \cdot y)^m = x^m \cdot y^m$$

Example 2   **A Power of a Quotient**

$$\left(\frac{8}{2}\right)^3 = \left(\frac{8}{2}\right)\left(\frac{8}{2}\right)\left(\frac{8}{2}\right) \qquad \text{by definition}$$

$$= \frac{8 \cdot 8 \cdot 8}{2 \cdot 2 \cdot 2} \qquad \text{by Cases 2 and 3 in Section 2.4}$$

$$= \frac{8^3}{2^3} \qquad \text{by definition}$$

Thus a *power of a quotient* is equivalent to a *quotient of powers*. Here is the general rule:

Power of a Quotient

$$\left(\frac{x}{y}\right)^m = \frac{x^m}{y^m}$$

Taking a power of a product or a quotient illustrates new **distributive** properties. We see that raising to a power distributes over multiplication and division. Note that the distributive properties relate *adjacent* levels in Figure 5.1. In particular, exponential operators do *not* distribute over sums and differences.

Study Tip:

Powers distribute over products and quotients.
Powers **do not** distribute over sums and differences.

Example 3   **Powers Do Not Distribute Over sums**

$(3 + 2)^2 = 5^2 = 25$, but $3^2 + 2^2 = 9 + 4 = 13$. Thus $(3 + 2)^2 \neq 3^2 + 2^2$.

$(5 - 2)^2 = 3^2 = 9$, but $5^2 - 2^2 = 25 - 4 = 21$. Thus $(5 - 2)^2 \neq 5^2 - 2^2$.

For our final property of powers, we look at what happens when we take a power of a power.

Example 4   A Power of a Power

$$(7^3)^2 = (7^3)(7^3) \qquad \text{by definition}$$
$$= 7^{3+3} \qquad \text{by Property P}_1$$
$$= 7^{2 \cdot 3} = 7^6 \qquad \text{by definition of a product}$$

Thus a *power of a power* is equivalent to a *power* with the same base.

Power of a Power

$$(x^m)^n = x^{mn}$$

Study Tip:

To take a power of a power, multiply the exponents.

It is also possible to combine the above properties of powers to extend their use. For example,

$$(x^p \cdot y^q)^m = x^{pm} \cdot y^{qm} \quad \text{and} \quad \left(\frac{x^p}{y^q}\right)^m = \frac{x^{pm}}{y^{qm}}.$$

Example 5   Change a Product or a Quotient to a Power

Replace the product and the quotient with an equivalent power. Do not compute.

(a) $w^3 x^3$ (b) $\dfrac{35^4}{7^4}$

(a) The product $w^3 x^3$ is equivalent to the power $(wx)^3$.

(b) The quotient $\dfrac{35^4}{7^4}$ is equivalent to the power $\left(\dfrac{35}{7}\right)^4$.

> **Example 6**   **Change Power to a Product or a Quotient**
>
> Replace each power with an equivalent product or quotient. Do not compute, except as needed for exponents.
>
> $$\text{(a)} \quad (3 \cdot 5)^6 \qquad \text{(b)} \quad (x^2 \cdot y^3)^4 \qquad \text{(c)} \quad \left(\frac{x^3}{y^4}\right)^5$$
>
> (a) The power $(3 \cdot 5)^6$ is equivalent to the product $3^6 \cdot 5^6$.
>
> (b) The power $(x^2 \cdot y^3)^4$ is equivalent to the product
> $$(x^2)^4 (y^3)^4 \;=\; (x^{2 \cdot 4})(y^{3 \cdot 4}) \;=\; x^8 \cdot y^{12}.$$
>
> (c) The power $\left(\dfrac{x^3}{y^4}\right)^5$ is equivalent to the quotient $\dfrac{(x^3)^5}{(y^4)^5} = \dfrac{x^{3 \cdot 5}}{y^{4 \cdot 5}} = \dfrac{x^{15}}{y^{20}}$.

EXERCISE 5.4

DEVELOP YOUR SKILL

Replace each power of a product with an equivalent product of powers and each product of powers by an equivalent power of a product. Do not compute, except as needed for exponents.

1. $(3 \cdot 5)^2$

2. $2^4 \cdot 5^4$

3. $4^3 s^3 t^3$

4. $(x^2 \cdot y)^2$

Replace each power of a quotient with an equivalent quotient of powers and each quotient of powers by an equivalent power of a quotient. Do not compute, except as needed for exponents.

5. $\dfrac{12^2}{2^2}$

6. $\dfrac{x^3}{y^3}$

7. $\left(\dfrac{a}{b^2}\right)^3$

8. $\left(\dfrac{10}{5}\right)^2$

Write an equivalent expression in the form 3^n, when possible. Otherwise, write "not possible."

9. $3^5 - 3^2$

10. $3^5 \cdot 3^2$

11. $\dfrac{3^2}{3^2}$

12. $3^3 + 3^3$

13. $(3^2)^3$

14. $\dfrac{3^6}{3^2 \cdot 3^3}$

Maintain Your Skill

Write the corresponding equation that is matched to it by the definition of subtraction or the definition of division. [1.3, 3.2]

15. $m - a = b$

16. $x + y = c$

17. $\dfrac{c}{x} = m$

18. $ay = b$

Do not compute, but write equivalent expressions with parentheses around a sum or a difference. Do not change the first term. When possible, give a second alternate form. [2.4]

19. $41 + 16 - 30$

20. $72 - 34 + 58$

21. $21 + 37 - 15$

22. $30 - 22 - 5$

List all the factors of each number. [3.3]

23. 42

24. 54

Name each form and compute the basic numeral. [5.2]

25. $\dfrac{(3 \cdot 6)^2}{2}$

26. $\left(\dfrac{2 \cdot 9}{6}\right)^2$

27. $\left(\dfrac{3 \cdot 6}{2}\right)^2$

28. $\dfrac{2 \cdot 9^2}{6}$

29. $\dfrac{3 \cdot 6^2}{2}$

30. $2 \cdot 9^2$

Extend Your Skill

31. Give an example to show how powers distribute over products.

32. When taking a power of a power, explain what to do with the exponents.

5.5 – PRIME FACTORED FORM

OBJECTIVE

1. Write the prime factorizations of composite numbers.

Study Tip:

A natural number greater than one is **prime** if its only factors are one and itself. Otherwise, it is **composite**.

The numbers 0 and 1 are neither prime nor composite.

The natural numbers greater than one have a useful and characteristic structure when they are considered as products. For example, the number 15 can be written as a product of natural numbers in two ways:

$$1 \times 15 = 15 \quad \text{and} \quad 3 \times 5 = 15.$$

We see that 15 has four factors: 1, 3, 5, and 15. Likewise, the number 9 can be factored as

$$1 \times 9 = 9 \quad \text{and} \quad 3 \times 3 = 9,$$

so the number 9 has three factors: 1, 3, and 9. The number 7, on the other hand can only be written as a product by multiplying 1 and 7:

$$1 \times 7 = 7.$$

The only factors of 7 are 1 and 7.

The numbers 15 and 9 are examples of **composite** numbers: they can be written as a product of two natural numbers each greater than 1. The number 7 is an example of a **prime** number: it cannot be written as a product of natural numbers each greater than 1. The numbers 0 and 1 are neither prime nor composite.

The following result, called the **Fundamental Theorem of Arithmetic**, enables us to decompose composite numbers into their prime factors:

Fundamental Theorem of Arithmetic

> Every natural number greater than 1 is either prime or it can be written as a product of primes. This product is unique except for the order of writing the prime factors.

If we decide on the order of writing the prime factors, then we have just one way of writing each number, called the **prime factored form**. This is illustrated in Example 1 for the numbers 2 through 20.

Example 1   **Prime Factored Form**

Basic Numeral	Prime Factored Form	Basic Numeral	Prime Factored Form
		11	11
2	2	12	$2^2 \cdot 3$
3	3	13	13
4	2^2	14	$2 \cdot 7$
5	5	15	$3 \cdot 5$
6	$2 \cdot 3$	16	2^4
7	7	17	17
8	2^3	18	$2 \cdot 3^2$
9	3^2	19	19
10	$2 \cdot 5$	20	$2^2 \cdot 5$

The following rules are used to standardize the writing of the prime factored form:

Rules for Prime Factored Form

Rule	Example
1. A prime is written as a prime.	1. $3 = 3$
2. A power of a prime is written as a power of a prime.	2. $8 = 2^3$
3. If there are two or more prime factors, the prime factors are arranged in order of increasing size and appear only once, using exponents as needed.	3. $18 = 2 \cdot 3^2$

Example 2   **Prime Factored Form**

In what way does each of the following fail to be the prime factored form for 36?

   (a) $2^2 \cdot 9$ (b) $(2 \cdot 3)^2$ (c) $3^2 \cdot 2^2$ (d) $2 \cdot 2 \cdot 3^2$

(a) 9 is not a prime.

(b) This is a power of a product, not a product of powers.

(c) The prime 2 should be to the left of prime 3.

(d) It should be 2^2 instead of $2 \cdot 2$.

    When the basic numeral is known for a number, its prime factored form can be found by repeatedly factoring until all the factors are prime. Then like primes are grouped together using powers, and the terms are arranged so that the factors (and the base of the powers) increase in size from left to right.

Study Tip:

In part (a), be sure to write $2^3 \cdot 3^2$ and not $3^2 \cdot 2^3$. The prime bases increase from left to right.

Example 3   **Prime Factored Form**

Find the prime factored form for each number.

   (a) 72   (b) 200   (c) 420

(a) $72 = 6 \cdot 12 = (2 \cdot 3)(3 \cdot 4) = (2 \cdot 3)[3 \cdot (2 \cdot 2)] = 2^3 \cdot 3^2$

(b) $200 = 2 \cdot 100 = 2 \cdot (10 \cdot 10) = 2 \cdot [(2 \cdot 5)(2 \cdot 5)] = 2^3 \cdot 5^2$

Note that it does not matter how we begin the factoring. The final form will be the same. For example, we could have factored 200 as $20 \cdot 10$:

$$20 \cdot 10 = (4 \cdot 5)(2 \cdot 5) = [(2 \cdot 2) \cdot 5](2 \cdot 5) = 2^3 \cdot 5^2$$

(c) $420 = 42 \cdot 10 = (2 \cdot 21)(2 \cdot 5) = [2 \cdot (3 \cdot 7)](2 \cdot 5) = 2^2 \cdot 3 \cdot 5 \cdot 7$

Example 4   **Prime Factored Form**

Find the prime factored form for 181.

    Trials will show that none of the primes 2, 3, 5, 7, 11, or 13 will divide 181. The next prime to try is 17, but $17 \cdot 17 = 289$ and $289 > 181$. Hence if

181 were to be a product of two numbers, then one of these would have to be less than 17. Since trials have shown that 181 does not have a prime divisor less than 17, then 181 must itself be a prime. Thus the prime factored form is 181.

Example 5   **Prime Factored Form**

Assume that the variables are distinct primes with $x < y$ and $y < z$. Write equivalent expressions that meet the conditions for prime factored form.

(a) $x \cdot y^2 \cdot z \cdot y$ (b) $y \cdot x^2 \cdot z \cdot y$

(a) $x \cdot y^2 \cdot z \cdot y = x \cdot y^2 \cdot y \cdot z$ Order the bases in increasing size.
$\qquad\qquad = x \cdot y^3 \cdot z$ Group the like bases together as a power.

(b) $y \cdot x^2 \cdot z \cdot y = x^2 \cdot y \cdot y \cdot z$ Order the bases in increasing size.
$\qquad\qquad = x^2 \cdot y^2 \cdot z$ Group the like bases together as a power.

EXERCISE 5.5

DEVELOP YOUR SKILL

Write each number in prime factored form.

1. 26   **2.** 27   **3.** 28   **4.** 29

5. 32   **6.** 60   **7.** 75   **8.** 400

In Exercises 9 – 14, assume the variables are distinct primes with $x < y$ and $y < z$. Write equivalent expressions that meet the conditions for prime factored form.

9. $x^2 \cdot x^2$ **10.** $z \cdot y^4$ **11.** $y^2 \cdot z \cdot x$

12. $x \cdot y \cdot x^3 \cdot y$ **13.** $x \cdot z \cdot y^2 \cdot x$ **14.** $y \cdot x \cdot y \cdot z^2$

MAINTAIN YOUR SKILL

Show that each statement is true by writing the equation required by its definition. [1.1 and 1.2]

15. 52 is an even number.   **16.** $45 > 38$

Construct a vector model for the composition of the operators. [2.3]

17. $+3 - 7$ **18.** $-6 + 4$

Write an equivalent operator in basic form, when this is defined. If this basic form is not yet defined, write "not defined." [4.2]

19. $3(6(\ ))$

20. $\dfrac{2(\ )}{9}$

21. $3\left(\dfrac{(\ )}{8}\right)$

22. $\dfrac{2(\ )}{10}$

23. $\dfrac{\dfrac{(\ )}{9}}{2}$

24. $4\left(\dfrac{(\ )}{8}\right)$

Replace each expression with an equivalent one in which the multipliers, dividers, and sign operators have been distributed. Do not compute. [4.7]

25. $11 - (8 + 3)$

26. $30 - 3(8 - 6)$

27. $20 - \dfrac{16 + 12}{4}$

28. $17 + \dfrac{15 - 3}{3}$

29. $12 + 5(10 - 4)$

30. $25 - 2(4 + 6)$

Expand Your Skill

31. Can a composite number have exactly two factors? Explain.

32. Explain how a number can have an odd number of factors.

5.6 – Factoring Composite Expressions

OBJECTIVE

1. Use the distributive principle to factor composite expressions.

For numbers that are not written in their basic form, the prime factored form can sometimes be obtained without even computing the basic form. For example, if the number is written as a product, we can simply continue the factoring. If the number is written as a power, we can factor the base first and then apply the power.

Example 1   **Prime Factored Form**

The entire expression is a numeral for a single number. Write this number in prime factored form.

(a) $10 \cdot 18$ (b) 12^3 (c) $(6 \cdot 20)^2$

(a) $10 \cdot 18 = (2 \cdot 5)(2 \cdot 9) = (2 \cdot 5)(2 \cdot 3^2) = 2^2 \cdot 3^2 \cdot 5$

(b) $12^3 = (2 \cdot 6)^3 = (2 \cdot 2 \cdot 3)^3 = (2^2 \cdot 3)^3 = 2^6 \cdot 3^3$

(c) $(6 \cdot 20)^2 = (2 \cdot 3 \cdot 2^2 \cdot 5)^2 = (2^3 \cdot 3 \cdot 5)^2 = 2^6 \cdot 3^2 \cdot 5^2$

If the number to be factored is a sum or a difference, it may be that the first step should be the computation of its basic numeral. But in certain special cases, this can be avoided by using the distributive principle to go directly to a product form.

Example 2   **Prime Factored form**

The entire expression is a numeral for a single number. Write this number in prime factored form.

$$\text{(a)} \quad 5 \cdot 13 - 2 \cdot 13 \qquad \text{(b)} \quad 5 \cdot 11 - 2 \cdot 3 \qquad \text{(c)} \quad 7^2 \cdot 5 - 7^2 \cdot 3$$

(a) Since 13 is a factor of both terms, we can use the distributive principle to factor it out: $5 \cdot 13 - 2 \cdot 13 = (5 - 2)13 = 3 \cdot 13$

(b) This time there are no common factors in the two terms. We need to compute the basic numeral before factoring:

$$5 \cdot 11 - 2 \cdot 3 = 55 - 6 = 49 = 7^2$$

(c) Begin by factoring 7^2 from both terms:

$$7^2 \cdot 5 - 7^2 \cdot 3 = 7^2(5 - 3) = 7^2 \cdot 2 = 2 \cdot 7^2$$

Study Tip:

Remember that every number *n* can be written as the product $1 \cdot n$. This is useful in factoring.

Example 3   **Prime Factored form**

The entire expression is a numeral for a single number. Write this number in prime factored form.

$$\text{(a)} \quad 21 \cdot 13 + 13 \qquad \text{(b)} \quad 7^4 - 7^2$$

(a) If we see the second term as $1 \cdot 13$, then we can factor 13 out of both terms:

$$21 \cdot 13 + 13 = 21 \cdot 13 + 1 \cdot 13$$
$$= (21 + 1)13 = (22)(13) = 2 \cdot 11 \cdot 13$$

(b) This time the largest common factor is 7^2:

$$7^4 - 7^2 = 7^2 \cdot 7^2 - 1 \cdot 7^2$$
$$= (7^2 - 1)7^2 = 48 \cdot 7^2 = 2^4 \cdot 3 \cdot 7^2$$

Since $x^{2n} = (x^n)^2$, we see that any natural number x to an even power will be a perfect square. If a given natural number is not a square but its prime factored form has at least one factor whose exponent is 2 or more, then the number must have a factor (greater than 1) that is a square. By looking at the prime factored form of the number, we can easily find the largest square factor.

Example 4   **Find the Largest Square Factor**

Find the largest square factor of each expression.

(a) $972 = 2^2 \cdot 3^5$ (b) $w^3 \cdot x \cdot y^2 \cdot z^7$

(a) We see that 2^2 divides 972. The highest even power of 3 that divides 972 is 3^4. Thus the largest square factor of 972 is $2^2 \cdot 3^4 = 324$.

(b) The largest square factor of $w^3 \cdot x \cdot y^2 \cdot z^7$ is $w^2 \cdot y^2 \cdot z^6$.

EXERCISE 5.6

DEVELOP YOUR SKILL

In Exercises 1 – 8, the entire expression is a numeral for a single number. Write this number in prime factored form.

1. $8 \cdot 18$

2. $12 \cdot 20$

3. 20^2

4. $(10 \cdot 12)^2$

5. $3^3 \cdot 18^2$

6. $13 + 17 \cdot 13$

7. $19 \cdot 31 - 13 \cdot 31$

8. $17^2 + 17^3$

Find the largest square factor of each expression. Write your answer in factored form.

9. $2 \cdot 5^3$

10. $3^2 \cdot 5 \cdot 7^3$

11. $x^4 \cdot y$

12. $w \cdot x^3 \cdot y^5$

MAINTAIN YOUR SKILL

Write the composition of the two given operators as an equivalent single operator. [2.3, 4.2]

13. $-5-7$

14. $+6-10$

15. $2\left(\dfrac{(\ )}{16}\right)$

16. $12\left(\dfrac{(\ )}{4}\right)$

17. $\dfrac{\dfrac{(\ )}{3}}{5}$

18. $2(6(\ ))$

19. $\dfrac{24(\ )}{3}$

20. $\dfrac{5(\ )}{30}$

Write the inverse of each operator. [2.3, 4.2]

21. $+23$

22. -35

23. $6(\ )$

24. $\dfrac{(\ )}{24}$

25. Find the largest x such that x divides both 24 and 30. [3.2]

26. Find the smallest nonzero x such that x is a multiple of both 8 and 12. [3.2]

Solve each equation by using an invariant principle. [3.6]

27. $36 \cdot 15 = 18 \cdot x$

28. $80 \cdot x = 24 \cdot 40$

29. $\dfrac{x}{14} = \dfrac{35}{7}$

30. $\dfrac{36}{9} = \dfrac{12}{x}$

EXTEND YOUR SKILL

31. Describe the first step in finding the prime factored form for $7^6 + 7^5$.

32. If a number is a perfect square, what can be said about the exponents in its prime factored form?

5.7 – COMMON FACTORS AND COMMON MULTIPLES

OBJECTIVE

1. Find the greatest common factor and the least common multiple of two or more numbers.

Since $25 = 5^2$ and $35 = 5 \cdot 7$, the numbers 25 and 35 have the factor 5 in common. We say that 5 is a **common factor** of 25 and 35. The largest of the common factors of two or more numbers is called the **greatest common factor (GCF)**. One way to find the GCF of two numbers is to list all their factors and see what is the largest factor in common. For example, for 25 and 35 we have

Factors of 25: 1, 5, 25

Factors of 35: 1, 5, 7, 35

This works well for small numbers, but with larger numbers it can be quite tedious. A better way is to examine the prime factored form for each number. The common factors show up clearly if the prime factors of the numbers are arranged in rows and columns as in Example 1. Here we have spread out the prime factors so that each column has at most one prime factor, and within each column all the factors are the same. The factors of the GCF come from the columns that are full—i.e., that contain a factor for each of the original numbers.

Example 1   **Find the Greatest Common Factor**

Find the GCF of 210, 196, and 294.

Make a chart that shows the prime factors.

$210 = 2 \cdot 3 \cdot 5 \cdot 7$	2		3	5	7	
$196 = 2^2 \cdot 7^2$	2	2			7	7
$294 = 2 \cdot 3 \cdot 7^2$	2		3		7	7
	2				7		← GCF

The first "2" column and the first "7" column are full, meaning that 2 and 7 are factors of all three numbers. We have placed a 2 and a 7 at the bottom of their respective full columns (below the solid line). The GCF comes from their product: $2 \cdot 7$ or 14. This is the largest number that is a factor of all three original numbers.

Study Tip:

Don't be frightened by the letters. Remember, each letter just represents a number.

Example 2   **Find the Greatest Common Factor**

Find the GCF of $abcd^2$, a^2cd^2, and c^2d^3.

Make a chart as in Example 1.

$abcd^2$	a		b	c		d	d	
a^2cd^2	a	a		c		d	d	
c^2d^3				c	c	d	d	d
				c		d	d		← GCF

From the three columns that are full, we see that the GCF is cd^2.

Just as two numbers will have at least one divisor in common, they will also have multiples in common. The least of the *nonzero* common multiples is called the **least common multiple (LCM).** For example, by listing the nonzero multiples of 25 and 35 we see that the LCM of 25 and 35 is 175:

Nonzero multiples of 25: 25, 50, 75, 100, 125, 150, **175**, 200, ...

Nonzero multiples of 35: 35, 70, 105, 140, **175**, 210, 245, ...

Once again, the process is simplified by using the prime factored form for each number. The next example is a repeat of Example 1 with their LCM included. We see that the factors of the LCM come from each of the columns.

Example 3   **Find the Least Common Multiple**

Find the LCM *of* 210, 196, *and* 294.

Repeat the chart from Example 1 and label each column at the top with its prime number. The LCM comes from taking all these labels.

	2	2	3	5	7	7	← LCM
$210 = 2 \cdot 3 \cdot 5 \cdot 7$	2		3	5	7		
$196 = 2^2 \cdot 7^2$	2	2			7	7	
$294 = 2 \cdot 3 \cdot 7^2$	2		3		7	7	
	2				7		← GCF

The LCM is $2 \cdot 2 \cdot 3 \cdot 5 \cdot 7 \cdot 7$, or $2^2 \cdot 3 \cdot 5 \cdot 7^2$, or 2940.

Example 4   **Find the Least Common Multiple**

Find the LCM *of* $abcd^2$, a^2cd^2, *and* c^2d^3.

Complete the chart from Example 2.

	a	a	b	c	c	d	d	d	← LCM
$abcd^2$	a		b	c		d	d		
a^2cd^2	a	a		c		d	d		
c^2d^3				c	c	d	d	d	
				c		d	d		← GCF

By taking all the columns we see that the LCM is $a^2bc^2d^3$.

There is a short hand way of finding the GCF and LCM without making a chart. Write each number in prime factored form. If a prime occurs in each factorization, take that prime with its smallest exponent. All of these together form the GCF. For the LCM, take each prime that occurs in at least one of the factored forms, and give it the largest exponent that occurs in any form.

A chart is helpful, but sometimes it is easy to do without a chart.

Example 5   Find the GCF and LCM

Find the GCF *and* LCM *of* 1176, *and* 1680.

Begin with the prime factored forms:

$$1176 = 2^3 \cdot 3 \cdot 7^2$$
$$1680 = 2^4 \cdot 3 \cdot 5 \cdot 7$$

The prime 2 occurs in each factored form. The smallest exponent on 2 is 3. The prime 3 occurs in each factored form. The smallest exponent on 3 is 1. The prime 7 occurs in each factored form. The smallest exponent on 7 is 1. This means the GCF of the numbers is $2^3 \cdot 3 \cdot 7$.

The largest exponent on 2 is 4. The largest exponent on 3 is 1. The largest exponent on 5 is 1. The largest exponent on 7 is 2. Thus the LCM is $2^4 \cdot 3 \cdot 5 \cdot 7^2$.

If the GCF of two numbers is 1, the numbers are said to be **relatively prime**. For example, 4 and 15 are relatively prime. Since $4 = 2^2$ and $15 = 3 \cdot 5$, we see that they have no common prime factors and their GCF is 1.

Example 6   Relatively Prime

Determine whether the numbers in each pair are relatively prime. If they are not relatively prime, find their GCF.

   (a) 35 and 48   (b) 35 and 49

(a) $35 = 5 \cdot 7$ and $48 = 2^4 \cdot 3$, so their GCF is 1. They are relatively prime.

(b) $35 = 5 \cdot 7$ and $49 = 7^2$, so their GCF is 7. They are <u>not</u> relatively prime.

EXERCISE 5.7

DEVELOP YOUR SKILL

Find the GCF and the LCM of each set of numbers. Write your answers in prime factored form. Assume $r < s < t < u$.

1. $\begin{cases} 5^2 \\ 2 \cdot 5 \\ 3 \cdot 5 \end{cases}$

2. $\begin{cases} 3 \cdot 5 \\ 5 \cdot 7 \\ 2 \cdot 3 \end{cases}$

3. $\begin{cases} 2 \cdot 3 \\ 3^2 \cdot 5 \\ 3^3 \end{cases}$

4. $\begin{cases} 3^3 \cdot 5 \\ 3 \cdot 5 \cdot 7^2 \\ 3 \cdot 5 \cdot 7 \end{cases}$

5. $\begin{cases} rs^3u \\ r^2s^2t \\ rs^4t^2 \end{cases}$

6. $\begin{cases} r^2s^2u \\ s^2t \\ s^3tu^3 \end{cases}$

Determine whether the numbers in each pair are relatively prime. If they are not relatively prime, find their GCF.

7. 8 and 9

8. 10 and 12

9. 9 and 11

10. 14 and 21

11. Three separate strings of lights are used on a Christmas tree. Each has a blinker device. One string flashes off and on every 24 seconds, another every 30 seconds, and another every 36 seconds. If they are all seen to blink together at one time, how long will it be until this happens again?

MAINTAIN YOUR SKILL

Write the corresponding equation that is matched to it by the definition of subtraction or the definition of division. [1.3, 3.2]

12. $x - n = a$

13. $c + m = b$

14. $2b = M$

15. $\dfrac{k}{3} = R$

Use composition of operators to write an equivalent single operator. [2.3, 4.2]

16. $-r + s$, if $s \geq r$

17. $-r + s$, if $r \geq s$

18. $s\left(\dfrac{(\ )}{r}\right)$, if r divides s

19. $s\left(\dfrac{(\ )}{r}\right)$, if s divides r

In Exercises 20 and 21, state the key phrase and the operator equation that correspond to the situation described. [4.7]

Key Phrase	Operator Equation
"If you receive more, you will have more."	$+(+a) = +a$
"If you receive less, you will have less."	$+(-a) = -a$
"If you give more away, you will have less left."	$-(+a) = -a$
"If you give less away, you will have more left."	$-(-a) = +a$

20. Emily went to the mall to buy a Christmas present. She was planning on putting 50¢ in the Christmas kettle to help the homeless. But when she got there she found she didn't have any change, so she gave a dollar. How did her lack of change affect the amount of money she had for her shopping?

21. Frank needed to buy new tires for his car. He was expecting to buy a new set of four tires, but the salesman told him that the rear tires were still good and did not need to be replaced. So instead of buying four tires he only had to buy two. How did the good rear tires affect the amount of money he had when he finished shopping?

Name each form and compute the basic numeral. [5.2]

22. $2 \cdot 3^2$

23. $3 + 4^2$

24. $(2 + 4)^2$

25. $2(8 - 5)^2$

26. $\dfrac{(2 \cdot 5)^2}{5}$

27. $5 \cdot 8 - 3^2$

Find the largest square factor of each expression. Write your answer in factored form. [5.6]

28. $2^3 \cdot 5^4$

29. $x^2 \cdot y^6$

30. $x^4 \cdot x \cdot y^5$

EXTEND YOUR SKILL

31. What is the least common factor of 8 and 12? Explain your answer.

32. Do 8 and 12 have a greatest common multiple? Explain your answer.

5.8 – FACTORING WITH THE GCF

OBJECTIVE

1. Use the GCF to factor an algebraic expression.

The process of finding the GCF is useful in factoring algebraic expressions. This is like using the distributive property "in reverse." For example, the distributive property says that $3x(4 + 5y)$ is equal to $12x + 15xy$. To go in the other direction, we look for the GCF of $12x$ and $15xy$, and factor it out of each term. The GCF of 12 and 15 is 3, and the GCF of x and xy is x, so the GCF of $12x$ and $15xy$ is $3x$.

$$12x + 15xy = (3x)(4) + (3x)(5y)$$
$$= (3x)(4 + 5y)$$

Example 1   **Use the GCF to Factor an Expression**

Factor $12xy^2 + 30wxy$ by finding the GCF.

We can use a chart to find the GCF of the two terms, but when the numbers are small it's not too hard to do mentally. Checking the factors of 12 and 30 we see that the GCF of 12 and 30 is 6.

The GCF of xy^2 and wxy can be found easily by comparing the exponents in each term. w is a factor of of wxy, but not of xy^2. x is a factor of both terms, as is y. So the GCF of xy^2 and wxy is xy. Combining these together, the GCF of $12xy^2$ and $30wxy$ is $6xy$. Now factor this out of both terms:

$$12xy^2 + 30wxy = (6xy)(2y) + (6xy)(5w)$$
$$= 6xy(2y + 5w)$$

Don't forget to write the 1 here.

Example 2   **Use the GCF to Factor an Expression**

Factor $24x^3y + 8x^2$ by finding the GCF.

Since $8x^2$ divides $24x^3y$, the GCF is $8x^2$. When factoring $8x^2$ out of the first term we ask "what times $8x^2$ is equal to $24x^3y$?" The answer is $3xy$.

When factoring $8x^2$ out of the second term we ask "what times $8x^2$ is equal to $8x^2$?" The answer is 1.

$$24x^3y + 8x^2 = 8x^2(3xy + 1)$$

EXERCISE 5.8

DEVELOP YOUR SKILL

Use the GCF to factor each expression.

1. $8x + 28y$

2. $12xy + 18x$

3. $20xy^2 - 16y^3$

4. $21x^3y^2 - 12xy^2$

5. $16x^3y^2 - 4xy^2$

6. $5xy + 15x^2y$

7. $9x^2y + 3xy^2 + 6xy$

8. $4x^3y^3 - 8x^2y^3 + 2xy^3$

9. $2xy + 8w^2y - 5wxy$

10. $12x^2 + 6xy + 15y^2$

MAINTAIN YOUR SKILL

Simplify each expression. Compute as needed. [4.5]

11. $20\left(\dfrac{x}{4}\right)$

12. $\dfrac{4x}{20}$

13. $\dfrac{\frac{10}{x}}{5}$

14. $\dfrac{10}{\frac{x}{5}}$

Replace each expression with an equivalent one in which the multipliers, dividers, and sign operators have been distributed. Do not compute. [4.7]

15. $56 - 2(x + y)$

16. $37 + 4(a - b)$

17. $15 + \dfrac{m+n}{3}$

18. $80 - \dfrac{r-s}{4}$

Write an equivalent expression in the form 7^n, when possible. Otherwise, write "not possible." [5.4]

19. $7^5 \cdot 7^3$

20. $(7^5)^3$

21. $7^5 + 7^3$

22. $\dfrac{7^5}{7^3}$

In Exercises 23 to 30, the entire expression is a numeral for a single number. Write this number in prime factored form. [5.5]

23. 16^2

24. $33 \cdot 35$

25. $6^4 \cdot 2^5$

26. $17 \cdot 25 - 14 \cdot 25$

27. $3 \cdot 5 + 4 \cdot 7$

28. $(4^2 \cdot 6^3)^2$

29. $11^4 - 11^3$

30. $21(24 + 25)$

EXTEND YOUR SKILL

31. Factoring an expression that is in the form of a sum changes the sum into what form?

32. If one of the terms in an expression is $6x^2y$ and you factor $6x^2y$ out of each term, what is left in the $6x^2y$ term? Explain your answer.

CHAPTER 5 REVIEW

Write each expression using exponents. [5.1]

1. $7 \cdot 7 \cdot 7 \cdot 7 \cdot 7$

2. $m \cdot n \cdot m \cdot n \cdot n$

Evaluate each expression as indicated. [5.2]

3. $x^2 + y^0 - z^1$ when $x = 4$, $y = 5$, and $z = 6$

4. $x^3 - yz^2$ when $x = 3$, $y = 5$, and $z = 1$

Name each form and compute the basic numeral. [5.2]

5. $3 + 5^2$

6. $10 - 3^2$

7. $3(7 - 5)^2$

8. $3 \cdot 5 - 2^3$

9. $2 + 3 \cdot 5$

10. $\dfrac{5 + 7}{4}$

11. $\left(\dfrac{2^2 + 5}{3} \right)^3$

12. $2 \cdot 4^2$

Replace each product or quotient with an equivalent power. [5.3]

13. $(w + x)^4 (w + x)$

14. $\dfrac{(m - 6)^7}{(m - 6)^0}$

Write an equivalent expression in the form 5^n, when possible. Otherwise, write "not possible." [5.4]

15. $5^2 + 5^7$

16. $5^4 \cdot 5^3 \cdot 5^0$

17. $(5^3)^4$

18. $5^5 - 5^4$

Write equivalent expressions that meet the conditions for prime factored form, assuming that the variables are distinct primes with $x < y$ and $y < z$. [5.5]

19. $(x \cdot y^2)^4$

20. $x \cdot y^2 \cdot z \cdot y \cdot x^3$

The entire expression is a numeral for a single number. Write this number in prime factored form. [5.6]

21. $8 \cdot 15$

22. $12 \cdot 24$

23. 20^5

24. $11 + 25 \cdot 11$

25. $(3 \cdot 27)^4$

26. $17^2 - 17$

27. Find the GCF and the LCM of the numbers $2 \cdot 5 \cdot 7^2$, $2^2 \cdot 3 \cdot 7$, and $2 \cdot 5^2 \cdot 7$. Write your answers in prime factored form. [5.7]

28. List all the divisors of 50 that are relatively prime to 2. [5.7]

Use the GCF to factor each expression. [5.8]

29. $6xy + 15y$

30. $25xy^2 + 35x^2 y$

Chapter 6 — Solving Equations

6.1 – EQUIVALENT EQUATIONS: SUMS AND DIFFERENCES

OBJECTIVE

1. Identify and solve equations involving a sum and two addends.

Equations are mathematical sentences formed by a string of symbols that meet certain conditions. For a single equation, the equality sign "=" is used exactly once. Thus

$$a = b = c \quad \text{or} \quad \begin{aligned} a &= b \\ &= c \end{aligned}$$

is a way of writing several equations: $a = b$, $b = c$, and $a = c$.

If all the symbols used for an equation are constants, then the equation will be either a true statement or a false one. A true statement is said to have a **truth value** of true; a false statement has a truth value of false. Equations containing variables may have the form of a statement even though they lack a truth value. The equations

$$3 + 2 = x, \quad 3 + 2 = ?, \quad \text{and} \quad 3 + 2 = [\ ]$$

are called **conditional equations**. Each becomes a true statement only on the condition that the placeholder be replaced by a numeral for 5.

In the equation $x = y$, the first or left member is x and the second or right member is y. If $x = y$ is to be true, it is required that x and y be names for the same object. In this case, either x or y can replace the other in any statement about the object they name.

The truth value of an equation is not changed by an interchange of its left and right members. This is known as the symmetric property of equality.

Symmetric Property

If $x = y$, then $y = x$.

The equations $x + y = z$ and $z - x = y$ are related to each other by the definition of subtraction (Lesson 1.3). That is, if three numbers are chosen for x, y and z so that one of the equations becomes a true statement, then the other equation will also be true for these values of x, y and z. Likewise, if the three numbers should give a false statement for one equation, then the other equation will also be false. Equations which have the same truth value as each other for any choice of the variables are said to be **equivalent equations**.

The equation $x + y = z$ is said to be solved **explicitly** for z. That is, z appears only once in the equation, and it is one of the members by itself. To **solve** an equation for a variable (or a constant) means to find an equivalent equation that is solved explicitly for the desired variable (or constant).

We begin the process of solving equations by looking at the eight ways in which three numbers can be related by addition or subtraction. In Figure 6.1 we display these eight equations for the numbers 3, 5, and 8. The equations are arranged in a way designed to emphasize how the equations are related to each other. The three properties that relate them are

s: symmetric property of equality

c: commutative property of addition

d: definition of subtraction

Figure 6.1

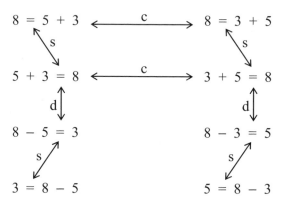

The top four equations in Figure 6.1 are solved explicitly for 8. The numbers 5 and 3 that are added together to get 8 are called **addends**. Thus the top four equations all say that 8 is the sum of the two addends 5 and 3. The lower four equations are each solved explicitly for one of the addends. The lower left pair are explicit for 3, and the lower right pair are explicit for 5. In each case we see that one addend is the sum minus the other addend.

We may summarize the two basic types of equations as follows:

Key Point

(S) The sum equals one addend plus the other addend.
      (See the top four equations in Figure 6.1.)

(A) One addend equals the sum minus the other addend.
      (See the bottom four equations in Figure 6.1.)

Once we have identified the role of each number in an equation, any of the other equations can be written, as desired, simply by following the pattern of the appropriate basic type.

Example 1   **Solve an Equation**

Construct a set of equivalent equations, solving explicitly for each number that is now implicit, but do not compute.

  (a) $4 + 7 = 11$ (b) $6 = 15 - 9$

(a) The equation is solved explicitly for the sum 11. To solve for the addend 4, we write the sum 11 minus the other addend 7:

$$4 = 11 - 7.$$

To solve for the addend 7, we write the sum 11 minus the other addend 4:

$$7 = 11 - 4.$$

(b) The equation is solved explicitly for the addend 6. To solve for the sum 15, we add the two addends 9 and 6 together, in either order:

$$15 = 9 + 6 \quad \text{or} \quad 15 = 6 + 9.$$

To solve for the addend 9, we write the sum 15 minus the other addend 6:

$$9 = 15 - 6.$$

EXERCISE 6.1

DEVELOP YOUR SKILL

Construct a set of equivalent equations, solving explicitly for each number that is now implicit, but do not compute.

1. $12 = 4 + 8$

2. $5 = 21 - 16$

3. $13 - 7 = 6$

4. $14 + 3 = 17$

5. $25 + 37 = 62$

6. $44 - 26 = 18$

7. $189 = 314 - 125$

8. $634 = 351 + 283$

MAINTAIN YOUR SKILL

Construct graphical models for the composition of the operators. [2.3, 4.2]

9. $-2 + 8$

10. $-3 + 6$

11. $8\left(\dfrac{(\ )}{2}\right)$

12. $6\left(\dfrac{(\ )}{3}\right)$

Simplify each expression. If no simpler form is possible, write "not possible." [4.4]

13. $\dfrac{2x+3}{x+3}$

14. $\dfrac{4(x-y)}{x-y}$

15. $\dfrac{x+2}{x-2}$

16. $5 + \dfrac{x}{5} - 5$

17. $(x+7) \div 7$

18. $2 + y - \dfrac{2x}{x}$

In Exercises 19 – 20, an operand number is given, followed by operators to be used in succession in the order stated. Construct this form. If the form defines a counting number, then compute this number. If it does not, write "not defined." [4.3]

19. $22; +3, \dfrac{(\ )}{5}, -2$

20. $11; 2(\ ), -4, \dfrac{(\ )}{3}$

Analyze each expression by stating an operand and then listing a sequence of operators that can be joined one at a time to produce the given expression. If more than one operand and sequence of operators can be used, give the alternate possibilities. [4.3, 5.2]

21. $(9 + 3 \cdot 4)^2$

22. $(8 - 3)^2 + 4$

23. $\dfrac{20-5}{3} + 4$

24. $7 + \dfrac{8}{2} - 3$

Write an equivalent expression in the form 5^n when possible. Otherwise, write "not possible." [5.4]

25. $(5^2 \cdot 5^0)^3$

26. $5^4 + 5^4$

27. $5^7 - 5^6$

28. $\dfrac{5^2}{5^2}$

29. $\dfrac{5^3 \cdot 5}{5^2}$

30. $\left(\dfrac{5^5}{5 \cdot 5}\right)^4$

EXTEND YOUR SKILL

31. If there is a plus sign on one side of an addition/subtraction equation, where is the sum term?

32. If there is a minus sign on one side of an addition/subtraction equation, where is the sum term?

6.2 – SUMS AND DIFFERENCES WITH VARIABLES

OBJECTIVE

1. Solve sum and difference equations that contain a variable.

In Lesson 6.1 it was easy to identify the sum term in an equation: it was the largest of the three numbers. If an equation contains a variable, then it may not be obvious which term is the largest. But we can still identify the sum term by its role in the equation. Recall the two basic types of equations:

Basic Types of Equations	Example
(S) The sum equals one addend plus the other addend.	$8 = 5 + 3$
[sum] = [one addend] + [other addend]	
(A) One addend equals the sum minus the other addend.	$5 = 8 - 3$
[one addend] = [sum] – [other addend]	

In Figure 6.2 we repeat the eight equations that relate sums and differences as in Figure 6.1, but this time using variables. The top four equations state explicitly that

z is the sum of the two addends x and y.

In the bottom four equations, it can be implied that z is the sum. For example, $z - x = y$ can be read as

The sum z minus one addend x is the other addend y.

Figure 6.2

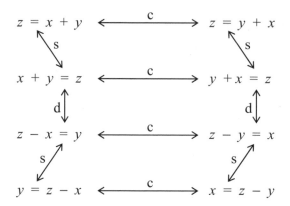

The lower four equations have also been paired by the commutative property because the two addends x and y exchange places. [They are commuted.] This gives the following extension of the commutative principle for addition:

The addends of a sum can be commuted.

If an equation only involves adding and subtracting, it can be thought of as a statement about *exactly three numbers*: a sum and two addends. Once these three terms have been identified, any of the other seven equation forms can be written by following the pattern of the appropriate basic type.

Study Tip:

If "+" is on one side of the equation, the sum term is on the other side of the equation.

If "−" is on one side of the equation, the sum term is the term to the left of "−".

Example 1   **Identify the Sum and the Addends**

Identify the sum term and the two addends in each equation.

   (a) $8 + m = t$ (b) $s = m - 4$ (c) $p - m = 7$ (d) $r = m + 2$

(a) We see the "+" on the left side. This means that t on the right side of the equation is the sum term. This is type (**S**). The addends are 8 and m.

(b) We see the "−" on the right side. This means that the m to the left of "−" is the sum term. The addends are s and 4. This is type (**A**).

(c) This is type (**A**) again. The sum term p minus the addend m is equal to the other addend 7.

(d) This follows type (**S**), where r is the sum, and the addends are m and 2.

Example 2 **Solve an Equation**

Solve each equation for m.

(a) $8 + m = t$ (b) $s = m - 4$ (c) $p - m = 7$ (d) $r = m + 2$

These are the same equations we had in Example 1. We have already identified m in each equation as the sum term or one of the addends. If m is the sum term, then it is equal to the sum of the addends. If m is one addend, then it is equal to the sum term minus the other addend.

(a) m is an addend, so it is equal to the sum t minus the other addend 8:
$$m = t - 8.$$

(b) m is the sum, so it is the sum of the two addends s and 4: $m = s + 4$.

(c) m is an addend. It equals the sum p minus the other addend 7:
$$m = p - 7.$$

(d) m is an addend and r is the sum. We have $m = r - 2$.

Study Tip:

This way of solving equations is very helpful in part (c). It would take several steps to solve it any other way.

If an equation involves several operations, sometimes the terms can be grouped together into one of the basic types of addition-subtraction equations.

Example 3 **Solve an Equation**

Solve each equation for x.

(a) $3y = x - 7$ (b) $25 + x = \dfrac{m}{4}$ (c) $16 = 5y - x$

(a) We group $3y$ together as one number, and see that x is the sum of the two addends $3y$ and 7: $x = 3y + 7$.

(b) We think of $\dfrac{m}{4}$ as one number. It is the sum of the addends 25 and x. Thus $x = \dfrac{m}{4} - 25$.

(c) $5y$ is the sum and the addends are 16 and x. Thus $x = 5y - 16$.

This is really important!

Remember:

[sum] = [one addend] + [other addend]

[one addend] = [sum] − [other addend]

EXERCISE 6.2

DEVELOP YOUR SKILL

Identify the sum term in each equation.

1. $a + x = 23$ **2.** $17 - x = n$ **3.** $30 = x - 4m$

4. $ab = 5 + x$ **5.** $\frac{a}{b} - x = 2$ **6.** $\frac{m}{n} = x - 5$

Solve each equation for x. These are the same equations used in Exercises 1 – 6.

7. $a + x = 23$ **8.** $17 - x = n$ **9.** $30 = x - 4m$

10. $ab = 5 + x$ **11.** $\frac{a}{b} - x = 2$ **12.** $\frac{m}{n} = x - 5$

Solve each equation for x and compute the basic numeral.

13. $x + 7 = 15$ **14.** $22 - x = 10$ **15.** $13 = x - 4$

16. $20 = x + 6$ **17.** $11 + x = 29$ **18.** $10 = 24 - x$

MAINTAIN YOUR SKILL

Write the corresponding equation that is matched to it by the definition of subtraction or the definition of division. [1.3, 3.2]

19. $x - y = m$ **20.** $a + k = s$

21. $cx = t$ **22.** $\frac{x}{a} = n$

In Exercises 23 – 26, the entire expression is a numeral for a single number. Write this number in prime factored form. [5.6]

23. 18^2 **24.** $33 \cdot 22$

25. $2^3 \cdot 12^2$ **26.** $23 \cdot 7 - 9 \cdot 7$

Use the GCF to factor each expression. [5.8]

27. $18xy^2 - 15y^3$

28. $16x^2y^5 + 18x^4y^3$

29. $4x^3 + 10x^2 + 12x$

30. $4x^3y - 3x^2y^2 - xy^3$

EXTEND YOUR SKILL

31. What property describes the relationship between the equations $5 = 12 - 7$ and $7 = 12 - 5$?

32. Write 16 as many ways as possible in the form $x + x^y$, where x and y are counting numbers.

6.3 – EQUIVALENT EQUATIONS: PRODUCTS AND QUOTIENTS

OBJECTIVE

1. Identify and solve equations involving a product and two factors.

The study of equivalent equations for products and quotients is similar to that for sums and differences. We now use the commutative property of multiplication (instead of addition), and the definition of division is used instead of that for subtraction.

s: symmetric property of equality

c: commutative property of multiplication

d: definition of division

Figure 6.3

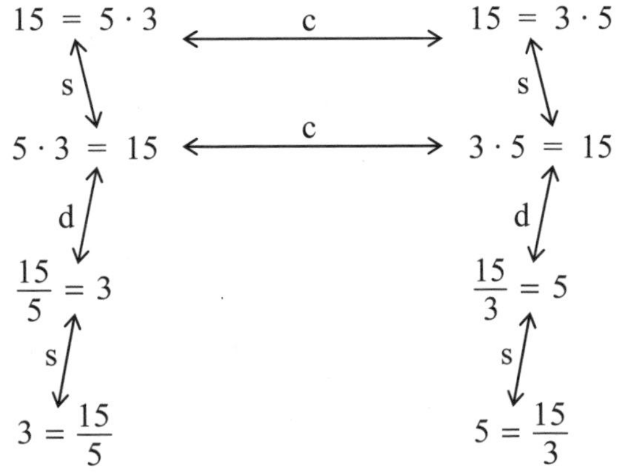

$$15 = 5 \cdot 3 \xleftrightarrow{\quad c \quad} 15 = 3 \cdot 5$$

$$\downarrow s \qquad\qquad \downarrow s$$

$$5 \cdot 3 = 15 \xleftrightarrow{\quad c \quad} 3 \cdot 5 = 15$$

$$\uparrow d \qquad\qquad \uparrow d$$

$$\frac{15}{5} = 3 \qquad\qquad \frac{15}{3} = 5$$

$$\uparrow s \qquad\qquad \uparrow s$$

$$3 = \frac{15}{5} \qquad\qquad 5 = \frac{15}{3}$$

The numbers chosen for Figure 6.3 are all different and greater than 1. The product is then larger than either of the two factors. However, the product can always be recognized just by its usage in the equation. In the upper four equations, the product is shown explicitly as a one factor times the other factor. In the lower four equations, the product is implied. In these equations, one of the factors is equal to the product divided by the other factor.

Figure 6.4

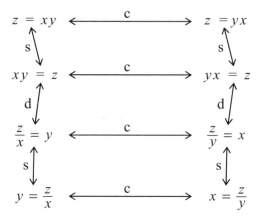

Once again the four lower equations have been paired by the commutative property. This is because the two factors x and y have been commuted (interchanged). This gives us the following extension of the commutative principle for multiplication.

> The factors of a product can be commuted.

The 3-number method may be used to transform equations built with products and quotients in a manner similar to that used in Lessons 6.1 and 6.2 with sums and differences. There are two types of equations:

Key Point

> (P) The product equals one factor times the other factor.
>   (See the top four equations in Figure 6.4.)
>
> (F) One factor equals the product divided by the other factor.
>   (See the bottom four equations in Figure 6.4.)

Study Tip:

If there is multiplying on one side of the equation, the product term is the other side of the equation.

If there is dividing on one side of the equation, the product term is the dividend in the quotient.

Example 1   Identify the Product Term

Identify the expression that is the product of two factors.

  (a) $8m = t$ (b) $s = \dfrac{m}{4}$ (c) $\dfrac{p}{m} = 7$ (d) $a + b = (m)(2)$

(a) This is type (**P**), and the product is t.

(b) This is type (**F**), and m is the product.

(c) This time p is the product (of the factors m and 7).

(d) View $a + b$ as one number. It is the product (of the factors m and 2.)

Example 2   Solve an Equation

Solve each equation for m.

  (a) $8m = t$ (b) $s = \dfrac{m}{4}$ (c) $\dfrac{p}{m} = 7$ (d) $a + b = (m)(2)$

    These are the same equations we had in Example 1. We have already identified m in each equation as the product term or one of the factors. If m is the product term, then it is equal to the product of the factors. If m is one factor, then it is equal to the product term divided by the other factor.

(a) Since m is a factor, and it equals the product divided by the other factor: $m = \dfrac{t}{8}$.

(b) m is the product and we have $m = 4s$.

(c) This time m is a factor, so $m = \dfrac{p}{7}$.

(d) The factor m equals the product $(a + b)$ divided by the other factor 2. That is, $m = \dfrac{a+b}{2}$.

This is really important!

Remember:

    [product] = [one factor] × [other factor]

    [one factor] $= \dfrac{\text{[product]}}{\text{[other factor]}}$

EXERCISE 6.3

DEVELOP YOUR SKILL

Identify the expression that is the product of the other two.

1. $3y = x$

2. $15 = \dfrac{n}{y}$

3. $12 = \dfrac{y}{b-c}$

4. $y(b+c) = 36$

5. $\dfrac{m+n}{y} = t$

6. $a-b = \dfrac{y}{x}$

Solve each equation for y. These are the same equations used in Exercises 1 – 6.

7. $3y = x$

8. $15 = \dfrac{n}{y}$

9. $12 = \dfrac{y}{b-c}$

10. $y(b+c) = 36$

11. $\dfrac{m+n}{y} = t$

12. $a-b = \dfrac{y}{x}$

Solve each equation for x and compute the basic numeral.

13. $x \cdot 4 = 12$

14. $\dfrac{15}{x} = 5$

15. $10 = \dfrac{x}{5}$

16. $30 = x \cdot 5$

17. $3 \cdot x = 24$

18. $7 = \dfrac{35}{x}$

MAINTAIN YOUR SKILL

In Exercises 19 – 22, use commutativity to interchange the order of the two operators. [2.3, 4.2]

19. $-r - s$

20. $-u + v$

21. $a\left(\dfrac{(\ )}{b}\right)$

22. $\dfrac{x(\ )}{y}$

Find the largest square divisor in each expression. Write your answer in prime factored form. [5.6]

23. $2 \cdot 3^5$

24. $3^3 \cdot 5 \cdot 7$

25. $5^3 \cdot 7^2$

26. $2 \cdot 3^4 \cdot 5^3$

Use the GCF to factor each expression. [5.8]

27. $18x + 21x$

28. $20wy - 15xy$

29. $6y^2 + 8xy$

30. $15x^2y + 21x^2y^2$

EXTEND YOUR SKILL

31. If there is a multiplying on one side of a multiplication/division equation, where is the product term?

32. If there is a dividing on one side of a multiplication/division equation, where is the product term?

6.4 – MIXED EQUATIONS

OBJECTIVE

1. Solve equations involving various operations.

    The 3-number method that we have studied in the last three lessons also extends to combinations of sums, differences, products, and quotients. First we identify three terms, grouping as necessary to put them into a sum or a product relationship. Then we solve for the other terms, as desired. By regrouping the terms, we may shift back and forth from a sum and two addends to a product and two factors, if needed.

Example 1   **Solve an Equation**

Solve explicitly for each number in $\dfrac{28}{4} = 13 - 6$. *Do not compute.*

If we group the equation as $\left(\dfrac{28}{4}\right) = (13) - (6)$, then 13 is seen to be the

sum of the two addends $\dfrac{28}{4}$ and 6. Thus $13 = \left(\dfrac{28}{4}\right) + 6$ and $6 = 13 - \left(\dfrac{28}{4}\right)$.

If we group the original equation as $\dfrac{(28)}{(4)} = (13 - 6)$, then 28 is the

product of the two factors 4 and 13 – 6. We have $28 = 4(13 - 6)$ and

$4 = \dfrac{28}{13 - 6}$.

> **Example 2**   **Solve an Equation**
>
> *Solve for x in* $18 = 2x + y$.
>
> There is only one way to view this equation: 18 is the sum of the addends $2x$ and y. Since we cannot make x a term by itself, we first solve for the term containing x. We have
>
> $$(2x) = (18) - (y),$$
>
> where we have emphasized the role of each term by using parentheses. Now group $18 - y$ together and separate 2 and x, so that
>
> $$(2)(x) = (18 - y).$$
>
> Here we see $(18 - y)$ as the product of the factors 2 and x. Thus
>
> $$x = \frac{(18 - y)}{2} \quad \text{or} \quad x = \frac{18 - y}{2}.$$

Study Tip:

The parentheses here help us see the terms when we regroup, but it is not necessary to use them. If you can regroup the terms mentally without using parentheses, that's OK.

EXERCISE 6.4

DEVELOP YOUR SKILL

Solve explicitly for each number in the equation, but do not compute.

1. $880 - 29 = 23 \cdot 37$

2. $19 \cdot 14 = 258 + 8$

3. $\dfrac{899}{31} = 17 + 12$

4. $54 - 11 = \dfrac{989}{23}$

Solve each equation for x and compute the basic numeral.

5. $3x - 8 = 10$

6. $2x + 3 = 15$

7. $24 - 5x = 9$

8. $11 = 25 - 2x$

9. $\dfrac{x+3}{2} = 8$

10. $20 = \dfrac{x}{3} + 5$

11. $16 = \dfrac{18}{x} + 7$

12. $\dfrac{x}{4} - 7 = 3$

13. $2(15 - x) = 16$

14. $17 - \dfrac{15}{x} = 14$

MAINTAIN YOUR SKILL

Find the inverse of each operator. [2.3, 4.2]

15. $+ 24$

16. $- 13$

17. $15(\ )$

18. $\dfrac{(\ )}{9}$

Replace each expression with an equivalent one in which the multipliers, dividers, and sign operators have been distributed. Do not compute. [4.7]

19. $17 + 3(12 - 5)$

20. $82 - 4(15 - 3)$

21. $50 - \dfrac{48 + 8}{4}$

22. $23 + \dfrac{20 + 22}{2}$

Name each form and compute the basic numeral. [5.2]

23. $4 + 5^2$

24. $(3 + 4)^2$

25. $2(7 - 3)^2$

26. $4 \cdot 9 - 2^3$

27. $\dfrac{16}{2} - 3$

28. $(8 - 3 \cdot 2)^2$

29. Evaluate $xy^2 - y$ when $x = 2$ and $y = -3$. [5.2]

30. List all the divisors of 50 that are relatively prime to 2. [5.7]

EXTEND YOUR SKILL

Exercises 31 and 32 relate to the equation $\dfrac{357}{17} = 55 - 34$.

31. If you were asked to solve the equation for 17 without computing, would it be better to view the equation as a sum and two addends, or as a product and two factors. Explain your answer.

32. If you were asked to solve the equation for 34 without computing, would it be better to view the equation as a sum and two addends, or as a product and two factors. Explain your answer.

6.5 – USING THE DISTRIBUTIVE PROPERTY

OBJECTIVE

1. Solve an equation for a variable that appears in more than one place.

If a variable appears in more than one place in an equation, then the distributive property must be used to factor it out of each term before we can solve for it.

Example 1   **Solve an Equation**

Solve for x in the equation $5x - 2x = 18$.

We begin by using the distributive property to factor out x from the two terms on the left side:

$$(5 - 2)x = 18 \quad \text{or} \quad 3x = 18.$$

Now we see 18 as the product of the factors 3 and x, so

$$x = \frac{18}{3} \quad \text{or} \quad x = 6.$$

When the solution of an equation is a numerical value, then the answer can be checked easily by substituting it back into the original equation. For example, in Example 1 we found $x = 6$. Substituting this into the left side of the original equation gives

$$5x - 2x = 5(6) - 2(6) = 30 - 12 = 18,$$

as desired.

Example 2   Solve an Equation and Check the Solution

Solve for x in each equation and check the solution.

  (a) $3x = 24 - 5x$ (b) $7x = 3x + 20$

(a) In order to factor x out of the two terms containing x, they must be on the same side of the equation. Getting $3x$ and $5x$ together is the same as solving for the sum term 24. We have

$$24 = 3x + 5x.$$

Now factor out the x:

$$24 = (3 + 5)x \quad \text{or} \quad 24 = 8x.$$

Then solve for the factor x:

$$x = \frac{24}{8} \quad \text{or} \quad x = 3.$$

To check this solution, substitute $x = 3$ into the original equation. The left side becomes $3x = 3(3) = 9$, and the right side is $24 - 5x = 24 - 5(3) = 24 - 15 = 9$, as desired.

(b) This time we solve for the addend 20 in order to get the two x-terms together:

$20 = 7x - 3x$	Solve for the addend 20.
$20 = (7 - 3)x$	Factor out x.
$20 = 4x$	Compute $7 - 3 = 4$.
$x = \dfrac{20}{4}$ or $x = 5$.	Solve for the factor x and compute.

To check this solution, substitute $x = 5$ in the original equation. The left side gives 35 and the right side is $20 + (3)(5) = 20 + 15 = 35$, as desired.

EXERCISE 6.5

DEVELOP YOUR SKILL

Solve each equation and check your answer.

1. $2x + 5x = 21$

2. $8y - 3y = 20$

3. $7x - 5x = 16$

4. $2y + 4y = 30$

5. $18 - 4d = 5d$

6. $3x + 12 = 7x$

7. $2a = 35 - 3a$

8. $m = 18 - 5m$

9. $4n = n + 15$

10. $4c - 20 = 2c$

MAINTAIN YOUR SKILL

Do not compute, but write equivalent expressions with parentheses around a sum or a difference. Do not change the first term. When possible, give a second alternate form. [2.4]

11. $46 + 24 - 35$

12. $28 - 15 - 6$

13. $25 + 29 - 13$

14. $43 - 21 + 30$

Simplify. Compute as needed. [4.5]

15. $5\left(\dfrac{x}{15}\right)$

16. $15\left(\dfrac{x}{5}\right)$

17. $\dfrac{\dfrac{x}{15}}{5}$

18. $\dfrac{\dfrac{15}{5}}{x}$

19. $\dfrac{15}{\dfrac{x}{5}}$

20. $\dfrac{\dfrac{15}{x}}{5}$

Construct each expression by stating an operand and then listing a sequence of basic operators that can be joined one at a time to produce the given expression. [4.3, 5.2]

21. $3 + 5^3 \cdot 7$

22. $3 \cdot 7^2 - 4$

23. $\dfrac{3^4 + 1}{2}$

24. $\left(\dfrac{26 - 5}{3}\right)^2$

Use the GCF to factor each expression. [5.8]

25. $14wx + 21x$

26. $24wx + 36xy$

27. $15x^2 + 20xy^2$

28. $3x^2y - 18x^2y^2$

29. $30xy^2 - 40xy$

30. $12wx^2 - 9x^2y$

EXTEND YOUR SKILL

In Exercises 31 to 34, write each number in the form $(n + 1)^2$, where n is a natural number, and then in the form $n^2 + 2n + 1$.

31. 25

32. 49

33. 64

34. 100

MID-CHAPTER 6 REVIEW

Solve each equation for the number 15, but do not compute. [6.1, 6.4]

1. $27 = 15 + 12$

2. $15 - 4 = 11$

3. $33 - 15 = 18$

4. $\dfrac{15 - 7}{4} = 2$

5. $4(15 - 3) = 48$

6. $\dfrac{37 - 15}{2} = 11$

Each equation is to be viewed as containing exactly three component expressions: a sum and two addends. Identify the expression that is the sum term. [6.2]

7. $\dfrac{m}{n} - x = bk$

8. $\dfrac{r}{s} = x + mn$

9. $am = bk + \dfrac{x}{y}$

10. $mk - \dfrac{a}{b} = \dfrac{x}{n}$

Each equation is to be viewed as containing exactly three component expressions: a product and two factors. Identify the expression that is the product term. [6.3]

11. $\dfrac{m}{n} - x = bk$

12. $\dfrac{r}{s} = x + mn$

13. $am = bk + \dfrac{x}{y}$

14. $mk - \dfrac{a}{b} = \dfrac{x}{n}$

Solve each equation for x and compute the basic numeral. [6.4, 6.5]

15. $4x - 5 = 23$

16. $7 + 3x = 22$

17. $\dfrac{x}{4} - 12 = 3$

18. $\dfrac{24}{x} - 2 = 6$

19. $25 - 2x = 17$

20. $8 + \dfrac{x}{3} = 17$

21. $11 - \dfrac{35}{x} = 6$

22. $2(x - 3) = 12$

23. $\dfrac{x - 1}{5} = 7$

24. $9x - 5x = 20$

25. $4x + 5x = 36$

26. $32 = 12x - 4x$

27. $2x + 18 = 5x$

28. $x = 24 - 7x$

29. $4x = 27 - 5x$

30. $5x - 12 = 3x$

6.6 – REMOVING INCREASES AND DECREASES

OBJECTIVES

1. Identify the accessible operator in an expression.

2. Solve an equation by removing increases and decreases.

The problem of simplifying an equation or solving explicitly for a particular variable is central to the study of algebra. In Lessons 6.1 – 6.3 we introduced a technique based on identifying a sum or a product relationship within the equation. In this lesson and the next we use the concept of operators to develop an additional way of solving equations.

To solve an equation such as $2x - 5 = 7$, we seek to simplify the equation so that the left side is just x by itself. The expression $2x - 5$ can be built by starting with the operand x and joining the operators $2(\ )$ and -5, in that order.

$$x \xrightarrow{\text{join } 2(\ )} 2x \xrightarrow{\text{join } -5} 2x - 5$$

Solving the equation can be thought of as reversing this process:

$$2x - 5 \xrightarrow{\text{remove } -5} 2x \xrightarrow{\text{remove } 2(\ )} x$$

Note that removing the operators is done in the reverse order from joining them. That is, the only operator that can be removed is the last operator that was joined.

An operator is **accessible for removal** from an expression if it is the *last* operator that was joined in constructing that expression. This is the operator that gives the expression its name as a form. In some cases (with sums and products), there will be two operators that are accessible.

Study Tip:

The only operator that is accessible for removal is from the *last* operation performed when computing. It identifies the name of the form.

┌───┐

Example 1   **Identify the Accessible Operators**

Name each form. Then indicate which operators are accessible for removal.

(a) $3(5 + 7)$ (b) $\dfrac{3 + 7}{2}$ (c) $6 + 3 \cdot 8$ (d) $(7 - 4)^2$

(a) This is a product. Both multiplication operators $3(\ )$ and $(\ )(5 + 7)$ are accessible for removal.

(b) This is a quotient. Only the division operator is accessible: $\dfrac{(\ )}{2}$.

(c) This is a sum. Both increases $6 +$ and $+ (3 \cdot 8)$ are accessible.

(d) This is a power. Only the exponent is accessible for removal: $(\ )^2$.

└───┘

The effect of removing (and joining) operators can be seen by comparing the values before and after the changes.

Example 2   **Effect of Joining or Removing Operators**

Before	After	Change
4	4 + 5	4 is increased by 5 by joining the operator $+5$.
8 − 5	8	3 is increased by 5 by removing the operator -5.
8	8 − 5	8 is decreased by 5 by joining the operator -5.
4 + 5	4	9 is decreased by 5 by removing the operator $+5$.

We see that removing an operator makes the same change as joining the inverse operator of the same magnitude.

Joining $+x$ or $x+$ results in an increase of x.

Removing $-x$ results in an increase of x.

Joining $-x$ results in a decrease of x.

Removing $+x$ or $x+$ results in a decrease of x.

If we have an equation and we make equivalent changes to both sides of the equation, then the truth value of the equation will not be changed. That is, the original equation and the equation after the change will be equivalent. We can make these changes by joining operators or removing operators (if they are accessible). In fact, we can remove an accessible operator from one side and join the inverse operator to the other side, since both changes have exactly the same effect.

Two equations are equivalent if one can be changed into the other by removing an accessible operator from one side and then joining the inverse operator to the other side.

Study Tip:

When you remove an accessible operator from one side of an equation, you join the *inverse* operator to the other side of the equation.

Example 3 **Remove an Operator and Join its Inverse**

Compare $\quad x + 3 = 5$

with $\quad x \quad = 5 - 3.$

Both sides of the first equation are decreased by 3. The left side is decreased by removing $+ 3$ and the right side by joining $- 3$. Thus the two equations are equivalent.

Study Tip:

You can think of subtracting 5 from both sides of the equation.
  You subtract 5 from the left side by removing + 5.
  You subtract 5 from the right side by joining – 5.

Example 4 **Solve an Equation**

Solve each equation for x by removing and joining operators.

(a) $x + 5 = 8$ (b) $9 = x - 4$

(a) Remove the increase of 5 from the left side and join its inverse, a decrease of 5, to the right side:

$$x + 5 = 8 \qquad \text{Write the equation.}$$
$$x \quad = 8 - 5 \qquad \text{Remove + 5 from the left side}$$
$$\text{and join} - 5 \text{ to the right side.}$$
$$x = 3 \qquad \text{Compute } 8 - 5.$$

(b) Remove the decrease of 4 from the right side and join its inverse, an increase of 4, to the left side.

$$9 = x - 4 \qquad \text{Write the equation.}$$
$$9 + 4 = x \qquad \text{Remove} - 4 \text{ from the right side}$$
$$\text{and join} + 4 \text{ to the left side.}$$
$$13 = x \qquad \text{Compute } 9 + 4.$$
$$x = 13 \qquad \text{Use the symmetric property of equality.}$$

EXERCISE 6.6

DEVELOP YOUR SKILL

Name each form (sum, difference, product, quotient, or power). Then indicate which operators are accessible for removal.

1. $\dfrac{12}{3} + 7$

2. $(12 - 8)2$

3. $24 - 13$

4. $\dfrac{2(5+4)}{3}$

5. $3\left(\dfrac{5+7}{4}\right)$

6. $\left(x - \dfrac{a}{b}\right)^2$

7. $8 + 5^2$

8. $n - xy$

9. $\dfrac{ab^2}{m}$

Solve each equation for x by removing and joining operators. Compute the basic numeral when possible.

10. $x + 7 = 12$

11. $x - 5 = 8$

12. $m = x + 8$

13. $3 + x = 18$

14. $10 = 4 + x$

15. $7 = x - a$

16. $15 = x - 12$

17. $x - 4 = 9$

18. $x - y = c$

MAINTAIN YOUR SKILL

Simplify each expression. If no simpler form is possible, write "not possible." [4.4]

19. $\dfrac{a(b-c)}{a}$

20. $\dfrac{xy}{x} + \dfrac{yz}{y}$

21. $\dfrac{ab-c}{a}$

22. $\dfrac{a+b}{a-b}$

23. $rs - (rt - t)$

24. $\dfrac{b(c-d)}{c} + d$

Evaluate each expression as indicated. [3.4, 5.2]

25. $x^3 - y^3$ when $x = 4$ and $y = 2$

26. $x^2 - y^2$ when $x = 7$ and $y = 6$

27. $(x - y)^3$ when $x = 4$ and $y = 2$

28. $(x - y)^2$ when $x = 7$ and $y = 6$

29. $x + y \cdot z$ when $x = 7$, $y = 5$, and $z = 3$

30. $x - y \cdot z$ when $x = 25$, $y = 2$, and $z = 3$

EXTEND YOUR SKILL

31. Explain what determines which operator is accessible for removal.

32. State two ways to subtract 7 from an expression by using operators.

33. Which forms (sum, difference, product, quotient, or power) have more than one accessible operator?

6.7 – REMOVING EXPANSIONS AND CONTRACTIONS

OBJECTIVE

1. Solve an equation by removing expansions and contractions.

Since expansions and contractions are inverse operations, we would expect that removing an expansion would have the same effect as joining a contraction.

Example 1		**Effect of Joining or Removing Operators**
Before	After	Change
8	5(8)	8 is multiplied by 5 by joining the operator 5( ).
$\dfrac{10}{5}$	10	2 is multiplied by 5 by removing the operator $\dfrac{(\ )}{5}$.
5(8)	8	40 is divided by 5 by removing the operator 5( ).
10	$\dfrac{10}{5}$	10 is divided by 5 by joining the operator $\dfrac{(\ )}{5}$.

If $x \neq 0$, multiplication by x results if the operators $x(\ )$ or $(\ )x$ are joined or if $\dfrac{(\ )}{x}$ is removed. Division by x results if the operator $\dfrac{(\ )}{x}$ is joined or if the operators $x(\ )$ or $(\ )x$ are removed. Of course, we do not want to join or remove the operator $0(\ )$, since it has no inverse.

Example 2   **Remove an Operator and Join its Inverse**

Compare $4 = \dfrac{x}{2}$

with $4 \cdot 2 = x.$

Both members of the first equation are multiplied by 2. The left member is multiplied by 2 by joining the operator $\cdot\, 2$, and the right member is multiplied by 2 by removing the operator $\dfrac{(\ )}{2}$. Thus the two equations are equivalent.

The first step in using operators to derive equivalent equations is to decide which operators are accessible for removal. If there is more than one choice, we consider the change that will give an equation that seems a step closer to the desired form.

Example 3   **Solve an Equation by Removing Operators**

Solve explicitly for each number in $\dfrac{28}{4} = 13 - 6$. *Do not compute.*

(Compare with Example 1 in Lesson 6.4.)

The accessible operators are $\dfrac{(\ )}{4}$ and $-\,6$. By removing $\dfrac{(\ )}{4}$ and joining $4(\ )$ we have

$$28 = 4(13 - 6).$$

By removing $-\,6$ and joining $+\,6$ we obtain

$$\dfrac{28}{4} + 6 = 13.$$

In the equation $28 = 4(13 - 6)$, the operator $(\ )(13 - 6)$ is accessible, so that

$$\dfrac{28}{13 - 6} = 4.$$

In the equation $\dfrac{28}{4} + 6 = 13$, the operator $\dfrac{28}{4} +$ is accessible, so that

$$6 = 13 - \dfrac{28}{4}.$$

Study Tip:

When $4(\ )$ is joined to $13 - 6$, parentheses must be used to group $13 - 6$ together as one term.

When operators are used with equations, we think of each member as representing just *one* number. Hence when operators are joined to a member of an equation, the change must be to that member as a whole. For expansions, the parentheses for $n(\ )$ or $(\ )n$ must enclose *all* of the member to which they are applied. Likewise for contractions, the bar of the division operator $\dfrac{(\ )}{n}$ is written underneath the *entire* member.

Example 4   **Solve an Equation**

Solve for x in $18 = 2x + y$. (*Compare with Example* 2 *in Lesson* 6.4.)

The operators $2(\ )$ and $(\ )x$ are *not* accessible here. The right side of the equation is a *sum*, so the accessible operators are $2x +$ and $+y$. Thus we may obtain

$$18 - 2x = y \quad \text{or} \quad 18 - y = 2x.$$

The second equation is closer to what we want since it has the term involving x by itself on the right side. In $18 - y = 2x$, the operator $2(\ )$ is now accessible so that

$$\frac{18 - y}{2} = x.$$

In this chapter we have studied two different ways of solving equations. These two methods use different thought patterns, and hence each is a good check on the other.

The first method identifies three numbers, either as a sum and two addends, or as a product and two factors. The given statement is always explicit for one of these three numbers, and two more explicit statements can always be made about these same three numbers. Further changes can be made whenever a different choice of three numbers (or variables) is available.

The second method makes changes by removing accessible operators from one member of the equation and joining the inverse operator to the other member. An accessible operator is the last one used in constructing that member, and is the one that determines the name of its form.

In any particular problem, it may be a combination of both methods that will be most effective in reaching the solution.

Here is a quick review.

Example 5   **Solve an Equation**

Solve each equation for x.

(a) $20 = (7 - x)y$.   (b) $\dfrac{12}{x} + 5 = y$

(a) First divide both members by y: $\dfrac{20}{y} = 7 - x$. Then see 7 as the sum

term and solve for the addend x: $x = 7 - \dfrac{20}{y}$.

(b) First subtract 5 from both members: $\dfrac{12}{x} = y - 5$. Then see 12 as

the product term and solve for the factor x: $x = \dfrac{12}{y - 5}$.

EXERCISE 6.7

DEVELOP YOUR SKILL

Solve explicitly for each number in the equation, but do not compute.

1. $15 + 7 = \dfrac{66}{3}$

2. $\dfrac{50}{2} = 38 - 13$

3. $(5)(8) = 23 + 17$

4. $26 - 5 = (3)(7)$

Solve each equation for y.

5. $x = 13 + 2y$

6. $8y - 3 = 5x$

7. $3(y + 5) = x$

8. $24 = x + 5y$

9. $\dfrac{2y - 3}{5} = x$

10. $\dfrac{16 - y}{2} = x$

Exercises 11 – 14 are from some of the many fields where algebraic formulas are used. They are stated in explicit form for one of the variables. Give explicit forms for each of the other variables.

11. If P represents the principal borrowed or invested (in dollars), R represents the interest rate, and I represents the interest, then $I = PR$ is a formula for computing the amount of interest when the principal and the rate of interest are known.

12. If r represents a constant rate of motion, t represents the time, and d represents the distance traveled, then $d = r \cdot t$ is a formula for computing the distance when the rate and time are known.

13. Let C represent the total cost, P represent the price per item, N represent the number of items, and let T represent the tax on a sale. Then $C = PN + T$.

14. Let E represent a salesperson's total earnings, S equal the amount of sales, R represent the commission rate on these sales, and let B represent the base salary. Then $E = SR + B$.

MAINTAIN YOUR SKILL

Construct graphical models for the composition of the operators. [1.9 and 2.8]

15. $-8 + 4$

16. $-2 + 6$

17. $4\left(\dfrac{(\ )}{8}\right)$

18. $6\left(\dfrac{(\ )}{2}\right)$

In Exercises 19 – 26, the entire expression is a numeral for a single number. Write this number in prime factored form. [5.6]

19. 24^2

20. $50 \cdot 55$

21. $2 \cdot 3 + 3 \cdot 4$

22. $21 \cdot 5^2 - 5^2$

23. $3^2 \cdot 6^2$

24. $5(22 + 3)$

25. $17^3 + 17^2$

26. $(2^3 \cdot 4^5)^2$

Solve each equation for x and compute the basic numeral. [6.5]

27. $5x - 3x = 18$

28. $4x = 30 - x$

29. $21 + 2x = 5x$

30. $7x - 15 = 4x$

EXTEND YOUR SKILL

31. State two ways to multiply an expression by 8 by using operators.

32. State two ways to divide an expression by 6 by using operators.

6.8 – READING ALGEBRA

One of the great advantages of algebra over arithmetic is that it enables us to solve more complicated problems. By using different letters as variables, we can consider several related ideas at the same time. The equations (or inequalities) that we construct form an algebraic model for the original problem. In this lesson we see how the rules for naming a form are a guide to reading algebraic expressions.

When an algebraic expression only involves one operation, it is easy to read in English: give the name of the form and then name the two terms being combined. For example:

$$x + y \longrightarrow \text{the sum of } x \text{ and } y$$

$$x - y \longrightarrow \text{the difference of } x \text{ and } y$$

$$xy \longrightarrow \text{the product of } x \text{ and } y$$

$$\frac{x}{y} \longrightarrow \text{the quotient of } x \text{ and } y$$

When an expression involves more than one operation, the first operation mentioned must correspond to the name of the form. For example, $2x + 3$ is a sum because the last operation is addition. In translating this into an English phrase, we begin by identifying it as a sum. Then we name the two parts of the sum, separating them by the word "and."

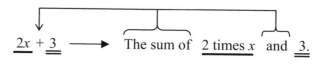

$$2x + 3 \longrightarrow \text{The sum of } \underline{2 \text{ times } x} \text{ and } \underline{3}.$$

Example 1   **Translate Algebra into English**

Write the English phrase that corresponds to $2(x + 3)$.

This is a product, since the last operation is multiplying. We have

$$2(x + 3) \longrightarrow \text{The product of } \underline{2} \text{ and } \underline{\text{the sum of } x \text{ and } 3}$$

A simple expression such as $x - 5$ can also be read as "5 less than x." (Think of starting with x and decreasing by 5.) Likewise, $x + 5$ becomes "5 more than x" and $5x$ is "5 times x." With a compound statement, these abbreviations may be used within the parts that are being combined, but they should not be used for the parts and the whole expression. For example, what does "3 more than x times y" mean? It could either refer to a sum or a product:

"3 more than x times y" as a sum $\longrightarrow$ $xy + 3$

"3 more than x times y" as a product $\longrightarrow$ $(x + 3)y$

By being careful to begin with the actual name of the form, this kind of ambiguity can be avoided.

In casual conversation it is all right to read an increase or decrease operator as written:

$$x + 9 \longrightarrow \text{"x plus 9"}$$

$$y - 2 \longrightarrow \text{"y minus 2"}$$

But this is not acceptable in a proper translation. The name of the form or "more than" or "less than" should be used.

Example 2   **Translate Algebra into English**

Write the English phrase that corresponds to each expression.

(a) $y + 7$ (b) $m(a - 2)$ (c) $x + 4y$

(a) "The sum of y and 7" or "7 more than y."

(b) "The product of m and the difference of a and 2" or "the product of m and 2 less than a."

(c) "The sum of x and the product of 4 and y" or "the sum of x and 4 times y."

EXERCISE 6.8

DEVELOP YOUR SKILL

Write the English phrase that corresponds to each expression.

1. $x + 10$

2. $y - 5$

3. $3x$

4. $\dfrac{12}{n}$

5. $\dfrac{x}{y+1}$

6. $4(x + 3)$

7. $x - 3n$

8. $5x + 3$

9. $(x + y)^2$

10. $x + y^2$

11. $x^2 - y$

12. $x^2(y - 5)$

MAINTAIN YOUR SKILL

List all the factors of each number. [3.3]

13. 36

14. 40

Use the GCF to factor each expression. [5.8]

15. $15x^2y + 18xy$

16. $18xy^3 - 12x^2y^2$

17. $3x^2y - xy$

18. $2x^2y + 8x^2y^2$

19. $12x^3 - 4x^2 + 8x$

20. $10x^2 + 6xy + 4y^2$

Solve each equation for x. [6.5, 6.7]

21. $3x + 4x = 56$

22. $x = 20 - 4x$

23. $3x = x + 18$

24. $8x - 21 = 5x$

25. $y = 12 - 3x$

26. $4 + 7x = y$

27. $6x - 11 = 5y$

28. $15 - x = \dfrac{y}{3}$

29. $\dfrac{5 + x}{2} = y$

30. $\dfrac{14 - x}{3} = y$

EXTEND YOUR SKILL

31. Write 12 as the sum of an even number of odd numbers, all equal to each other and greater than one.

32. Write 12 as the sum of an odd number of even numbers, all equal to each other.

6.9 – WRITING ALGEBRA

OBJECTIVE

1. Translate English phrases and sentences into algebraic expressions.

In Lesson 6.8 we explained how to read an algebraic expression. In this lesson we go the other direction: we take an English phrase or sentence and translate it into an algebraic expression.

Example 1   **Translate English into Algebra**

Translate each word phrase into a mathematical expression. If you are not given some other name for it, use the letter x to represent the "number."

    (a) twice a number

    (b) 7 more than a number

    (c) 5 less than a number

    (d) the product of 4 and the sum of x and y

(a) We can write either $2x$ or $(x)(2)$. While either answer is acceptable, the first is preferred for two reasons: it follows the same order as the word phrase, and we may omit the parentheses when writing the numeral to the left of the variable.

(b) We have $x + 7$ or $7 + x$. This time the form $x + 7$ is preferable, even though it seems to reverse the word order. The idea is that we start with a number, x, and increase it by 7. By so doing we end up with "7 more than a number." But the *process* is really "a number increased by 7."

(c) In this case, the *only* correct answer is $x - 5$. To end up with 5 less than a number, we must start with the number and decrease it by 5. The mathematical expression must tell us how to do this computation.

(d) We have $4(x + y)$. In a phrase like this that combines two operations, the *first* operation mentioned in English gives the name of the form. (Recall that this will be the *last* operation to be performed in the computation.) Thus our answer must be in the form of a product. The first factor is 4 and the second factor is the sum of x and y.

Study Tip:

Parentheses are necessary in part (d). The expression
$4x + y$
is the **sum** of 4 times x and y.

In the following table we list the algebraic equivalent of several common English phrases. We have used x as the name for the variable, but any other letter would be equally acceptable.

Table 6.1

English Phrase	Algebraic Expression
Addition	
A number increased by 7	$x + 7$
The sum of a number and 5	$x + 5$
Six more than a number	$x + 6$
A number plus 8	$x + 8$
Subtraction	
A number decreased by 3	$x - 3$
The difference of a number and 8	$x - 8$
The difference of 9 and a number	$9 - x$
Seven less than a number	$x - 7$
Three fewer than a number	$x - 3$
Five minus a number	$5 - x$
Multiplication	
The product of 4 and a number	$4x$
Six times a number	$6x$
A number multiplied by 8	$8x$
Twice a number	$2x$
Two-thirds of a number (used with fractions)	$\frac{2}{3}x$
Division	
The quotient of a number and 5	$\frac{x}{5}$
The quotient of 5 and a number	$\frac{5}{x}$
A number divided by 3	$\frac{x}{3}$

Do I have to memorize all these?

No, but read them over until they make sense to you.

Power	
A number to the fourth power	x^4
The square of a number	x^2
The cube of a number	x^3
More than one operation	
The sum of twice a number and 3	$2x + 3$
Twice the sum of a number and 3	$2(x + 3)$
Five less than 7 times a number	$7x - 5$
Three times the sum of a number and 6	$3(x + 6)$
The sum of 3 times a number and 6	$3x + 6$
Three times a number, increased by 6	$3x + 6$
The product of 4 and 3 less than a number	$4(x - 3)$

It is only a small step from writing a mathematical expression to writing a mathematical equation. The key is to recognize that the English word "is" means "is equal to," and it is therefore represented by an equal sign.

Example 2   **Translate English into Algebra**

Write each statement as a mathematical equation.

(a) Seven is four more than a number.

(b) Three less than twice a number is eleven.

(c) The product of 3 and x is the sum of y and 5.

(a) $7 = x + 4$

seven is four more than a number
$$7 \quad = \quad x + 4$$

(b) $2x - 3 = 11$

3 less than twice a number is eleven
$$2x - 3 \quad = \quad 11$$

(c) $3x = y + 5$

the product of 3 and x is the sum of y and 5
$$3x \quad = \quad y + 5$$

EXERCISE 6.9

DEVELOP YOUR SKILL

Translate each word phrase into an algebraic expression.

1. The sum of x and 5
2. 9 less than y
3. The square of the difference of m and n
4. The sum of 4 and the square of y
5. 5 less than the product of 3 and y
6. 7 increased by the quotient of 10 and x
7. The product of 5 less than x and y
8. The quotient of x and 2 more than y

Write each statement as an algebraic equation, using x as the variable. Do not solve the equation.

9. The sum of 3 times a number and 5 is 26.
10. The quotient of 10 more than a number and 5 is 6.
11. The product of 4 and 2 more than a number is 20.
12. Three more than twice a number is 11.
13. Three times a number is 16 more than this number.
14. A number divided by 5 is 12 less than this number.

MAINTAIN YOUR SKILL

Name each form and compute the basic numeral. [5.2]

15. $\dfrac{(4 \cdot 5)^2}{2}$

16. $\dfrac{4 \cdot 5^2}{2}$

17. $4 + 5^2$

18. $(4 + 5)^2$

19. $\left(\dfrac{4 \cdot 5}{2}\right)^2$

20. $4^2 + 5^2$

Find the largest square divisor in each expression. Write your answer in prime factored form. Assume the variables are distinct primes with $w < x < y < z$. [5.6]

21. $3^5 \cdot 5^2$

22. $2 \cdot 3^6 \cdot 5^3$

23. $x^2 \cdot y^3$

24. $x \cdot y^5 \cdot z^2$

25. $w^2 \cdot y \cdot z^3$

26. $w \cdot x^6 \cdot y^2 \cdot z^3$

Exercises 27 – 30 are from some of the many fields where algebraic formulas are used. They are stated in explicit form for one of the variables. Give explicit forms for each of the other variables. [6.8]

27. If h is the number of hits and b is the number of a player's official times at bat, then the batting average A is given by $A = \dfrac{h}{b}$.

28. If U is the unit cost, N is the units made, and F is the fixed cost, then the total cost of production T is given by $T = U \cdot N + F$.

29. If v_0 is the initial velocity of a falling object, and t is the time the object is falling, then the final velocity v of the falling object is given approximately by $v = v_0 + 32t$.

30. If C is the cost of an item, and M is the markup rate, then the selling price S is given by $S = C + MC$.

EXTEND YOUR SKILL

31. Name the form that is obtained when "7 more than the product of x and y" is written as an algebraic expression.

32. Name the form that is obtained when "y times the sum of x and 7" is written as an algebraic expression.

$A = \dfrac{h}{b}$

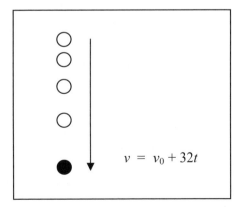

$v = v_0 + 32t$

6.10 – MODELING WITH EQUATIONS

OBJECTIVE

1. Use equations to model real-world situations.

When given a real-world situation, there is a 3-step strategy to setting up an equation (or an inequality) as a model:

1. Write a model of the situation using simple words.
2. Define a variable for the unknown quantity.
3. Translate the words into an algebraic expression.

In step 1, try to write a sentence using a form of the verb "is." This will make step 3 easier: the word "is" becomes the equal sign in the equation.

We've rewritten the sentence to help you set up the equation. You don't have to do this.

Example 1   **Write an Equation**

Bob is 183 cm tall. If Bob is 8 cm taller than Frank, write an equation to find Frank's height.

Words: Bob's height is 8 cm more than Frank's height.

Variable: Let F represent Frank's height.

Bob's height   is   8 more than Frank's height.

Equation: 183   = $F + 8$

Example 2   **Write an Equation**

Ruth is twice as old as Mary. If Ruth is 52 years old, write an equation to find Mary's age.

Words: Ruth's age is twice Mary's age.

Variable: Let M represent Mary's age.

Ruth's age   is   twice Mary's age.

Equation: 52   = $2M$

Sometimes there is more than one reasonable way to model a given situation. This is illustrated in the next example.

Example 3   **Write an Equation**

Write an algebraic equation as a model for the following problem:

> *Tom has just made a purchase of 47¢. How much change should he receive from a dollar bill if there is no sales tax?*

There are two ways of thinking about this problem. We might think of subtracting his purchase from the dollar to get the change:

Words: A dollar minus the amount he spent equals his change.

Variable: Let *C* represent his change.

	A dollar	minus	the amount he spent	equals	his change.
Equation:	100	−	47	=	C

Or we might think of "counting out" the change as the sales clerk might do. We could start with the purchase and add on the change to get a dollar.

Words: The amount he spent plus his change is a dollar.

Variable: Let *C* represent his change.

	The amount he spent	plus	his change	is	a dollar.
Equation:	47	+	C	=	100

The first equation has the advantage of being explicit for *C*, but either equation is an acceptable model for the problem. Of course, the two equations are really equivalent. (Do you see why?)

They are related by the definition of subtraction.

EXERCISE 6.10

DEVELOP YOUR SKILL

In Exercises 1 – 6, you are to do two things: (a) Define a variable. (b) Write an equation to model the situation. [You do not need to solve the equation.]

1. Fernando weighs 28 pounds more than his sister Maria. If Fernando weighs 152 pounds, how much does Maria weigh?

2. Jacki ran in a marathon last week. She finished the race 12 minutes faster than she expected. If she finished in 258 minutes, how long did she expect the race to take?

3. Bob plays guard on the basketball team. In his last game he scored 15 points. This was 7 points below his average for the season. What is his average for the season?

4. Mt. Everest is known as the highest mountain on earth, but Mauna Kea in Hawaii is actually taller in one way. Measured from its base on the bottom of the Pacific Ocean, Mauna Kea's height (above the ocean floor) is 1357 meters more than Mt. Everest's height (above sea level). If the top of Mauna Kea is 10,205 meters above its base, how high is Mt. Everest?

5. Jennifer's savings are 3 less than twice Nicole's savings. If Jennifer has saved $165, how much has Nicole saved?

6. The Missouri river is the longest river in the United States. It is 264 miles more than 4 times the length of the Porcupine River in Alaska. If the Missouri River is 2540 miles long, how long is the Porcupine River?

MAINTAIN YOUR SKILL

Write the composition of the two given operators as an equivalent single operator in basic form. [2.3, 4.2]

7. $-17 + 4$

8. $-3 + 8$

9. $\dfrac{4(\ \ )}{8}$

10. $12\left(\dfrac{(\ \ )}{3}\right)$

11. $5\left(\dfrac{(\ \ )}{15}\right)$

12. $\dfrac{21(\ \ )}{7}$

Find the number for x that will give a true statement. [5.4]

13. $\dfrac{3^x}{3^6} = 3^2$

14. $5^x \cdot 5^3 = 5^3$

15. $\dfrac{13^8}{13^x} = 13^4$

16. $\left(19^x\right)^2 = 19^6$

Determine whether the numbers in each pair are relatively prime. If they are not relatively prime, find their GCF. [5.8]

17. 15 and 22

18. 21 and 27

Use the GCF to factor each expression. [5.8]

19. $15x^2 - 21xy$

20. $25xy + 18y^2$

21. $24wxy - 12wx^2$

22. $5xy + 10x^2y$

Solve each equation for x. [6.5]

23. $32 - 3x = 5x$

24. $x = 4x - 15$

Name each form (sum, difference, product, quotient, or power). Then indicate which operators are accessible for removal. [6.6]

25. $(a - b)c$

26. $r - \dfrac{s}{t}$

27. $(a \cdot b)^r$

28. $\dfrac{m \cdot n^2}{p}$

29. $\dfrac{m(a+b)}{c}$

30. $ab + bc$

EXTEND YOUR SKILL

31. In Exercise 1, what is wrong with letting the variable M represent Maria?

32. If p is a prime number, what can be said about the numbers that are relatively prime to p? [5.8]

CHAPTER 6 REVIEW

Solve each equation for the number 23, but do not compute. [6.1]

1. $68 = 45 + 23$

2. $23 - 14 = 9$

Each equation is to be viewed as containing exactly three component expressions. Identify the expression that is the sum of the other two. [6.2]

3. $xy = ab + \dfrac{c}{d}$

4. $am - y = \dfrac{x}{n}$

Each equation is to be viewed as containing exactly three component expressions. Identify the expression that is the product of the other two. [6.3]

5. $xy = ab + \dfrac{c}{d}$

6. $am - y = \dfrac{x}{n}$

Name each form. Then indicate which operators are accessible for removal. [6.6]

7. $28 - \dfrac{14}{7}$

8. $\dfrac{8 + 7}{3}$

9. $5(3 + 7)$

10. $745 - 23 \cdot 15$

Solve each equation for x. [6.2 – 6.7]

11. $3x + 8 = 29$

12. $21 - 4x = 5$

13. $7 + \dfrac{x}{2} = 18$

14. $\dfrac{35}{x} + 8 = 15$

15. $3x + 6x = 45$

16. $25 + 2x = 37$

17. $2x = 30 - 8x$

18. $16 + x = 3x$

19. $y = 20 - 3x$

20. $15 = 2x + y$

21. $5(x - 3) = y$

22. $3 = \dfrac{y + 7}{x}$

23. $24 = x(y + 3)$

Write the English phrase that corresponds to each expression. [6.8]

24. $5x - 2$

25. $2x + 3y$

26. $(x - y)^2$

Translate each statement into a mathematical equation. [6.9]

27. The square of the sum of 3 and 5 is x.

28. The sum of the squares of 3 and 5 is y.

29. The product of 3 and y is 12 more than twice x.

Define a variable and write an equation to model the situation. Then solve the equation. [6.10]

30. Bill's age is 5 less than twice Mark's age. If Bill is 47 years old, how old is Mark?

Chapter 7 — Rational Numbers

7.1 – QUOTIENTS AND FRACTIONS

OBJECTIVES

1. Understand the meaning of a fraction and represent it graphically.

2. Reduce a fraction to lowest terms.

Up to this point we have confined our attention to the counting numbers. While this has simplified the ideas, it has also meant that some differences and most quotients were undefined. There are many practical situations, however, for which the counting numbers are inadequate. This prompts us to extend our notion of a number to include other possibilities. In this chapter we introduce fractions, and in Chapter 8, we consider negative numbers.

The quotient $\frac{2}{3}$ cannot be a counting number, since there is no counting number x such that $3x = 2$, as required by the definition of division. But the *need* for such a number can be seen in the following problem.

Suppose we have a line segment that is two units long:

If we divide this line segment into 3 equal parts, how long will each part be?

The symbols that we use to describe the length above are the same symbols that were used to state the problem. Namely, when 2 is divided by 3, the result is $\frac{2}{3}$. That is to say, the number $\frac{2}{3}$ is precisely the number that when multiplied by 3 is equal to 2.

**Definition
of a
Rational
Number**

> The numbers x that are solutions of the equation $(n)(x) = m$, where m and n are counting numbers with $n \neq 0$, are called **rational numbers**. The number x can be represented by a numeral, the **fraction** $\frac{m}{n}$. Thus we have
>
> $$(n)\left(\frac{m}{n}\right) = m.$$
>
> The set of numbers given by this definition is denoted by $\mathbb{Q}^+$ (the set of nonnegative quotients).

There are two helpful ways to visualize the fraction $\frac{2}{3}$. In the introduction we started with 1, multiplied by 2 (to get a line segment of length 2), and then we divided by 3. That is,

$$\frac{2}{3} = \frac{2 \cdot 1}{3}.$$

We can also think of $\frac{2}{3}$ as starting with 1, dividing by 3 (to get $\frac{1}{3}$), and then multiplying by 2. That is,

$$\frac{2}{3} = (2)\left(\frac{1}{3}\right).$$

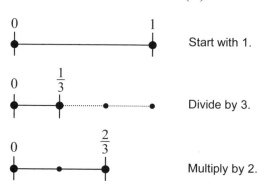

Notice that the length obtained here for $\frac{2}{3}$ is the same as the length obtained by taking 2 and dividing by 3:

Having defined the number $\frac{2}{3}$ as above, the operator $\frac{2}{3}(\ )$ can also be defined. We let the operator $\frac{2}{3}(\ )$ be the composite, in either order, of $2(\ )$ and $\frac{(\ )}{3}$. That is, multiplying by the fraction $\frac{2}{3}$ is the composition of multiplying by 2 and dividing by 3, in either order.

$$\frac{m}{n}(\ ) = \frac{m(\ )}{n} = m\frac{(\ )}{n}.$$

When $\frac{2}{3}$ is viewed as a quotient, we have called 2 the dividend and 3 the divisor. When $\frac{2}{3}$ is viewed as a fraction, then 2 is called the **numerator** and 3 is called the **denominator**.

Quotient   Fraction

dividend $\longrightarrow$ $\dfrac{2}{3}$ $\longleftarrow$ divisor $\dfrac{2}{3}$ $\longleftarrow$ numerator / denominator

These new names come from the second model above where we first divide by 3 and then multiply by 2. The denominator identifies (or denominates) the kind of a fraction—in this case thirds. The numerator enumerates how many of the thirds we have—in this case two.

If counting numbers are used for m and n, then $\frac{m}{n}$ is a **simple** fraction. If $m < n$, then $\frac{m}{n}$ is a **proper** fraction, but if $m \geq n$, then $\frac{m}{n}$ is called an **improper** fraction.

Example 1   **Simple Fractions and Proper Fractions**

$\frac{2}{3}$, $\frac{4}{8}$, and $\frac{7}{12}$ are simple proper fractions.

$\frac{5}{3}$, $\frac{10}{2}$, and $\frac{7}{7}$ are simple improper fractions.

$\frac{2 \cdot 3}{4}$, $\frac{\frac{2}{3}}{4}$, and $\frac{5}{3+8}$ are not simple fractions.

Every rational number has an infinite set of fraction names by which it can be represented. For example,

$$\frac{2}{3} = \frac{4}{6} = \frac{6}{9} = \frac{8}{12} = \cdots$$

These equalities all follow from the invariant principle for quotients:

$$\frac{2}{3} = \frac{2 \cdot 2}{3 \cdot 2} = \frac{4}{6}, \quad \frac{2}{3} = \frac{2 \cdot 3}{3 \cdot 3} = \frac{6}{9}, \quad \frac{2}{3} = \frac{2 \cdot 4}{3 \cdot 4} = \frac{8}{12}, \cdots$$

Among all the equivalent fractions that represent the same rational number $\frac{x}{y}$, the **basic numeral** is the simple fraction with x and y as small as possible. Such a fraction is said to be in **lowest terms**. In reducing a fraction to lowest terms, the invariant principle for quotients is very useful. Recall that

$$\frac{x}{y} = \frac{nx}{ny} \quad \text{and} \quad \frac{x}{y} = \frac{\dfrac{x}{n}}{\dfrac{y}{n}}, \text{ for } n \neq 0.$$

The problem of reducing a fraction to lowest terms is often made easier by writing both the numerator and the denominator in factored form. Then the basic numeral can be obtained by removing the same operator $\cdot\, n$ from the numerator and the denominator. This has the effect of dividing both the numerator and the denominator by n. Or equivalently, we may think of canceling a multiplying by n (in the numerator) with a dividing by n (in the denominator).

Study Tip:

Removing the $\cdot\, 17$ operators has the effect of dividing both the numerator and the denominator by 17.

Example 2   **Reduce a Fraction**

$$\frac{51}{68} = \frac{3 \cdot 17}{4 \cdot 17}$$

Factor the numerator and the denominator.

$$= \frac{3 \cdot \cancel{17}}{4 \cdot \cancel{17}} = \frac{3}{4}$$

Remove the $\cdot\, 17$ operators. Or, cancel a multiplying by 17 (in the numerator) with a dividing by 17 (in the denominator).

When reducing a fraction, it is helpful to look for the GCF of the numerator and the denominator:

$$\frac{30}{42} = \frac{5 \cdot 6}{7 \cdot 6} = \frac{5}{7}$$

But if the GCF is not used, the process can be done in repeated steps:

$$\frac{30}{42} = \frac{15 \cdot 2}{21 \cdot 2} = \frac{15}{21} = \frac{5 \cdot 3}{7 \cdot 3} = \frac{5}{7}$$

When the denominator of a fraction is 1, the fraction can be simplified to a counting number.

Remember:

You are **not** canceling the 19's. You are canceling a multiplying by 19 with a dividing by 19.

Example 3   **Reduce a Fraction**

$$\frac{38}{19} = \frac{2 \cdot 19}{1 \cdot 19} = \frac{2}{1} = 2$$

Notice how 19 was replaced by 1 · 19 so that 19 is seen to be a factor in the denominator. Both the numerator and the denominator can then be divided by 19 by removing the operator · 19.

EXERCISE 7.1
DEVELOP YOUR SKILL

Construct a graphical model for each interpretation of the fraction $\frac{3}{4}$.

1. $\dfrac{3}{4} = \dfrac{3 \cdot 1}{4}$

2. $\dfrac{3}{4} = 3\left(\dfrac{1}{4}\right)$

Reduce each fraction to lowest terms.

3. $\dfrac{15}{20}$

4. $\dfrac{28}{35}$

5. $\dfrac{60}{36}$

6. $\dfrac{25}{45}$

7. $\dfrac{27}{54}$

8. $\dfrac{48}{32}$

MAINTAIN YOUR SKILL

Do not compute, but write equivalent expressions without parentheses. Do not change the first term. When possible, give a second alternate form. [2.4]

9. $9 + (8 - 3)$

10. $11 - (7 - 4)$

11. $15 - (5 + 6)$

12. $7 + (12 - 9)$ **13.** $8 - (12 - 10)$ **14.** $14 - (3 + 8)$

In Exercises 15 – 20, the entire expression is a numeral for a single number. Write this number in prime factored form. [5.6]

15. $15 \cdot 24$ **16.** $8 \cdot 32$ **17.** $(6 \cdot 14)^2$

18. 34^3 **19.** $9 \cdot 19 + 19$ **20.** $2 \cdot 17 + 11 \cdot 17$

21. If x divides y, what is the greatest common divisor of x and y? [5.7]

22. If x divides y, what is the least common multiple of x and y? [5.7]

In Exercises 23 – 30, each equation can be viewed as consisting of exactly three components. Identify the expression that is the sum (S) or the product (P) of the other two expressions. Give all possible interpretations. [6.4]

23. $x - y = w + z$ **24.** $r - s = p - q$ **25.** $m + n = \frac{s}{t}$

26. $cd = e + f$ **27.** $g - h = ef$ **28.** $\frac{r}{s} = m - n$

29. $\frac{u}{v} = xy$ **30.** $\frac{w}{x} = \frac{y}{z}$

EXTEND YOUR SKILL

31. Use the definition to explain what the fraction $\frac{3}{4}$ is.

32. Explain how multiplying by $\frac{3}{4}$ can be viewed as the composition of two operators.

7.2 – MULTIPLYING FRACTIONS

OBJECTIVES

1. Compute the product of two or more fractions.

2. Find the reciprocal of a rational number.

To compute the product of two rational numbers, we use the fact that multiplying by $\frac{m}{n}$ has the same effect as multiplying by m and dividing by n.

$$\left(\frac{m}{n}\right)\left(\frac{x}{y}\right) = \frac{m\left(\frac{x}{y}\right)}{n}$$ Multiply $\frac{x}{y}$ by m and divide by n.

$$= \frac{\frac{mx}{y}}{n}$$ Interchange the order of dividing by y and multiplying by m.

$$= \frac{mx}{ny}$$ The composition of dividing by y and dividing by n is dividing by ny.

This gives us the following formula.

Product of Rational Numbers

The product of the rational number $\frac{m}{n}$ and the rational number $\frac{x}{y}$ is the rational number $\frac{mx}{ny}$. Thus $\left(\frac{m}{n}\right)\left(\frac{x}{y}\right) = \frac{mx}{ny}$.

In the above formula, note how the expansions $m(\ )$ and $(\ )x$ work together to give mx, and how the contractions $\frac{(\ )}{n}$ and $\frac{(\ )}{y}$ help each other to give the contraction $\frac{(\ )}{ny}$.

Example 1   **Multiply Fractions**

$$\left(\frac{2}{3}\right)\left(\frac{4}{5}\right) = \frac{2\cdot 4}{3\cdot 5} = \frac{8}{15} \qquad \left(\frac{3}{4}\right)\left(\frac{7}{8}\right) = \frac{3\cdot 7}{4\cdot 8} = \frac{21}{32}$$

Sometimes when two fractions are multiplied, the result is a basic numeral as above. Other times, the result is not a basic numeral and it must then be reduced to lowest terms. The key to doing this is to write all the numerators and denominators in factored form. Then we can cancel inverse operators to simplify the expression. This can be done after multiplying, as in part (a) of the next example, or before multiplying, as in part (b).

Example 2   **Multiply Fractions**

Compute the product and simplify: $\left(\frac{5}{6}\right)\left(\frac{4}{15}\right)$.

We factor the numerators and denominators and cancel inverse operators.

(a)
$$\left(\frac{5}{6}\right)\left(\frac{4}{15}\right) = \left(\frac{5}{2\cdot 3}\right)\left(\frac{2\cdot 2}{3\cdot 5}\right) = \frac{\cancel{5}\cdot \cancel{2}\cdot 2}{\cancel{2}\cdot 3\cdot 3\cdot \cancel{5}} = \frac{2}{9}$$

(b)
$$\left(\frac{5}{6}\right)\left(\frac{4}{15}\right) = \left(\frac{1\,\cancel{5}}{\cancel{2}\cdot 3}\right)\left(\frac{\cancel{2}\cdot 2}{3\,\cancel{5}}\right) = \frac{2}{9}$$

We could also have simplified the computation by dividing both 5 and 15 by 5 (their greatest common factor), and by dividing both 6 and 4 by 2 (their GCF), before multiplying numerators and denominators.

$$\left(\frac{\overset{1}{\cancel{5}}}{\underset{3}{\cancel{6}}}\right)\left(\frac{\overset{2}{\cancel{4}}}{\underset{3}{\cancel{15}}}\right) = \frac{2}{9}$$

When multiplying two fractions that have variables, we treat the variables as if they were numbers and remove any common factors from the numerator and denominator.

Example 3   **Multiply Fractions with Variables**

Compute the product and simplify: $\left(\dfrac{6y}{5x}\right)\left(\dfrac{15}{4xy^2}\right)$.

$$\left(\frac{6y}{5x}\right)\left(\frac{15}{4xy^2}\right) = \frac{(\overset{3}{\cancel{6}})(\overset{1}{\cancel{y}})(\overset{3}{\cancel{15}})}{(\underset{1}{\cancel{5}})(x)(\underset{2}{\cancel{4}})(x)(\underset{y}{\cancel{y^2}})} = \frac{3\cdot 1\cdot 3}{1\cdot x\cdot 2\cdot x\cdot y} = \frac{9}{2x^2 y}$$

Reduce $\dfrac{6}{4}$ *to* $\dfrac{3}{2}$, $\dfrac{15}{5}$ *to* $\dfrac{3}{1}$, *and* $\dfrac{y}{y^2}$ *to* $\dfrac{1}{y}$.

A mixed number like $2\frac{1}{2}$ is really the sum of two numbers:

$$2\frac{1}{2} \quad \text{means} \quad 2+\frac{1}{2}.$$

Because of this, we change mixed numbers into improper fractions before multiplying.

Example 4   **Multiply Mixed Numbers**

(a) $$\left(2\frac{1}{2}\right)\left(3\frac{2}{3}\right) = \left(\frac{5}{2}\right)\left(\frac{11}{3}\right) = \frac{55}{6} \quad \text{or} \quad 9\frac{1}{6}$$

(b) $$(6)\left(4\frac{1}{8}\right) = \left(\overset{3}{\cancel{6}}\right)\left(\frac{33}{\underset{4}{\cancel{8}}}\right) = \frac{99}{4} \quad \text{or} \quad 24\frac{3}{4}$$

Study Tip:

Zero does not have a reciprocal.

When the numerator and the denominator of a fraction are interchanged, the new fraction and the original fraction are called **reciprocals** of each other. The product of a number and its reciprocal is always equal to 1. If a rational number is in the form of a simple fraction $\frac{x}{y}$, then its reciprocal is $\frac{y}{x}$ and $\left(\frac{x}{y}\right)\left(\frac{y}{x}\right) = 1$. The number zero has a fraction or quotient form of $\frac{0}{1}$. But zero *does not* have a reciprocal, since the quotient $\frac{1}{0}$ is undefined. If the reciprocal of a mixed number is needed, we first change it into an equivalent improper fraction.

Example 5   **Find a Reciprocal**

Find the reciprocal of each number.

(a) $\dfrac{3}{5}$ (b) $\dfrac{9}{4}$ (c) $\dfrac{1}{2}$ (d) 4 (e) $1\dfrac{3}{4}$

(a) The reciprocal of $\dfrac{3}{5}$ is $\dfrac{5}{3}$. $\left(\dfrac{3}{5}\right)\left(\dfrac{5}{3}\right) = \dfrac{15}{15} = 1$

(b) The reciprocal of $\frac{9}{4}$ is $\frac{4}{9}$. $\left(\frac{9}{4}\right)\left(\frac{4}{9}\right) = \frac{36}{36} = 1$

(c) The reciprocal of $\frac{1}{2}$ is $\frac{2}{1}$, or 2. $\left(\frac{2}{1}\right)(2) = \left(\frac{1}{2}\right)\left(\frac{2}{1}\right) = \frac{2}{2} = 1$

(d) The reciprocal of 4 (or $\frac{4}{1}$) is $\frac{1}{4}$. $(4)\left(\frac{1}{4}\right) = \left(\frac{4}{1}\right)\left(\frac{1}{4}\right) = \frac{4}{4} = 1$

(e) To find the reciprocal of $1\frac{3}{4}$, we first write $1\frac{3}{4} = \frac{7}{4}$. Since $\frac{7}{4}$ and $\frac{4}{7}$ are reciprocals of each other, we see that the reciprocal of $1\frac{3}{4}$ is also $\frac{4}{7}$:

$$\left(1\frac{3}{4}\right)\left(\frac{4}{7}\right) = \left(\frac{7}{4}\right)\left(\frac{4}{7}\right) = \frac{28}{28} = 1.$$

EXERCISE 7.2

DEVELOP YOUR SKILL

Compute the product and simplify.

1. $\left(\frac{12}{35}\right)\left(\frac{25}{28}\right)$ 2. $\left(\frac{8}{63}\right)\left(\frac{45}{44}\right)$ 3. $\left(\frac{35}{22}\right)\left(\frac{33}{50}\right)$

4. $\left(\frac{28}{45}\right)\left(\frac{30}{77}\right)$ 5. $\left(\frac{7}{12}\right)\left(\frac{4}{5}\right)\left(\frac{45}{56}\right)$ 6. $\left(\frac{2xy^2}{21}\right)\left(\frac{3x}{y^5}\right)$

Write the reciprocal as a simple fraction or a natural number.

7. 13   8. $\frac{4}{7}$ 9. $3\frac{1}{2}$

10. $\frac{1}{9}$ 11. $3+5$ 12. $\frac{\frac{1}{8}}{3}$

Compute the basic numeral. Use the mixed number form for your answer.

13. $\left(3\frac{2}{3}\right)\left(4\frac{1}{2}\right)$ 14. $\left(2\frac{2}{5}\right)\left(3\frac{1}{4}\right)$

Maintain Your Skill

Simplify each expression, if possible. If no simpler form is possible, write "not possible." [4.4]

15. $s + \dfrac{t}{s}$

16. $\dfrac{x+y}{x}$

17. $s\left(\dfrac{t}{s}\right)$

18. $\dfrac{x \cdot y}{x}$

19. $\dfrac{(x-y)y}{x-y} - x$

20. $\dfrac{r(r-s)}{r} + s$

Construct each expression by stating an operand and then listing a sequence of basic operators that can be joined one at a time to produce the given expression. [4.3, 5.2]

21. $\left(\dfrac{13-7}{3}\right)^2$

22. $\dfrac{5^2 - 4}{7}$

23. $\dfrac{5 + 3^2}{2}$

24. $6 + 3 \cdot 4^2$

25. Find the LCM of 15 and 20. [5.7]

26. Find the LCM of 18 and 27. [5.7]

Translate each statement into a mathematical equation. [6.9]

27. x is $\frac{2}{3}$ of y.

28. y is $\frac{3}{5}$ of z.

29. y is 3 more than x.

30. z is 9 less than y.

Extend Your Skill

31. Describe in words how to compute the product of two fractions.

32. Explain the steps in finding the reciprocal of a mixed number.

7.3 – DIVIDING FRACTIONS

Since division in the set $\mathbb{Q}^+$ of nonnegative quotients is just a matter of writing the quotient, we would expect that division should be a simple operation with fractions. Thus to divide $\frac{2}{3}$ by $\frac{5}{7}$, we get the quotient just by writing

$$\frac{2}{3} \div \frac{5}{7} = \frac{\frac{2}{3}}{\frac{5}{7}}.$$

While the form at the right does represent the correct quotient number, it is not a basic numeral. In order to compute the basic numeral we use the invariant principle for division, which we now extend to rational numbers.

Invariant Principle for Division

If x, y, and n are rational numbers with $y \neq 0$ and $n \neq 0$, then

$$\frac{x}{y} = \frac{xn}{yn} \quad \text{and} \quad \frac{x}{y} = \frac{\frac{x}{n}}{\frac{y}{n}}.$$

To simplify the quotient $\frac{2}{3} \div \frac{5}{7}$, we seek an appropriate rational number n to use as a multiplier in the numerator and the denominator:

$$\frac{\frac{2}{3}}{\frac{5}{7}} = \frac{\left(\frac{2}{3}\right)n}{\left(\frac{5}{7}\right)n}$$

The choice of the multiplier ( )n can be made in one of two ways:

(A) If $\left(\frac{2}{3}\right)n$ is to be a natural number, then n must be a multiple of 3. If $\left(\frac{5}{7}\right)n$ is to be a natural number, then n must be a multiple of 7. The smallest choice for such an n is 21, the least common multiple (LCM) of 3 and 7. We have

$$\frac{\frac{2}{3}}{\frac{5}{7}} = \frac{\left(\frac{2}{3}\right)21}{\left(\frac{5}{7}\right)21} = \frac{14}{15}.$$

(B)   We may let n be the reciprocal of the denominator. This gives us

$$\frac{\dfrac{2}{3}}{\dfrac{5}{7}} = \frac{\left(\dfrac{2}{3}\right)\left(\dfrac{7}{5}\right)}{\left(\dfrac{5}{7}\right)\left(\dfrac{7}{5}\right)} = \frac{\dfrac{14}{15}}{1} = \frac{14}{15}.$$

Since $\frac{x}{1} = x$ for all x, the reciprocal method in (B) can be shortened to

$$\frac{\dfrac{2}{3}}{\dfrac{5}{7}} = \left(\dfrac{2}{3}\right)\left(\dfrac{7}{5}\right) = \frac{14}{15}.$$

Thus, dividing by a fraction gives the same quotient as multiplying by its reciprocal:

$$\frac{2}{3} \div \frac{5}{7} = \frac{2}{3} \times \frac{7}{5} = \frac{14}{15}.$$

Division of Fractions

> To divide by a fraction, we may multiply by its reciprocal:
>
> $$\frac{a}{b} \div \frac{c}{d} = \frac{a}{b} \times \frac{d}{c} = \frac{ad}{bc}, \qquad \text{where } b, c, \text{ and } d \text{ are not } 0.$$

This rule should come as no surprise, given our work with expansions and contractions. For example,

$$\frac{2}{8}(\ ) = \frac{2(\ )}{8}$$

since multiplying by $\frac{2}{8}$ is the same as multiplying by 2 and dividing by 8. But

$$\frac{2(\ )}{8} = \frac{(\ )}{\dfrac{8}{2}}$$

since the composition of an expansion by 2 and a contraction by 8 is a contraction by $\frac{8}{2}$. Once again we see that dividing by a fraction has the same effect as multiplying by its reciprocal.

Example 1   **Divide Mixed Numbers**

Simplify $1\frac{3}{4} \div 2\frac{1}{4}$.

   We will illustrate both methods of simplifying, and begin by writing each mixed number as an improper fraction.

(A) $\dfrac{1\frac{3}{4}}{2\frac{1}{4}} = \dfrac{\frac{7}{4}}{\frac{9}{4}} = \dfrac{\left(\frac{7}{4}\right)4}{\left(\frac{9}{4}\right)4} = \dfrac{7}{9}$

(B) $\dfrac{1\frac{3}{4}}{2\frac{1}{4}} = \dfrac{\frac{7}{4}}{\frac{9}{4}} = \left(\dfrac{7}{\cancel{4}}\right)\left(\dfrac{\cancel{4}^{\,1}}{9}\right) = \dfrac{7}{9}$

In this case, method (A) is probably easier since the multiplying by 4 can easily be done mentally.

   If a rational number $\frac{x}{y}$ is to be multiplied by a natural number n, there is a choice between two possible computations: the numerator x may be multiplied by n, or the denominator y may be divided by n. Thus

Here are a couple of useful tips.

$$n\left(\frac{x}{y}\right) = \frac{n \cdot x}{y} \quad \text{and} \quad n\left(\frac{x}{y}\right) = \frac{x}{\frac{y}{n}}.$$

If n does not divide y, then the first choice is preferable. But if n divides y, then the second is usually simpler.

Example 2   **Multiply a Fraction by Natural Number**

To multiply $\frac{5}{11}$ by 2, we multiply the 5 by 2 to obtain $\frac{10}{11}$. This interchanges the order of dividing by 11 and multiplying by 2.

$$\left(\frac{5}{11}\right)(2) = \frac{5 \cdot 2}{11} = \frac{10}{11}.$$

But to multiply $\frac{5}{12}$ by 2, we divide the 12 by 2 to obtain $\frac{5}{6}$. In this way we obtain the basic numeral without having to reduce the fraction.

$$\left(\frac{5}{12}\right)(2) = \frac{5}{\frac{12}{2}} = \frac{5}{6}.$$

Recall from Lesson 4.2 that the composition of dividing by 12 and multiplying by 2 is dividing by $\frac{12}{2}$ or 6.

Similarly, if a rational number $\frac{x}{y}$ is to be divided by a natural number n, there is also a choice between two possible computations: the numerator x may be divided by n, or the denominator may be multiplied by n. Thus

$$\frac{\frac{x}{y}}{n} = \frac{\frac{x}{n}}{y} \quad \text{and} \quad \frac{\frac{x}{y}}{n} = \frac{x}{n \cdot y}.$$

If n divides x, then the first choice is preferable. But if n does not divide x, then the second choice is better.

Example 3 **Divide a Fraction by a Natural Number**

To divide $\frac{6}{11}$ by 2, we divide the 6 by 2 to obtain $\frac{3}{11}$. We can think of this as interchanging the order of dividing by 11 and dividing by 2.

$$\frac{\frac{6}{11}}{2} = \frac{\frac{6}{2}}{11} = \frac{3}{11}.$$

To divide $\frac{5}{11}$ by 2, we multiply the 11 by 2 to obtain $\frac{5}{22}$. Recall that the composition of dividing by 11 and dividing by 2 is dividing by 22.

$$\frac{\frac{5}{11}}{2} = \frac{5}{11 \cdot 2} = \frac{5}{22}.$$

When solving an equation with fractions, we can use either method from Chapter 6.

Example 4   Solve an Equation with Fractions

Solve the equation $\frac{3}{4}x = \frac{2}{5}$ *for x.*

We will do this both ways.

(a) x is a factor. It is equal to the product $\frac{2}{5}$ divided by the other factor $\frac{3}{4}$.

$$x = \frac{\frac{2}{5}}{\frac{3}{4}} = \frac{2}{5} \cdot \frac{4}{3} = \frac{8}{15}$$

(b) To get x by itself, we want to remove the multiplying by $\frac{3}{4}$ from the left side. When doing this we must join a dividing by $\frac{3}{4}$ to the right side.

$$\frac{3}{4}x = \frac{2}{5}$$

$$x = \frac{2}{5} \div \frac{3}{4} = \frac{2}{5} \cdot \frac{4}{3} = \frac{8}{15}$$

This second approach can be shortened somewhat if we realize that dividing by $\frac{3}{4}$ is the same as multiplying by its reciprocal $\frac{4}{3}$.

$$\frac{3}{4}x = \frac{2}{5}$$

$$\frac{4}{3}\left(\frac{3}{4}x\right) = \frac{2}{5} \cdot \frac{4}{3} \qquad \text{Multiply both sides by } \frac{4}{3}.$$

$$x = \frac{8}{15} \qquad \text{Simplify and compute.}$$

Study Tip:

With practice you can do the middle steps mentally and go directly from

$$\frac{3}{4}x = \frac{2}{5}$$

to

$$x = \frac{2}{5} \cdot \frac{4}{3} = \frac{8}{15}.$$

EXERCISE 7.3

DEVELOP YOUR SKILL

Simplify each expression.

1. $\dfrac{\frac{2}{5}}{\frac{7}{11}}$ **2.** $\dfrac{\frac{3}{5}}{8}$ **3.** $\dfrac{3}{\frac{5}{8}}$ **4.** $\dfrac{5}{2\frac{1}{3}}$

5. $\dfrac{1\frac{1}{3}}{2\frac{1}{2}}$ **6.** $\dfrac{1+\frac{3}{4}}{4+\frac{1}{2}}$ **7.** $\dfrac{\frac{1}{r}}{s}$ **8.** $\dfrac{\frac{a}{b}}{c}$

Solve each equation for x.

9. $\dfrac{2}{3}x = \dfrac{5}{8}$ **10.** $\dfrac{5}{8}x = \dfrac{2}{3}$ **11.** $\dfrac{x}{\frac{2}{3}} = \dfrac{5}{8}$

12. $\dfrac{2}{3} = \dfrac{\frac{5}{8}}{x}$ **13.** $\dfrac{3}{5} = 1\dfrac{1}{4}x$ **14.** $\dfrac{3}{5}x = 1\dfrac{1}{4}$

MAINTAIN YOUR SKILL

Use composition of operators to write an equivalent single operator. Assume $m \geq n$. [2.3]

15. $-m+n$ **16.** $+n-m$ **17.** $-n+m$ **18.** $+m-n$

Simplify each expression. [4.5]

19. $3(12x)$ **20.** $3\left(\dfrac{x}{12}\right)$ **21.** $\dfrac{12}{3x}$

22. $\dfrac{\frac{3}{x}}{12}$ **23.** $\dfrac{\frac{12}{x}}{3}$ **24.** $\dfrac{\frac{3}{x}}{12}$

Replace each expression by an equivalent one in which the multipliers, dividers, and sign operators have been distributed. Do not compute. [4.7]

25. $14 - \dfrac{30+12}{6}$ **26.** $12 - \dfrac{18-15}{3}$ **27.** $15 + \dfrac{12-8}{4}$

28. $25 - 2(8+3)$ **29.** $27 - 3(8-2)$ **30.** $4 + 3(9-5)$

EXTEND YOUR SKILL

31. Suppose the fraction $\frac{x}{y}$ is to be multiplied by 3. Describe two ways to do this and explain how to decide which way to use.

32. Suppose the fraction $\frac{x}{y}$ is to be divided by 3. Describe two ways to do this and explain how to decide which way to use.

7.4 – RATIOS

OBJECTIVE

1. Find the ratio comparison of two numbers.

If x and y are not zero, then the quotient $\frac{x}{y}$ is said to express the **ratio** of x to y. Thus we say that 12 has the same ratio to 4 as 3 has to 1 since

$$\frac{12}{4} = \frac{3}{1}.$$

We can visualize these ratios by grouping 12 markers into 3 groups of 4. Then we see that

in the same way that

We can also model ratio comparisons with line segments. The values we get depend on the scales used. For example, the ratio comparison of m and n shown below depends on whether we use scale A, B, or C.

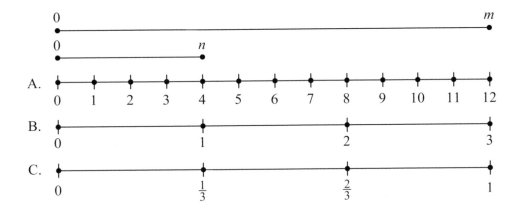

With scale A, the ratio of m to n is seen to be 12 to 4, or $\frac{12}{4}$.

With scale B, the ratio of m to n is 3 to 1, or $\frac{3}{1}$.

Since $\frac{12}{4} = \frac{3}{1}$, these two equivalent fractions represent the same ratio. Scale B, however, gives the simplest way of stating the ratio since the second line segment n has a measure of 1.

The number 1 is the usual basis for ratio comparisons, but we often use simpler statements that do not mention 1 explicitly. For example, instead of saying that "12 has the same ratio to 4 that 3 has to 1," it is easier to say that "12 is 3 times 4."

If we reverse the ratio and compare n to m, we use scale C, where m corresponds to 1. We see that n then corresponds to $\frac{1}{3}$. In other words, the ratio of 4 to 12 is the same as the ratio of $\frac{1}{3}$ to 1. This is usually stated more simply as "4 is $\frac{1}{3}$ of 12."

Ratio comparisons can be made with any two non-zero numbers. A first number is said to be so many times a second number, or equal to, or to be a certain part of the second. The phrases "3 times" and "$\frac{1}{3}$ of" are verbal statements for the operators 3( ) and $\frac{1}{3}$( ). When the ratio comparison is greater than 1 we usually use the word "times" and when the comparison is less than 1 we use "of." In both cases we are referring to multiplication.

In general, the ratio comparison of a first number to a second is given by stating the expansion or contraction that will change the *second* number into the *first*. This ratio is found by taking the first number, dividing it by the second number, and then simplifying.

Example 1   **Find a Ratio Comparison**

Write a sentence that states the ratio comparison of $\frac{5}{8}$ to $\frac{7}{8}$.

Compute the first number divided by the second number.

$$\frac{\frac{5}{8}}{\frac{7}{8}} = \frac{\left(\frac{5}{8}\right)8}{\left(\frac{7}{8}\right)8} = \frac{5}{7}.$$

The multiplication operator that will change $\frac{7}{8}$ to $\frac{5}{8}$ is $\frac{5}{7}(\ )$ or "$\frac{5}{7}$ of,"

and so we write "$\frac{5}{8}$ is $\frac{5}{7}$ of $\frac{7}{8}$."

Example 2   **Find a Ratio Comparison**

A box contains 200 crackers. If 80 of the crackers are broken, what fractional part of the crackers in the box are broken?

We can rephrase the question by asking, "80 is what part of 200?" We want the ratio comparison of 80 to 200:

$$\frac{80}{200} = \frac{2 \cdot 40}{5 \cdot 40} = \frac{2}{5}.$$

We see that $\frac{2}{5}$ of the crackers are broken.

Example 3   **Find a Ratio Comparison**

$2\frac{2}{3}$ is how many times $\frac{1}{2}$?

We want the ratio comparison of $2\frac{2}{3}$ to $\frac{1}{2}$, so we take the quotient

$$\frac{2\frac{2}{3}}{\frac{1}{2}} = \frac{\frac{8}{3}}{\frac{1}{2}} = \left(\frac{8}{3}\right)\left(\frac{2}{1}\right) = \frac{16}{3} = 5\frac{1}{3}.$$

The operator $5\frac{1}{3}(\ )$ or "$5\frac{1}{3}$ times" will change $\frac{1}{2}$ into $2\frac{2}{3}$. Thus $2\frac{2}{3}$ is $5\frac{1}{3}$ times $\frac{1}{2}$.

It is easy to check our answer by multiplying $5\frac{1}{3}$ (or $\frac{16}{3}$) times $\frac{1}{2}$.

We have

$$\left(\frac{\overset{8}{\cancel{16}}}{3}\right)\left(\frac{1}{\underset{1}{\cancel{2}}}\right) = \frac{8}{3} = 2\frac{2}{3},$$

as desired.

In Example 3 we found that

$$\frac{2\frac{2}{3}}{\frac{1}{2}} = \frac{16}{3}.$$

We now have three ways of thinking about this equation:

- $\frac{16}{3}$ is the simplest equivalent form for the **fraction** $\dfrac{2\frac{2}{3}}{\frac{1}{2}}$.

- When $2\frac{2}{3}$ is divided by $\frac{1}{2}$, the **quotient** is $\frac{16}{3}$.

- The **ratio** of $2\frac{2}{3}$ to $\frac{1}{2}$ is the same as the **ratio** of 16 to 3.

EXERCISE 7.4

DEVELOP YOUR SKILL

Write a sentence that states the ratio comparison of the first number to the second.

1. $\frac{2}{5}, \frac{3}{5}$

2. $\frac{4}{7}, \frac{2}{7}$

3. $\frac{3}{4}, \frac{3}{7}$

4. $1\frac{1}{4}, 2\frac{1}{4}$

5. $3\frac{1}{2}$ is how many times $2\frac{1}{2}$?

6. $4\frac{1}{3}$ is what part of $5\frac{1}{3}$?

7. If 18 out of 20 problems were correct on an assignment, what fractional part of the assignment was correct?

8. If 12 ounces of a 16-ounce solution are alcohol, what fractional part of the solution is alcohol?

MAINTAIN YOUR SKILL

Name each form and compute the basic numeral. [5.2]

9. $4 \cdot 3^2$

10. $3(7-3)^2$

11. $7 + 3^2$

12. $(8-2)^2$

13. $(5+6)^2$

14. $5 \cdot 2^2$

15. $2(5^2 - 4^2)$

16. $9^2 - 3^2$

In Exercises 17 – 22, the entire expression is a numeral for a single number. Write this number in prime factored form. [5.6]

17. $12 \cdot 15$

18. $21 \cdot 28$

19. $11 + 15 \cdot 11$

20. $(19 + 21)(25)$

21. $21^2 + 21^3$

22. $21^3 - 21^2$

In Exercises 23 –28, each equation can be viewed as consisting of exactly three terms. Identify the sum term (S) or the product term (P) as appropriate. Give all possible interpretations. [6.2, 6.3]

23. $rs - t = wx - y$

24. $bc - d = \dfrac{e}{f} + g$

25. $m + pq = \dfrac{a-b}{c}$

26. $m(n + p) = \dfrac{a}{b} + c$

27. $\dfrac{x}{y-z} = uv$

28. $\dfrac{p-q}{r+s} = \dfrac{w+x}{y-z}$

Construct a graphical model for each fraction. [7.1]

29. $\dfrac{4}{3} = \dfrac{4 \cdot 1}{3}$

30. $\dfrac{4}{3} = 4\left(\dfrac{1}{3}\right)$

EXTEND YOUR SKILL

31. What is the difference between a quotient, a fraction, and a ratio?

32. If $\dfrac{2x}{3y} = \dfrac{4}{7}$, what is the ratio of x to y? Explain how to find the answer.

7.5 – ADDING AND SUBTRACTING FRACTIONS

OBJECTIVE

1. Compute the sum or difference of fractions.

When two fractions have the same denominator, they can be added using the distributive property of division.

Example 1   **Add Like Fractions**

Compute the basic numeral: $\dfrac{2}{7} + \dfrac{3}{7}$.

$$\frac{2}{7} + \frac{3}{7} = \frac{2+3}{7} = \frac{5}{7}$$ Use the distributive property and compute.

In order to add two fractions with different denominators, we first change them into equivalent fractions having a common denominator. Then we add the numerators.

Example 2   **Add Unlike Fractions**

Compute the basic numeral: $\dfrac{1}{5} + \dfrac{2}{3}$

$$\frac{1}{5} + \frac{2}{3} = \frac{3}{15} + \frac{10}{15}$$ Replace $\frac{1}{5}$ by $\frac{3}{15}$ and $\frac{2}{3}$ by $\frac{10}{15}$.

$$= \frac{3+10}{15} = \frac{13}{15}$$ Use the distributive property and compute.

Since $\dfrac{a}{b} + \dfrac{c}{d} = \dfrac{ad}{bd} + \dfrac{bc}{bd} = \dfrac{ad+bc}{bd}$, we have the following general rule.

Addition of Fractions

The sum of the rational number $\dfrac{a}{b}$ and the rational number $\dfrac{c}{d}$ may be computed as $\dfrac{a}{b} + \dfrac{c}{d} = \dfrac{ad+bc}{bd}$.

While this rule always produces a correct sum, it may not be a fraction in lowest terms. We can save work in reducing our answer if we use the least common multiple of b and d as the common denominator instead of their product. We refer to this number as the least common denominator (LCD).

Example 3   **Add Unlike Fractions**

Compute the basic numeral: $\dfrac{5}{6} + \dfrac{8}{15}$.

We can find the sum by using the general rule:

$$\frac{5}{6} + \frac{8}{15} = \frac{5 \cdot 15 + 6 \cdot 8}{6 \cdot 15} = \frac{75 + 48}{90} = \frac{123}{90} = \frac{3 \cdot 41}{3 \cdot 30} = \frac{41}{30} = 1\frac{11}{30}.$$

But since the LCM of 6 and 15 is 30, we can shorten our work by using 30 as the common denominator:

$$\frac{5}{6} + \frac{8}{15} = \frac{25}{30} + \frac{16}{30} \qquad \text{The LCD is 30. Multiply } \tfrac{5}{6} \times \tfrac{5}{5} \text{ and } \tfrac{8}{15} \times \tfrac{2}{2}.$$

$$= \frac{41}{30} = 1\frac{11}{30}. \qquad \text{Add the numerators and write as a mixed number.}$$

Study Tip:

The LCM of 6 and 15 is 30, so the LCD of the fractions is 30.

While addition is always defined in $\mathbb{Q}^+$, subtraction is only a partial operation. If a first fraction is greater than or equal to a second fraction, then the difference of the two fractions will be defined. We have the following general rule:

Subtraction of Fractions

If $\dfrac{a}{b} \ge \dfrac{c}{d}$, then the difference $\dfrac{a}{b} - \dfrac{c}{d}$ is the rational number $\dfrac{ad - bc}{bd}$.

As in addition, the computational work in subtraction can be shortened by using the least common multiple of b and d as the common denominator instead of their product.

Study Tip:

It may be necessary to do some reducing even when the LCD is used.

Example 4 **Subtract Unlike Fractions**

Compute the basic numeral: $\dfrac{7}{2} - \dfrac{5}{6}$.

$$\frac{7}{2} - \frac{5}{6} = \frac{21}{6} - \frac{5}{6}$$ The LCD is 6. Replace $\frac{7}{2}$ by $\frac{21}{6}$.

$$= \frac{21-5}{6} = \frac{16}{6} = \frac{8}{3}$$ Subtract the numerators and simplify.

Example 5 **Add Mixed Numbers**

Compute the basic numeral: $2\dfrac{3}{4} + 3\dfrac{5}{6}$.

We can begin by changing the mixed numbers into improper fractions:

$$2\frac{3}{4} + 3\frac{5}{6} = \frac{11}{4} + \frac{23}{6}$$ Replace $2\frac{3}{4}$ by $\frac{11}{4}$ and $3\frac{5}{6}$ by $\frac{23}{6}$.

$$= \frac{33}{12} + \frac{46}{12}$$ The LCD is 12. Multiply $\frac{11}{4} \times \frac{3}{3}$ and $\frac{23}{6} \times \frac{2}{2}$.

$$= \frac{79}{12} = 6\frac{7}{12}$$ Add the numerators and write as a mixed number.

Or, we can combine the whole numbers and fractions separately.

$$2\frac{3}{4} + 3\frac{5}{6} = \left(2 + \frac{3}{4}\right) + \left(3 + \frac{5}{6}\right)$$ Expand the mixed numbers.

$$= (2+3) + \left(\frac{3}{4} + \frac{5}{6}\right)$$ Use the commutative and associative properties.

$$= 5 + \left(\frac{9}{12} + \frac{10}{12}\right)$$ Get a common denominator.

$$= 5 + \frac{19}{12}$$ Add the numerators.

$$= 5 + \left(1 + \frac{7}{12}\right) = 6\frac{7}{12}$$ Replace $\frac{19}{12}$ by a mixed number and add 5 + 1.

The second way may appear to be longer, but it keeps the fractions smaller and some of the steps may be done mentally without writing them down.

EXERCISE 7.5

DEVELOP YOUR SKILL

Compute the basic numeral.

1. $\dfrac{4}{5}+\dfrac{3}{7}$

2. $\dfrac{5}{3}-\dfrac{4}{5}$

3. $\dfrac{5}{4}-\dfrac{3}{8}$

4. $\dfrac{2}{3}+\dfrac{7}{6}$

5. $\dfrac{3}{10}+\dfrac{4}{15}$

6. $\dfrac{7}{12}+\dfrac{3}{16}$

7. $\dfrac{13}{15}-\dfrac{11}{24}$

8. $\dfrac{3}{4}-\dfrac{7}{16}$

9. $1\dfrac{1}{3}+4\dfrac{1}{2}$

10. $5\dfrac{2}{3}+2\dfrac{1}{4}$

MAINTAIN YOUR SKILL

Do not compute, but write equivalent expressions without parentheses. Do not change the first term.
When possible, give a second alternate form. [2.5]

11. $10+(24-15)$

12. $14-(37-25)$

13. $13-(22-19)$

14. $25-(10+11)$

Simplify each expression. If no simpler form is possible, write "not possible." [4.4]

15. $x+\dfrac{w(y-x)}{w}$

16. $\dfrac{6x+12y}{3}$

17. $2m-\dfrac{3(2m-4)}{2}$

18. $\dfrac{nx-xp}{p}$

Solve each equation for x and compute the basic numeral. [6.4]

19. $5x+3=21$

20. $24-3x=17$

21. $7x-5=20$

22. $\dfrac{x-1}{3}=5$

23. $10-\dfrac{x}{4}=7$

24. $\dfrac{3x+1}{4}=2$

Compute the basic numeral. [7.2, 7.3]

25. $\dfrac{3\dfrac{2}{3}}{2\dfrac{1}{6}}$

26. $\dfrac{1\dfrac{3}{5}}{5\dfrac{1}{3}}$

27. $\left(1\dfrac{1}{6}\right)\left(2\dfrac{2}{5}\right)$

28. $\left(3\dfrac{3}{4}\right)\left(2\dfrac{2}{5}\right)$

29. $5\frac{1}{2}$ is how many times $3\frac{1}{2}$? [7.4]

30. $7\frac{1}{2}$ is what part of $8\frac{1}{2}$? [7.4]

EXTEND YOUR SKILL

31. Which property (commutative, associative, or distributive) is used when computing $\frac{2}{9}+\frac{5}{9}=\frac{7}{9}$?

32. Explain why computing $\frac{a}{b}+\frac{c}{d}$ as $\frac{ad+bc}{bd}$ may not be the easiest way to do it.

7.6 – ORDERING FRACTIONS AND SOLVING EQUATIONS

OBJECTIVES

1. Compare the size of two fractions.

2. Solve equations with fractions.

If two fractions have the same denominator, then it is easy to see which one is larger: just compare their numerators:

$$\frac{3}{7} < \frac{4}{7} \quad \text{because} \quad 3 < 4.$$

When the denominators of two fractions are different, then to determine their relative sizes we compare equivalent fractions having a common denominator. Since $\frac{a}{b}=\frac{ad}{bd}$ and $\frac{c}{d}=\frac{bc}{bd}$, this process may be shortened by using the cross product rule.

Cross Product Rule

$$\frac{a}{b} < \frac{c}{d} \text{ if and only if } ad < bc,$$

$$\frac{a}{b} = \frac{c}{d} \text{ if and only if } ad = bc, \text{ and}$$

$$\frac{a}{b} > \frac{c}{d} \text{ if and only if } ad > bc.$$

Study Tip:

The name "cross product" rule comes from the ✕ in the diagram.

Example 1　　　**Compare the Size of Two Fractions**

Which is larger, $\frac{2}{3}$ or $\frac{5}{8}$?

We have $2 \cdot 8 = 16$ and $3 \cdot 5 = 15$. It is helpful to think of the computations as follows:

$$2 \cdot 8 = 16 \qquad 3 \cdot 5 = 15$$

$$\frac{2}{3} \times \frac{5}{8}$$

Since $16 > 15$, we have $\frac{2}{3} > \frac{5}{8}$.

In Example 1 we wrote the 16 above the $\frac{2}{3}$ and the 15 above the $\frac{5}{8}$. These numbers represent the numerators of the equivalent fractions with a common denominator:

$$\frac{2}{3} = \frac{16}{24} \quad \text{and} \quad \frac{5}{8} = \frac{15}{24}.$$

That's why we can compare the sizes of the fractions by comparing 16 and 15.

Example 2　　　**Compare the Size of Two Fractions**

Which is larger, $\frac{2}{3}$ or $\frac{12}{18}$?

$$2 \cdot 18 = 36 \qquad 3 \cdot 12 = 36$$

$$\frac{2}{3} \times \frac{12}{18}$$

Since the cross products are both equal to 36, we have $\frac{2}{3} = \frac{12}{18}$.

Example 3   **Combine Fractional Increases and Decreases**

Simplify: $x + \dfrac{3}{4} - \dfrac{2}{5}$.

Since $3 \cdot 5 > 4 \cdot 2$, we have $\dfrac{3}{4} > \dfrac{2}{5}$. So the combined change is an increase.

$$x + \frac{3}{4} - \frac{2}{5} = x + \left(\frac{3}{4} - \frac{2}{5} \right).$$ Combine the increase and the decrease.

$$= x + \left(\frac{15}{20} - \frac{8}{20} \right)$$ The LCD is 20. Multiply $\frac{3}{4} \times \frac{5}{5}$ and $\frac{2}{5} \times \frac{4}{4}$.

$$= x + \frac{7}{20}$$ Compute.

Study Tip:

The composition of an increase of $\dfrac{3}{4}$ and a decrease of $\dfrac{2}{5}$ is an increase of their difference:

$$+ \left(\frac{3}{4} - \frac{2}{5} \right).$$

Example 4   **Solve an Equation with Fractions**

Solve for x: $x + \dfrac{5}{7} = \dfrac{3}{4}$.

$$x + \frac{5}{7} = \frac{3}{4}$$ Write the equation.

$$x = \frac{3}{4} - \frac{5}{7}$$ The addend x is the sum minus the other addend.
Or, subtract $\frac{5}{7}$ from both sides.

$$x = \frac{21}{28} - \frac{20}{28}$$ The LCD is 28. Multiply $\frac{3}{4} \times \frac{7}{7}$ and $\frac{5}{7} \times \frac{4}{4}$.

$$x = \frac{1}{28}$$ Compute, by subtracting the numerators.

Sometimes an equation with fractions can be simplified by multiplying each term by the LCM of the denominators. This will produce an equivalent equation without fractions.

Example 5   **Solve an Equation with Fractions**

Solve for x: $\dfrac{x}{2} - \dfrac{1}{4} = \dfrac{1}{2}$

$$\frac{x}{2} - \frac{1}{4} = \frac{1}{2}$$ Write the equation.

$$2x - 1 = 2$$ Multiply each term by 4, the LCM of 2 and 4.

$$\left(\frac{x}{2}\right)(4) = 2x, \quad \left(\frac{1}{4}\right)(4) = 1, \quad \left(\frac{1}{2}\right)(4) = 2$$

$$2x = 2 + 1 = 3$$ Solve for $2x$ and compute.

$$x = \frac{3}{2}$$ Solve for the factor x, or divide both sides by 2.

EXERCISE 7.6

DEVELOP YOUR SKILL

1. Which is larger, $\frac{4}{9}$ or $\frac{2}{5}$?

2. Which is larger, $\frac{2}{5}$ or $\frac{3}{7}$?

Simplify each expression.

3. $x - \frac{2}{3} + \frac{4}{5}$

4. $x - \frac{5}{8} - \frac{1}{2}$

5. $x + \frac{3}{4} - \frac{1}{3}$

6. $x - 1\frac{1}{5} + \frac{1}{2}$

Solve each equation for x and compute the basic numeral. If such a number has not yet been defined, write "not defined."

7. $x + \frac{1}{3} = \frac{5}{8}$

8. $\frac{1}{2} = \frac{5}{6} - x$

9. $x - \frac{1}{5} = \frac{1}{6}$

10. $\frac{5}{8} + x = \frac{2}{3}$

11. $1 + \frac{x}{4} = \frac{5}{2}$

12. $\frac{x}{3} - \frac{5}{6} = \frac{5}{3}$

MAINTAIN YOUR SKILL

Solve each equation by using an invariant principle. [3.6]

13. $24 \cdot 15 = 8 \cdot x$

14. $60 \cdot x = 27 \cdot 20$

15. $\frac{x}{48} = \frac{60}{12}$

16. $\frac{35}{7} = \frac{70}{x}$

Name each form and compute the basic numeral. [5.2]

17. $3 \cdot 4^2$

18. $15 - 3 \cdot 2$

19. $2 + 3 \cdot 4$

20. $5 \cdot 2^2$

21. $\dfrac{5+6}{3^2}$

22. $\left(\dfrac{2 \cdot 3}{5}\right)^2$

Write an equivalent expression in the form 3^n when possible. Otherwise, write "not possible." [5.4]

23. $3^4 + 3^2$

24. $3^5 \cdot 3^3$

25. $(3 \cdot 3^4)^2$

26. $\dfrac{3 \cdot 3^4}{3^2}$

27. $(3^4 - 3^2)^2$

28. $\dfrac{3^2 \cdot 3^2}{3^4}$

Define a variable and write an equation to model each situation. [6.10]

29. Brian caught 5 fish less than Jason caught. If Brian caught 8 fish, how many fish did Jason catch?

30. John's age is 3 more than twice Frank's age. If John is 27, how old is Frank?

EXTEND YOUR SKILL

31. Why is it important to draw the arrows in the cross product from the bottom to the top.

32. If $3ad = 2bc$, which is larger, $\dfrac{a}{b}$ or $\dfrac{c}{d}$? Explain your answer.

7.7 – DECIMAL FRACTIONS

OBJECTIVES

1. Change fractions to decimals and decimals to fractions.

2. Solve equations with decimals.

A **decimal fraction** is a shorthand way of writing a fraction with a denominator that is a power of 10. The number of zeros in the denominator tells us how many digits should be to the right of the decimal point. For example,

$\dfrac{27}{10} = 2.7$ There is 1 zero in the denominator and 1 digit to the right of the decimal point.

$\dfrac{1538}{100} = 15.38$ There are 2 zeros in the denominator and 2 digits to the right of the decimal point.

$\dfrac{5}{1000} = 0.005$ There are 3 zeros in the denominator and 3 digits to the right of the decimal point.

The quotient notation for rational numbers is called the **common fraction** notation. To change from the decimal form into the common fraction form, first rewrite the decimal as a common fraction where the denominator is the appropriate power of ten. Then reduce, as needed.

Example 1   **Write a Decimal as a Common Fraction**

$$1.7 = \frac{17}{10} \qquad\qquad 0.043 = \frac{43}{1000} \qquad\qquad 0.15 = \frac{15}{100} = \frac{3}{20}$$

$$4.5 = \frac{45}{10} = \frac{9}{2} \quad \text{or} \quad 4.5 = 4 + 0.5 = 4 + \frac{1}{2} = \frac{9}{2}$$

To write a common fraction as a decimal, divide the denominator into the numerator. In simple cases, you can use long division. For larger numbers, use a calculator.

Study Tip:

We usually write 0.375 instead of .375 because the decimal point is easy to miss. Having a 0 to the left of the decimal point calls attention to it.

Example 2   **Write a Fraction as a Decimal**

Write $\frac{3}{8}$ *as a decimal.*

$$
\begin{array}{r}
0.375 \\
8\overline{)3.000} \\
\underline{2\,4} \\
60 \\
\underline{56} \\
40 \\
\underline{40} \\
0
\end{array}
$$

Add a decimal point and zeros as needed: 3 = 3.000

⟵ Division ends when the remainder is 0.

The fraction $\frac{3}{8}$ is equivalent to the decimal 0.375.

A decimal like 0.375 is called a **terminating decimal** because the division ends, or terminates, with a remainder of zero. For some fractions, the remainder never becomes zero. Instead, there is a repeating pattern of digits in the remainder and in the quotient. Such numbers are called **repeating decimals**.

Example 3   **Write a Fraction as a Decimal**

Write $\dfrac{5}{6}$ as a decimal.

$$
\begin{array}{r}
0.8\mathbf{33} \\
6\overline{)5.000} \\
\underline{4\,8} \\
20 \\
\underline{18} \\
20 \\
\underline{18} \\
\mathbf{2}
\end{array}
$$

← The digit 3 repeats.

← The remainder 2 repeats.

We indicate the repeating 3's by drawing a bar over the repeating part.

Thus $\dfrac{5}{6} = 0.8\overline{3}$.

Study Tip:

In algebra you will learn how to change a repeating decimal into a fraction.

If the only prime divisors of the denominator of a fraction are 2 and 5, then the fraction can be converted into a decimal without long division. The key is to change the denominator into a power of 10.

Study Tip:

Dividing by 100 has the effect of moving the decimal point 2 places to the left.

Example 4   **Write a Fraction as a Decimal**

Write $\dfrac{23}{50}$ as a decimal.

$$\frac{23}{50} = \frac{46}{100}$$ Multiply by $\frac{2}{2}$ to change the denominator into 100.

$$= 0.46$$

Study Tip:

You solve an equation with decimals the same way you would an equation with natural numbers.

Example 5   **Solve an Equation with Decimals**

Solve the equation for x: $\dfrac{x-1.3}{0.4} = 0.3$

$$x - 1.3 = (0.3)(0.4)$$ See $x - 1.3$ as the product of 0.4 and 0.3, or multiply both sides by 0.4.

$$x - 1.3 = 0.12 \qquad \text{Compute: } (0.3)(0.4) = 0.12$$

$$x = 0.12 + 1.3 \qquad \text{See } x \text{ as the sum of the addends 1.3 and 0.12,}$$
See x as the sum of the addends 1.3 and 0.12, or add 1.3 to both sides.

$$x = 1.42 \qquad \text{Compute: } 0.12 + 1.3 = 1.42$$

EXERCISE 7.7

DEVELOP YOUR SKILL

Replace each common fraction by an equivalent decimal fraction.

1. $\dfrac{17}{100}$ **2.** $\dfrac{17}{10}$ **3.** $\dfrac{2}{5}$

4. $\dfrac{1}{6}$ **5.** $\dfrac{11}{25}$ **6.** $\dfrac{17}{50}$

Replace each decimal fraction by an equivalent common fraction in lowest terms.

7. 0.75   **8.** 1.8   **9.** 0.125   **10.** 3.25

Solve each equation for x.

11. $3.4 + x = 9.2$ **12.** $12 - x = 4.7$

13. $\dfrac{2.5 - x}{0.6} = 3.0$ **14.** $\dfrac{0.9}{x} + 0.04 = 0.4$

MAINTAIN YOUR SKILL

Simplify each expression. [2.6, 4.7]

15. $8 - (3 - x)$ **16.** $12 - (x - 7)$ **17.** $15 + (x - 4)$

18. $7 + (5 - x)$ **19.** $9 - (12 - x)$ **20.** $8 + (x - 10)$

In Exercises 21 and 22, each equation can be viewed as consisting of exactly three components. Identify the expression that is the sum (S) or the product (P) of the other two expressions. Give all possible interpretations. [6.2, 6.3]

21. $ab - c = d(f - g)$ **22.** $\dfrac{rs}{t} = p - (u - v)$

Write the reciprocal as a simple fraction or a natural number. [7.2]

23. $\dfrac{4}{7}$ **24.** $5\dfrac{1}{3}$ **25.** 28   **26.** $\dfrac{1}{\frac{3}{5}}$

27. Which is larger, $\dfrac{3}{5}$ or $\dfrac{2}{3}$? [7.6]

28. Which is larger, $\dfrac{3}{5}$ or $\dfrac{4}{7}$? [7.6]

Simplify each expression. [7.6]

29. $x + \dfrac{1}{4} - \dfrac{2}{5}$

30. $x - \dfrac{4}{3} + \dfrac{7}{5}$

EXTEND YOUR SKILL

31. Explain what a decimal fraction is.

32. Why is writing 0.75 preferred to writing just .75?

7.8 – THE DISTANCE FORMULA AND DIMENSIONAL ANALYSIS

OBJECTIVES

1. Use the distance formula to solve real-world problems.

2. Use dimensional analysis to solve real-world problems.

3. Use unit price to compare costs.

When an object is moving at a constant rate r for a time t, then the distance d that it travels is given by the formula:

$$\text{distance} = \text{rate} \times \text{time}$$
$$d = r \cdot t$$

If the values of any two variables are known, then the third can be found by substituting into the formula and solving for the desired variable. When the distance and the time are known, then the formula gives the *average* rate or speed of the object.

Example 1 **Use the Distance Formula**

If a dolphin is swimming 23 miles an hour, how far will it swim in 4 hours?

$$d = r \cdot t \qquad \text{Write the formula.}$$
$$d = 23 \cdot 4 \qquad \text{Substitute the given values.}$$
$$d = 92 \qquad \text{Compute.}$$

It will swim 92 miles.

When a problem has its origin in a physical situation, some or even most of the numbers used will be associated with physical units or dimensions. In using the distance formula we often think of distance in miles, the time in hours, so that the rate will be in miles per hour. One way to be certain that we have the correct relationship between the variables is to write the dimensions into the $d = r \cdot t$ formula. In doing this we represent "miles per hour" by "miles" divided by "hour."

$$(\text{miles}) = \left(\frac{\text{miles}}{\text{hour}}\right)(\text{hours}).$$

Then think of $\dfrac{(\ \ )}{\text{hour}}$ and $(\ \ )$hours as canceling to give "(miles) = (miles)."

This kind of **dimensional analysis** is also useful when changing from one measuring system into another. The basic equivalences for measuring length in the American system are the following:

$$12 \text{ inches } = 1 \text{ foot} \qquad 3 \text{ feet } = 1 \text{ yard} \qquad 5280 \text{ feet } = 1 \text{ mile}$$

The ratio $\dfrac{12 \text{ in}}{1 \text{ ft}}$, for example, is called a **conversion factor** (or a unit multiplier). Its value is 1, since 12 in = 1 ft. Multiplying by a conversion factor can be used to change from one unit of measurement into another.

Study Tip:

Since $\dfrac{3 \text{ ft}}{1 \text{ yd}}$ has a value of 1, it changes the form, but not the value, when we multiply by it.

Example 2   **Use a Conversion Factor**

Use a conversion factor to convert 21 *yards to feet.*

We have a choice of two conversion factors:

$$\frac{3 \text{ ft}}{1 \text{ yd}} \quad \text{and} \quad \frac{1 \text{ yd}}{3 \text{ ft}}$$

If we multiply the 21 yards by the second factor, we obtain

$$(21 \text{ yd})\left(\frac{1 \text{ yd}}{3 \text{ ft}}\right) = \frac{21}{3}\frac{(\text{yd})(\text{yd})}{\text{ft}}.$$

The units have not become feet, so this is not what we want. If we multiply the 21 yards by the first conversion factor we have

$$(21 \text{ yd})\left(\frac{3 \text{ ft}}{1 \text{ yd}}\right) = (21)(3) \text{ ft } = 63 \text{ ft}.$$

This time the multiplying and dividing by "yd" cancel to give feet.

In the next example we are given a rate of 3 feet for 2 minutes and we want to change this into inches per minute. To change $\frac{\text{ft}}{\text{min}}$ into $\frac{\text{in}}{\text{min}}$ we need to multiply $\frac{\text{ft}}{\text{min}}$ by $\frac{\text{in}}{\text{ft}}$ so that the multiplying and dividing by feet cancel.

$$\left(\frac{\cancel{\text{ft}}}{\text{min}}\right)\left(\frac{\text{in}}{\cancel{\text{ft}}}\right) = \frac{\text{in}}{\text{min}}$$

Example 3   **Use Dimensional Analysis**

An ant walked 3 feet in 2 minutes. What was its speed in inches per minute?

We want to change the units of feet per minute into inches per minute. As explained in the dimensional analysis above, we have the following relationships:

$$\left(\frac{\cancel{\text{ft}}}{\text{min}}\right)\left(\frac{\text{in}}{\cancel{\text{ft}}}\right) = \frac{\text{in}}{\text{min}}$$

Using the data from this example we obtain

$$\left(\frac{3 \text{ ft}}{2 \text{ min}}\right)\left(\frac{12 \text{ in}}{1 \text{ ft}}\right) = \frac{36}{2} = 18 \text{ in/min}$$

When a ratio compares two measurements having different kinds of units, it is called a **rate**. When the second measurement is 1, it is called a **unit rate**. In Example 3, the given rate of 3 feet per 2 minutes was converted into a unit rate of 18 inches per 1 minute.

When a unit rate is used to compare the cost per item, it is called a **unit price**. Some markets give the unit price of an item to help shoppers compare the cost of different sizes of the same product.

Example 4   **Use Unit Price to Compare Costs**

Blank VCR videotapes can be purchased in a package of 3 for $2.78 or a package of 10 for $8.88. Which is the better buy?

We divide the package price by the number of tapes in the package to get the unit price per tape.

$$\frac{\text{price for package}}{\text{number of tapes}} = \frac{\$2.78}{3} \approx 93¢ \qquad \text{Unit price of the 3-pack}$$

$$\frac{\text{price for package}}{\text{number of tapes}} = \frac{\$8.88}{10} \approx 89¢ \qquad \text{Unit price of the 10-pack}$$

The better buy is the 10-pack.

EXERCISE 7.8

DEVELOP YOUR SKILL

1. If a person can keep up a pace of $3\frac{1}{2}$ miles per hour, how far can they walk in $2\frac{1}{3}$ hours?

2. If a car can be expected to average 21 miles per gallon, what is the maximum miles range if the tank holds $14\frac{1}{2}$ gallons?

3. What is the average speed (rate) in km/hr for a Canadian Goose that flies 180 kilometers in 3 hours?

4. Convert 7 feet to inches.

5. Convert 54 inches to yards.

6. Convert $\frac{1}{2}$ mile to feet.

7. What is the unit price for a 400 ml bottle of shampoo that costs $1.84?

8. A 2 quart carton of Flopicana orange juice costs $2.24 and a 3 quart carton of Second Made orange juice costs $3.45. Which is the better buy and what is its unit price?

MAINTAIN YOUR SKILL

Construct vector models for the composition of the operators. [2.3]

9. $+4-7$ 10. $-8+3$

Simplify each expression. If no simpler form is possible, write "not possible." [4.4]

11. $z - \dfrac{xz}{x}$

12. $\dfrac{ab - (ab - c)}{c}$

13. $\dfrac{x + a}{a} - x$

14. $\dfrac{x - (xb + b)}{bx}$

Name each form (sum, difference, produce, quotient, or power). Then indicate which operators are accessible for removal. [6.6]

15. $\dfrac{x + y}{x - y}$

16. $a\left(\dfrac{b + c}{y}\right)$

17. $\dfrac{a - b}{x} + y$

18. $\dfrac{a}{b} - \left(\dfrac{c}{d}\right)^2$

19. If one of two candidates got 12 votes and the other got 18 votes, what fractional part of the total vote did each receive? [7.4]

20. If a quarterback completed 60 out of 96 passes thrown, what fractional part of the total passes was completed? What part was not completed? [7.4]

Find the value of each expression when $x = \frac{1}{2}$, $y = \frac{2}{3}$, and $z = \frac{1}{5}$. [7.5]

21. $xy - z^2$

22. $x^2 y + z$

23. $x^2(y + z)$

24. $y^2(x - z)$

Replace each common fraction by an equivalent decimal fraction. [7.7]

25. $\dfrac{7}{5}$

26. $\dfrac{3}{25}$

27. $\dfrac{23}{10}$

Replace each decimal fraction by an equivalent common fraction in lowest terms. [7.7]

28. 0.35

29. 0.44

30. 2.4

EXTEND YOUR SKILL

31. If a certain distance is covered twice as fast, how has the time changed? What principle have you used in your answer?

32. What is the difference between and ratio and a rate?

CHAPTER 7 REVIEW

Reduce each fraction to lowest terms. [7.1]

1. $\dfrac{21}{49}$

2. $\dfrac{35}{45}$

3. $\dfrac{400}{600}$

Write the reciprocal of each number. [7.2]

4. $\dfrac{3}{8}$

5. $3\dfrac{1}{4}$.

Compute the basic numeral. [7.2, 7.3, and 7.5]

6. $\left(\dfrac{4}{9}\right)\left(\dfrac{15}{14}\right)$

7. $\dfrac{\frac{7}{9}}{\frac{5}{6}}$

8. $\dfrac{3}{4}+\dfrac{7}{6}$

9. $\dfrac{5}{4}-\dfrac{7}{8}$

10. $\left(3\dfrac{1}{3}\right)\left(4\dfrac{1}{2}\right)$

11. $(3)\left(\dfrac{1}{2}\right)-(2)\left(\dfrac{3}{4}\right)$

Solve each equation for x and compute the basic numeral. If such a number has not yet been defined, write "not defined."   [7.3, 7.6]

12. $x+\dfrac{3}{4}=\dfrac{9}{8}$

13. $3\dfrac{1}{2}-x=1\dfrac{2}{3}$

14. $\dfrac{2}{3}x=\dfrac{4}{5}$

15. $\dfrac{4-x}{3}=\dfrac{5}{6}$

Find the value of each expression when $x = \frac{1}{3}$ and $y = \frac{3}{2}$. Write your answer as a common fraction in lowest terms. [7.3, 7.5]

16. $\dfrac{x}{y}$

17. $y - x$

18. xy^2

19. $5x + 4y$

20. Write a sentence that states the ratio comparison of $\dfrac{3}{5}$ to $\dfrac{7}{10}$. [7.4]

21. $2\dfrac{1}{3}$ is what part of $3\dfrac{2}{3}$? [7.4]

22. Arrange the numbers $\dfrac{3}{4}, \dfrac{4}{5}, \dfrac{7}{9}$ in a list so that they increase in size from left to right. [7.6]

Replace each common fraction by an equivalent decimal fraction, and each decimal fraction by an equivalent common fraction in lowest terms. [7.7]

23. $\dfrac{57}{1000}$

24. $\dfrac{11}{20}$

25. 0.6

26. 0.35

Solve each equation for x and compute the basic numeral. Write your answer as a decimal. [7.7]

27. $0.4x = 0.6$

28. $5 - \dfrac{x}{0.4} = 0.8$

29. In 2000, Martin Strel from Slovenia set the world distance swimming record of 1,866 miles by swimming the length of the Danube River (and more) through 8 countries in 60 days. What was his average rate in miles per day? Source: Guinness World records, 2004. [7.8]

30. A 13 ounce bag of Mostitos tortilla chips costs $2.47 and a 16 ounce bag of Caliente tortilla chips costs $3.20. Which is the better buy and what is its unit price? [7.8]

Chapter 8 — Proportion and Percent

8.1 – PROPORTIONS

OBJECTIVES

1. Identify a proportion.

2. Solve a proportion.

A **proportion** is an equation stating that two ratios are equivalent. For example, when we say that the fraction $\frac{6}{8}$ equals the fraction $\frac{3}{4}$, we are stating a proportion:

$$\frac{6}{8} = \frac{3}{4}$$

We can use the cross product rule from Lesson 7.6 to determine whether a pair of ratios forms a proportion.

Study Tip:

If the two numbers in a quotient have no units or the same units, the quotient is called a **ratio**. It the numbers have different units, the quotient is called a **rate**.

Example 1   **Identify a Proportion**

Determine whether the ratios $\frac{3}{5}$ and $\frac{8}{13}$ form a proportion.

Check the cross products:

$$13 \cdot 3 = 39 \qquad 5 \cdot 8 = 40$$

$$\frac{3}{5} \diagdown \diagup \frac{8}{13}$$

Since $39 < 40$, the ratios are not equal. ($\frac{3}{5}$ is smaller than $\frac{8}{13}$.) Thus the ratios do not form a proportion.

When one of the numbers in a proportion is unknown, it can be found by using the cross product rule or the invariant principle for division from Lesson 3.6.

Example 2   **Solve a Proportion**

Solve the proportion $\dfrac{x}{20} = \dfrac{35}{100}$.

Since there is a simple relationship between 100 and 20, it will be easy to use the invariant principle for division. We recall that 35 changes into x in the same way that 100 changes into 20. Since we divide 100 by 5 to get 20, we must also divide 35 by 5 to get x. Thus,

$$x = \frac{35}{5} = 7.$$

Example 3   **Solve a Proportion**

Solve the proportion $\dfrac{x}{3} = \dfrac{7}{11}$.

Since 3 does not divide 11, it will be easier this time to use the cross product rule. We know that 11 times x must equal 3 times 7. Thus,

$$11x = (3)(7)$$ Set the cross products equal.

$$11x = 21$$ Multiply (3)(7).

$$x = \frac{21}{11}$$ Divide each side by 11.

EXERCISE 8.1

DEVELOP YOUR SKILL

Determine whether each pair of ratios form a proportion.

1. $\dfrac{2}{3}$ and $\dfrac{10}{15}$

2. $\dfrac{8}{5}$ and $\dfrac{5}{3}$

3. $\dfrac{1.2}{0.3}$ and $\dfrac{2.8}{7}$

4. $\dfrac{6}{16}$ and $\dfrac{3}{8}$

Solve each proportion.

5. $\dfrac{y}{66} = \dfrac{5}{11}$

6. $\dfrac{0.6}{n} = \dfrac{1.8}{27}$

7. $\dfrac{39}{75} = \dfrac{m}{25}$

8. $\dfrac{5}{7} = \dfrac{w}{10}$

9. $\dfrac{5}{3} = \dfrac{8}{k}$

10. $\dfrac{5}{4} = \dfrac{b+3}{28}$

11. Find the value of x that makes $\dfrac{3}{2}$ and $\dfrac{15}{x-4}$ a proportion.

MAINTAIN YOUR SKILL

In Exercises 12 – 16, the entire expression is a numeral for a single number. Write this number in prime factored form. [5.5]

12. $8 \cdot 28$

13. $6 \cdot 16$

14. $15 \cdot 27$

15. $3^{12} - 3^{10}$

16. $7^8 + 7^6$

Solve each equation for x. [6.4, 7.3]

17. $12 = \dfrac{5}{x} + 4$

18. $\dfrac{x-2}{5} = 7$

19. $3 + x = 5x$

20. $8x = 3x + 7$

21. $r = \dfrac{s}{x} + t$

22. $\dfrac{s-x}{r} = t$

23. $m + x = px$

24. $mx = nx + p$

Translate each statement into a mathematical equation. [6.9]

25. x is 3 more than y.

26. Twice y is 7 less than z.

Construct a graphical model for each fraction. [7.1]

27. $\dfrac{3}{5} = \dfrac{3 \cdot 1}{5}$

28. $\dfrac{3}{5} = 3\left(\dfrac{1}{5}\right)$

Compute the ratios. [7.4]

29. $5\frac{1}{4}$ is what part of $6\frac{3}{4}$?

30. $5\frac{2}{3}$ is how many times $4\frac{1}{3}$?

EXTEND YOUR SKILL

31. Explain what a proportion is.

32. Identify the two ways to solve a proportion and indicate how to know which to use.

8.2 – MODELING PROPORTIONS WITH LINEAR SCALES

OBJECTIVES

1. Use linear scales to model proportions.

2. Use proportions to solve applied problems.

Linear scales can be used to model many operations on real numbers. Up to this point we have used them as a background for vectors to show increases and decreases. We now show how two linear scales placed side by side can be used to model proportions. Different units of length are used on the two scales, but their zero points coincide. For example, consider the following pair of scales.

Note that the upper number is always twice the lower number. That is, the ratios

$$\frac{2}{1}, \ \frac{4}{2}, \ \frac{6}{3}, \ \frac{8}{4}$$

are all equal. Furthermore, if we look at the points corresponding to 4 and 6 on the upper scale (2 and 3 on the lower scale), we see that the ratio of the left number to the right number is the same on both scales.

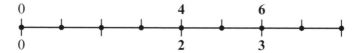

The left number **4** divided by the right number **6** on the top scale is equal to the left number **2** divided by the right number **3** on the bottom scale:

$$\frac{4}{6} = \frac{2}{3}.$$

These relationships hold in general when two linear scales are placed side by side with their zero points coinciding. If we focus on two points on the scale, a total of four proportions can be obtained:

Consider two linear scales with their zero points coinciding:

The following proportions all apply:

$$\frac{a}{b} = \frac{c}{d} \;\leftrightarrow\; \frac{\text{top}}{\text{bottom}} = \frac{\text{top}}{\text{bottom}} \qquad \frac{b}{a} = \frac{d}{c} \;\leftrightarrow\; \frac{\text{bottom}}{\text{top}} = \frac{\text{bottom}}{\text{top}}$$

$$\frac{a}{c} = \frac{b}{d} \;\leftrightarrow\; \frac{\text{left}}{\text{right}} = \frac{\text{left}}{\text{right}} \qquad \frac{c}{a} = \frac{d}{b} \;\leftrightarrow\; \frac{\text{right}}{\text{left}} = \frac{\text{right}}{\text{left}}$$

The next two examples show how linear models are useful in organizing a problem based on proportional reasoning. In setting up the proportion, we choose the form that is easiest to solve for the desired quantity.

Example 1   **Use Linear Scales to Model a Proportion**

A will requires that an estate of $500,000 be divided into $2\frac{1}{2}$ shares. What is the value of one share?

In setting up a model, we let one scale represent dollars and the other scale represent shares.

We have $500,000 on the upper scale corresponding to $2\frac{1}{2}$ shares on the lower scale. We want to find the number x that corresponds to 1 on the lower scale. The proportion will be easiest to solve for x if we have x divided by 1. Thus we use the relationship

$$(\text{top}) \div (\text{bottom}) = (\text{top}) \div (\text{bottom}).$$

This gives us the following proportion to solve.

$$\frac{x}{1} = \frac{500{,}000}{2\frac{1}{2}}$$

$$x = (500{,}000)\left(\frac{2}{5}\right) \qquad \text{Multiply by the reciprocal of } \frac{5}{2}.$$

$$x = \$200{,}000. \qquad \text{Compute.}$$

Example 2   **Use Linear Scales to Model a Proportion**

A home was purchased some years ago for $120,000. It is now appraised for $300,000. Its present value is how many times the original purchase price?

This problem is asking for a ratio comparison using $120,000 as the basis. We put the dollar amounts on the upper scale and show the multipliers on the lower scale.

Since 120,000 is the basis for the comparison, it is placed above the 1 on the lower scale. The number x that is sought corresponds to 300,000. This time the easiest proportion to solve will be of the form (right) ÷ (left). We have

$$\frac{x}{1} = \frac{300{,}000}{120{,}000} \quad \text{and} \quad x = 2\frac{1}{2}.$$

EXERCISE 8.2
DEVELOP YOUR SKILL

1. Write four proportions that can be obtained from the numbers on the linear scales.

Construct a linear scale to represent each problem. Then give an equation model for the problem and solve it.

2. Sally received an inheritance of $20,000. If this was $\frac{4}{7}$ of the total estate, how large was the total estate?

3. Jose bought some stock 3 years ago for $8 a share. The stock is now selling for $22 a share. Its present value is how many times its value 3 years ago?

4. A coat with a price tag of $90 was marked down to $75 for a sale. The sale price was what fractional part of the original price?

5. A football team has won 6 games, which was $\frac{2}{3}$ of the games played in the season. How many games were played during the season?

6. After driving 80 miles, Mrs. Edwards estimated she had covered about $\frac{2}{5}$ of the planned trip. If this is true, the entire trip would be how many miles?

7. A business had a profit of $4200 for its first year. The next year the profits were $9450. The second year profits were how many times those of the first year?

8. If a cross country runner has a time of 30 minutes for $3\frac{3}{4}$ miles, what has been his average rate in minutes per mile?

Maintain Your Skill

Do not compute, but write equivalent expressions without parentheses. Use only counting numbers and do not change the first term. When possible, give a second alternate form. [2.5]

9. $12 - (18 - 10)$

10. $17 - (23 - 15)$

11. $16 + (27 - 21)$

12. $32 - (12 + 17)$

Name each form and compute the basic numeral. [5.2]

13. $\dfrac{3+9}{2^3}$

14. $\left(\dfrac{7-3}{5}\right)^0$

15. $3\left(\dfrac{4+5}{6}\right)$

16. $\left(\dfrac{5}{9-7}\right)^2$

17. $\left(\dfrac{4\cdot 3}{5}\right)^2$

18. $\dfrac{8-3}{2^2}$

19. $4\cdot 5^2$

20. $5 + 2\cdot 3$

21. $14 - 2\cdot 3$

22. $4\cdot 3^2$

Solve each equation for x. [7.3]

23. $\dfrac{x}{4} = \dfrac{5}{8}$

24. $\dfrac{\frac{3}{4}}{x} = \dfrac{5}{8}$

25. $\dfrac{x}{\frac{3}{4}} = \dfrac{5}{8}$

26. $\dfrac{\frac{x}{3}}{4} = \dfrac{5}{8}$
    27. $\dfrac{3}{\frac{x}{4}} = \dfrac{5}{8}$
    28. $\dfrac{3}{\frac{4}{x}} = \dfrac{5}{8}$

29. In July, 2004, Philip Rabinowitz set a new world record in the 100 meter dash for a centenarian (a person at least 100 years old). His time was 30.86 seconds. This was 5.33 seconds faster than the previous world record. What was the previous world record? Source: www.guardian.co.uk [7.7]

30. A 3-pack of Memoless DVD-R disks costs $5.10. A 5-pack of Minwell DVD-R disks costs $8.75. Which is the better buy and what is its unit price? [7.8]

EXTEND YOUR SKILL

31. Explain what determines which of the four proportions should be used in solving a given problem.

32. Consider the problem: "If 3 apples cost $1.20, how much will 7 apples cost?" In setting up the linear scales, is it appropriate to put a 3 on the upper scale above a 7 on the lower scale? Why or why not?

8.3 – FRACTIONS, DECIMALS, AND PERCENTS

OBJECTIVES

1. Write percents as fractions and decimals and vice versa.

2. Use a percent to describe a relationship.

A **percent** is a ratio that compares a number to 100. Instead of writing a percent as a fraction with a denominator of 100, the symbol % is often used.

$$\frac{3}{100} = 3\%, \quad \frac{25}{100} = 25\%, \quad \frac{135}{100} = 135\%, \quad \text{etc.}$$

Since percent means "per hundred," we can change a percent into a fraction by dividing the percent by 100 and then simplifying.

Example 1   **Write a Percent as a Fraction**

Write each percent as a fraction in simplest form.

(a) 5%   (b) 28%   (c) 3.5%   (d) 150%

(a) $5\% = \dfrac{5}{100} = \dfrac{1}{20}$ (b) $28\% = \dfrac{28}{100} = \dfrac{7}{25}$

(c) $3.5\% = \dfrac{3.5}{100}$

$= \dfrac{35}{1000}$ Multiply the numerator and denominator by 10 to eliminate the decimal in the numerator.

$= \dfrac{7}{200}$ Reduce the fraction by dividing the numerator and denominator by 5.

(d) $150\% = \dfrac{150}{100}$

$= \dfrac{3}{2}$ Reduce the fraction by dividing the numerator and denominator by 50.

Changing a percent into a decimal is easy. Divide by a hundred and remove the percent symbol %. To divide by 100, just move the decimal point 2 places to the left.

Example 2   **Write a Percent as a Decimal**

Write each percent as a decimal.

(a) 65%   (b) 4.7%   (c) 230%

(a) 65% = 0.65   (b) 4.7% = 0.047   (c) 230% = 2.3

Changing from a decimal to a percent is also easy. Multiply the number by 100 and join the percent symbol %. To multiply by 100, move the decimal point 2 places to the right.

Example 3   **Write a Decimal as a Percent**

Write each decimal as a percent.

(a) 0.17   (b) 0.009   (c) 3.14

(a) 0.17 = 17%   (b) 0.009 = 0.9%   (c) 3.14 = 314%

One way to change a fraction into a percent is to change it into an equivalent fraction with a denominator of 100. This is easy to do if the denominator is a factor of 100. If the denominator is not a factor of 100, write the fraction as a decimal and then change the decimal into a percent.

Example 4   **Write a Fraction as a Percent**

Write each fraction as a percent.

   (a) $\dfrac{5}{4}$ (b) $\dfrac{5}{8}$ (c) $\dfrac{4}{3}$

(a) $\dfrac{5}{4} = \dfrac{125}{100}$ Multiply numerator and denominator by 25.

       $= 125\%$ Write as a percent.

(b) $\dfrac{5}{8} = 0.625$ Divide 5 by 8 and write it as a decimal.

       $= 62.5\%$ Change the decimal into a percent.

(c) $\dfrac{4}{3} = 1.33\overline{3}$ Divide 4 by 3 and write it as a decimal.

       $= 133.\overline{3}\%$ Change the decimal into a percent.

Example 5   **Using a Percent**

What percent of each figure is shaded?

(a)   (b)   (c)

(a) 7 of the 25 squares are shaded, so $\dfrac{7}{25} = \dfrac{28}{100} = 28\%$ is shaded.

(b) 4 squares are completely shaded and 8 squares are half shaded. So the equivalent of $4 + \dfrac{8}{2} = 4 + 4 = 8$ of the 25 squares are shaded. It follows that $\dfrac{8}{25} = \dfrac{32}{100} = 32\%$ of the figure is shaded.

(c) 3 of the 6 triangles are shaded, so $\dfrac{3}{6} = \dfrac{1}{2} = \dfrac{50}{100} = 50\%$ is shaded.

EXERCISE 8.3

DEVELOP YOUR SKILL

Write each percent as a decimal and as a fraction in lowest terms.

1. 42%   **2.** 3%   **3.** 140%   **4.** $\frac{1}{4}$%

Write each decimal or fraction as a percent.

5. 0.95   **6.** $\frac{3}{4}$ **7.** $\frac{3}{20}$ **8.** 2.45

9. 0.385   **10.** $\frac{4}{5}$ **11.** $1\frac{1}{4}$ **12.** 0.06

Determine what percent of each figure is shaded.

13.   **14.**

MAINTAIN YOUR SKILL

Simplify each expression. [4.5]

15. $5\left(\dfrac{x}{20}\right)$ **16.** $\dfrac{\frac{20}{x}}{5}$ **17.** $\dfrac{\frac{5}{x}}{20}$

18. $\dfrac{5}{\frac{x}{20}}$ **19.** $\dfrac{20}{\frac{x}{5}}$ **20.** $\dfrac{20}{\frac{5}{x}}$

Name each form and indicate which operators are accessible for removal. [6.6]

21. $35 + 17$ **22.** $25 - 8$

23. $\dfrac{12+6}{3}$ **24.** $2\left(\dfrac{7-5}{2}\right)$

25. Over several months the market index rose from 900 to 1050. This increase was what fractional part of the first figure? [7.4]

26. In one year the unemployment figure for a city dropped from 15,000 to 12,000. This decrease was what fractional part of the earlier number? [7.4]

27. Convert $5\frac{1}{2}$ feet to inches. [7.8]   **28.** Convert $2\frac{1}{4}$ yards to inches. [7.8]

Construct a linear scale to represent the problem. Then give an equation model for the problem and solve it. [8.2]

29. If peanuts are priced at $1.20 for 12 ounces ($\frac{3}{4}$ of a pound), what is the price per pound?

30. Bananas are on sale for 3 pounds for 84¢. How much will 5 pounds cost?

EXTEND YOUR SKILL

31. Explain what a percent is.

32. Explain how to change a decimal into a percent.

33. Explain how to change a percent into a fraction.

8.4 – PERCENT COMPARISONS

OBJECTIVES

1. Use linear scales to model percents.

2. Solve percent problems.

In the ratio comparison of two numbers, the second number is always the basis for the comparison. For example, when we say

$$4 \text{ is } \frac{4}{5} \text{ of } 5,$$

we identify 5 as the whole amount (called the **base** number), 4 is the **part** of the whole, and $\frac{4}{5}$ is the **rate**. If we write the rate as a percent, we have the equivalent statement

$$4 \text{ is } 80\% \text{ of } 5.$$

When used in an equation, the percent is *always* written as a decimal:

Part ⟶   ⟵ Base

$$4 = 0.80 \times 5$$

⟵ Percent rate as a decimal

This illustrates the fundamental **percent equation**.

$$\text{Part} = \text{Percent} \times \text{Base}$$

Caution

Percent must always be thought of as an operator. It does not stand by itself. We always mean percent of *something*. In order for the percent operator to be understood, the operand (or base number) must be determined. Sometimes it is not explicitly stated and must be inferred from the context.

When solving problems using percents, it is often helpful to draw linear scales as a model. To do this, locate the first number (the part) and the second number (the base) on the upper scale. In practical applications, these numbers usually have dimensions such as dollars, pounds, hours, etc. The lower scale has the ratio comparisons as percents, and these are numbers without dimensions.

Study Tip:

We have labeled the "Part," the "Base," and the "Percent Rate" to help you. It is not necessary to label them in your scales.

Example 1   **Draw a Linear Model for Percent**

Draw a linear model for the statement "4 is 80% of 5."

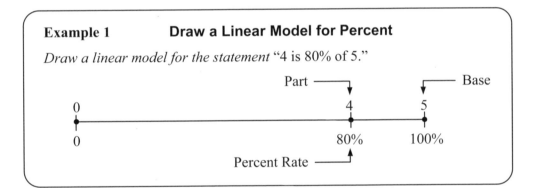

There are three typical problems that are modeled by the scales in Example 1. Each problem corresponds to omitting one piece of data.

(A) What is 80% of 5? $x = (0.80)(5)$ Answer: 4

(B) 4 is what percent of 5? $4 = (x)(5)$ Answer: 80%

(C) 4 is 80% of what number? $4 = (0.80)(x)$ Answer: 5

In (A), the part is unknown. In (B) the percent rate is unknown. And in (C), the base is unknown. Each of these problems can be solved by setting up a proportion from the scales and solving for the missing information. They can also be solved by translating the question directly into an equation.

Example 2   **Solve a Percent Problem**

Draw a linear model for the following problem. Then set up a conditional equation and solve it.

> "Fred made a down payment of $2550 on a car. This down payment was what percent of the total cost of $8500?"

The base amount is $8500 and the part is $2550. We are asked to find the percent rate. If we let x be the percent, then the linear model looks like this:

We choose to write a proportion of the form (left) ÷ (right), since this will be the easiest to solve:

$$\frac{x}{1} = \frac{2550}{8500} \qquad \text{and} \qquad x = 0.3 = 30\%.$$

Note that we have replaced 100% by its decimal equivalent 1 when setting up the proportion equation.

We could also solve this problem by setting up the percent equation. As an English sentence we have:

> 2550 is what percent of 8500?

This becomes the equation

$$2550 = (x)(8500),$$

which gives us

$$x = \frac{2550}{8500} \qquad \text{and} \quad x = 0.3 = 30\%, \text{ as before.}$$

If the first number in a ratio comparison is smaller than the second number, then the rate will be less than 1. That is, the rate is less than 100%. If the first number is larger than the second, as in the next example, then the rate will be more than 100%. In this case the "Part" is greater than the "Base."

Example 3   **Draw a Linear Model for Percent**

"5 is what percent of 4?"

This time the base is 4 and the "part" is 5. Let x be the desired percent rate.

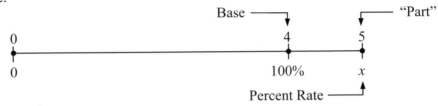

Don't forget to change the percents into decimals when you set up the equation.

We choose to write a proportion of the form (right) ÷ (left), since this will be the easiest to solve:

$$\frac{x}{1} = \frac{5}{4} \quad \text{and} \quad x = 1.25 = 125\%$$

Setting this up as a percent equation we have $5 = (x)(4)$, so that

$x = \frac{5}{4} = 1.25 = 125\%$, as before.

Don't forget to change the percents into decimals when you set up the equation.

When the "Part" of the Base is not known, the model looks like this:

Example 4   **Draw a Linear Model for Percent**

"What is 20% of 45?"

This time the base is 45 and the percent is 20%. Let x be the desired number.

To solve this we set up the proportion as (top) ÷ (bottom):

$$\frac{x}{0.2} = \frac{45}{1}$$

Cross multiply to find $x = (0.2)(45)$ and $x = 9$. Notice that the equation we obtain from the proportion simplifies to the percent equation: $x = (0.2)(45)$.

When the Base for the percent is not known, the model looks like this:

Example 5   **Draw a Linear Model for Percent**

"78 is 120% of what number?"

This time 78 is the "Part" and the Percent is 120%. Since the percent is more than 100%, the "Part" is larger than the Base. Let x be the unknown Base.

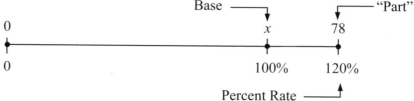

The easiest form of the proportion is (top) ÷ (bottom).

$$\frac{x}{1} = \frac{78}{1.2}$$

We solve to find $x = 65$.

If we set up the original problem as a percent equation we have

$$78 = 1.2x,$$

which also yields $x = \frac{78}{1.2} = 65$.

EXERCISE 8.4

DEVELOP YOUR SKILL

Exercises 1 – 6 give linear models for percent problems. Write a verbal statement of each problem. Then set up a conditional equation with x as the variable and solve.

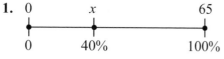

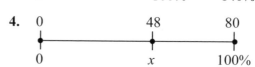

5.

0		84	x

0		80%	100%

6.

0		x	104

0		100%	$133\frac{1}{3}\%$

Draw a linear model to represent each problem. Then construct a conditional equation with x as the variable and solve.

7. If an automobile costing $22,000 depreciated 15% during the first year, what was the loss in value?

8. A tip of $6.00 was left for a $40.00 dinner bill. This tip was what percent of the bill?

9. A house valued at $180,000 rents for $14,400 a year. What percent of the value of the house is the annual rent income?

10. A family budget allows 22% for food. What is the planned expenditure if the monthly income is $3000?

MAINTAIN YOUR SKILL

Use an invariant principle to write an equivalent sum or difference that you would consider easier to compute. [1.6]

11. $437 + 98$

12. $451 - 95$

Write an equivalent expression in the form 5^n, when possible. Otherwise, write "not possible." [5.4]

13. $5^7 \cdot 5^3$

14. $5^7 - 5^3$

15. $(5^7)^3$

16. $\dfrac{5^7}{5^3}$

17. $5 \cdot 25$

18. $\dfrac{5^2}{25}$

Use the GCF to factor each expression. [5.8]

19. $12xy + 20xy^2$

20. $25xy + 35x^2$

21. $10x^2 - 12y^2$

22. $15xy - 16wx$

In Exercises 23 and 24, define a variable and write an equation to model each situation. Then solve the equation. [6.10]

23. U. S. astronaut Alan Bean spent a total of 69.66 days in space. This was 20.53 days more than astronaut Charles Conrad spent in space. How long was Conrad in space? Source: Kids' Almanac, 1999.

24. In 2000 there were about 207 million people whose native language was Arabic. This was 43 million less than twice the number who spoke Japanese. How many people spoke Japanese? Source: World Almanac for Kids, 2005

Write the reciprocal as a simple fraction or a natural number. [7.2]

25. $\dfrac{5}{3}$

26. $4\dfrac{2}{3}$

Write each fraction as a percent. [8.3]

27. $\dfrac{7}{10}$

28. $\dfrac{9}{20}$

29. $\dfrac{4}{25}$

30. $\dfrac{13}{50}$

EXTEND YOUR SKILL

31. Explain what it means for the percent rate to be more than 100%.

32. Explain what is wrong with this equation: $(75\%)(80) = 60$.

8.5 – ESTIMATING WITH PERCENTS

OBJECTIVES

1. Find simple percents mentally.

2. Estimate with percents.

Some percents are particularly simple when written as fractions. For example,

$$10\% = \frac{1}{10} \qquad 12\frac{1}{2}\% = \frac{1}{8} \qquad 20\% = \frac{1}{5} \qquad 25\% = \frac{1}{4} \qquad 30\% = \frac{3}{10}$$

$$33\frac{1}{3}\% = \frac{1}{3} \qquad 40\% = \frac{2}{5} \qquad 50\% = \frac{1}{2} \qquad 60\% = \frac{3}{5} \qquad 66\frac{2}{3}\% = \frac{2}{3}$$

$$75\% = \frac{3}{4} \qquad 80\% = \frac{4}{5} \qquad 90\% = \frac{9}{10} \qquad 125\% = \frac{5}{4} \qquad 150\% = \frac{3}{2}$$

Computations involving these percents can often by done mentally, treating the percent as a fraction.

Example 1   **Find a Percent Mentally**

Find the percent of each number mentally.

   (a) 50% of 28   (b) 25% of 800   (c) 60% of 35

(a) 50% is $\frac{1}{2}$, and $\frac{1}{2}$ of 28 is 14. So, 50% of 28 is 14.

(b) 25% is $\frac{1}{4}$, and $\frac{1}{4}$ of 800 is 200. So, 25% of 800 is 200.

(c) 60% is $\frac{3}{5}$. $\frac{1}{5}$ of 35 is 7, so $\frac{3}{5}$ of 35 is (3)(7) = 21.

Sometimes an exact answer is not needed in a problem. In these cases an estimate of the answer can be found by replacing the given numbers by nearby numbers that are easier to use in computing.

Example 2   **Use Estimation with Percents**

Estimate the percent of each number.

   (a) 33% of 61   (b) 27% of 39   (c) 76% of 79

(a) 33% is about $\frac{1}{3}$, and 61 is about 60. So, 33% of 61 is about $\frac{1}{3} \times 60 = 20$.

(b) 27% is about $\frac{1}{4}$, and 39 is about 40. So 27% of 39 is about $\frac{1}{4} \times 40 = 10$.

(c) 76% is about $\frac{3}{4}$, and 79 is about 80. Now, $\frac{1}{4}$ of 80 is 20, so 76% of 79 is about $3 \times 20 = 60$.

Estimations can also be used to approximate the value of a percent.

Example 3   **Use Estimation with Percents**

Estimate each percent.

   (a) 7 out of 22   (b) 17 out of 35   (c) 19 out of 80

(a) Since 22 is about 21, $\frac{7}{22} \approx \frac{7}{21} = \frac{1}{3}$, and $\frac{1}{3}$ is about 33%, so 7 out of 22 is about 33%.

(b) $\frac{17}{35} \approx \frac{17}{34} = \frac{1}{2} = 50\%$, so 17 out of 35 is about 50%.

(c) $\frac{19}{80} \approx \frac{20}{80} = \frac{1}{4} = 25\%$, so 19 out of 80 is about 25%.

Example 4   **Use Estimation to Solve a Problem**

Lisa had lunch with her friends and the bill came to $28.37. If they want to leave a 15% tip, what is a reasonable amount?

$28.37 is about $30, and 15% = 10% + 5%. We find

10% of $30 is $3.00.   Move the decimal point one place to the left.

5% of $30 is $1.50.   5% is one half of 10%.

So a reasonable tip is $3.00 + $1.50, or $4.50.

EXERCISE 8.5

DEVELOP YOUR SKILL

Find the percent of each number mentally.

1. $33\frac{1}{3}\%$ of 600

2. 75% of 84

3. 40% of 55

Estimate the percent of each number.

4. 9% of 348

5. 67% of 24

6. 21% of 49

Estimate each percent.

7. 7 out of 68

8. 11 out of 40

9. 39 out of 59

Exercises 10 – 12 are based on the following chart that gives the number of new registrations with the American Kennel Club for several popular dog breeds.

AKC Registrations in 2002			Source: World Almanac
German Shepherd	46,963	Cocker Spaniel	20,655
Beagle	44,610	Great Dane	8,975
Dachshund	42,571	Collie	6,252
Poodle	33,917	Saint Bernard	5,188

10. Which breed had about 30% of the registrations of the Cocker Spaniel?

11. Which breed had about 20% of the registrations of the Beagle?

12. Which breed had about 75% of the registrations of the Beagle?

MAINTAIN YOUR SKILL

Write the composition of the two given operators as an equivalent single operator in basic form. [2.3, 4.2]

13. $-3 + 10$

14. $-4 - 5$

15. $2\left(\dfrac{(\ )}{10}\right)$

16. $\dfrac{15(\ )}{5}$

Find the largest square factor of each expression. Write your answer in factored form. [5.6]

17. $3^2 \cdot 7^3$

18. $2^2 \cdot 3^5$

19. $x^3 \cdot y^4$

20. $x^7 \cdot y$

Each equation in Exercises 21 – 24 can be viewed as consisting of exactly three terms. Identify the sum term (S) or the product term (P) as appropriate. Give all possible interpretations. [6.2, 6.3]

21. $a - b = mn$

22. $\dfrac{a}{b} - c = m + n$

23. $xy = \dfrac{a}{b}$

24. $\dfrac{m}{p} = x - n$

Define a variable and write an equation to model each situation in Exercises 25 to 28. Do not solve the equation. [6.10]

25. When the Three Gorges Dam is completed in China, it will be able to generate 18,200 MW (megawatts) of electricity. This is about 7 times the largest hydroelectric plant in the U.S. About how large is the largest plant in the U.S.? Source: *The World Almanac*

26. In 2003, General Motors spent more money on advertising than any other company in the U.S. It was 1.2 billion dollars more than Ford Motor Company. If General Motors spent 3.4 billion dollars, how much did Ford Motors spend? Source: *The World Almanac*

27. Bob's age is 3 more than 4 times Fred's age. If Bob is 75 years old, how old is Fred?

28. The Akashi Channel bridge in Japan is the longest suspension bridge in the world. It is 1830 feet less than twice the span of the Golden Gate bridge in California. If the Akashi Channel bridge has a span of 6570 feet, what is the span of the Golden Gate bridge? Source: *The World Almanac*

Draw a linear model to represent each situation. Then construct a conditional equation with x as the variable and solve. [8.4]

29. Barbara baked a delicious apple pie and cut the pie into six equal pieces. After supper Bob ate $1\frac{1}{2}$ pieces for dessert. If the whole pie had 2280 calories, how many calories did Bob eat?

30. A town whose population was 12,000 some years ago now has a population of 40,000. The present population is how many times the former figure?

EXTEND YOUR SKILL

31. In Example 2(a), the number 61 was approximated by the number 60. Explain why this was better than using 62 as an approximation.

32. Explain an easy way to compute 150% of a number.

8.6 – PERCENT CHANGES

OBJECTIVE

1. Find the percent of increase and decrease.

When percents are applied to increases and decreases, we get the **percent of change**. This percent is computed as the ratio of the amount of change to the original amount. For example, suppose that a camera priced at $50 is on sale for $40. The decease in price can be described in several ways:

Words:

(A) 40 is 10 less than 50.

(B) 40 is $\frac{1}{5}$ of 50 less than 50.

(C) 40 is 20% of 50 less than 50.

(D) 40 is 20% less than 50.

Equation:

$40 = 50 - 10$

$40 = 50 - \left(\frac{1}{5}\right)(50)$

$40 = 50 - (0.20)(50)$

$40 = 50 - (0.20)(50)$

To obtain the 20%, we take the amount of the decrease ($10) and divide by the original amount before the change ($50):

$$\text{amount of change} \longrightarrow \frac{10}{50} = 0.2 = 20\%$$
$$\text{original amount} \longrightarrow$$

Here is the general rule:

Percent of Change

$$\text{percent of change} = \frac{\text{amount of change}}{\text{original amount}}$$

Notice in statement (D) above that the *base* for the percent is omitted. It must be determined from the context. Remember that the base for the percent is always the original amount *before* the change. When the new amount is less than the original amount, then the percent of change is called a **percent of decrease**.

Example 1   **Find the Percent of Decrease**

The cost of a new jacket was marked down from $80 to $56. Find the percent of decrease.

The amount of the decrease was $80 - $56 = $24. To find the percent of decrease, take the amount of the decrease and divide by the original amount:

$$\begin{array}{l}\text{amount of change} \longrightarrow \\ \text{original amount} \longrightarrow\end{array} \quad \frac{24}{80} = \frac{3}{10} = 30\%$$

The price decreased by 30%.

When an amount increases, then the percent of change is called a **percent of increase**.

Example 2   **Find the Percent of Increase**

The average price of regular unleaded gasoline in the U. S. increased from $1.11 a gallon in 1993 to $1.59 a gallon in 2003. Find the percent of increase.   Source: World Almanac

The amount of the increase was $1.59 - $1.11 = $0.48. To find the percent of increase, take the amount of the increase and divide by the original amount:

amount of change ⟶ $\dfrac{0.48}{1.11}$ ≈ 0.43 = 43%
original amount ⟶

The price increased about 43%.

When an item is marked for sale at a discount, then the sale price can be found by subtracting the amount of the discount from the original price:

$$\text{Sale Price} = \text{Original Price} - \text{Amount of Discount}$$

When the discount is given as a percent, it is always a percent of the original price before the discount is applied.

Remember:

The base for a percent of increase or decrease is always the amount before the change.

Example 3   Use the Percent of Change to Find a Price

Andrew purchased a television that was on sale for 30% *off the original price. If the original price was* $240, *what was the sale price?*

The decrease of 30% is a decrease of 30% of the original price. First, find the amount of this decrease:

(0.30)($240) = $72   Change 30% to 0.30 when computing.

Now subtract this decrease from the original price:

$240 - $72 = $168

The sale price was $168.

EXERCISE 8.6

DEVELOP YOUR SKILL

Find each percent of change to the nearest percent. State whether the percent of change is an *increase* or a *decrease*.

1. From 8 to 12

2. From 12 to 16

3. From 12 to 8

5. From 69 to 62

4. From 16 to 12

6. From 38 to 61

In Exercises 7 – 10, find the sale price of each item to the nearest cent.

7. lawn chair: $34.85, 25% off

9. floor lamp: $68.94, 15% off

8. video game: $69.50, 30% off

10. diamond necklace: $135, 40% off

11. In 1990, the population of Phoenix, Arizona, was 988,983. In 2002, the population was 1,371,960. Find the percent of change in the population from 1990 to 2002. Round to the nearest tenth.

12. Find the percent discount on a $295 gym set that regularly sells for $384. Round to the nearest tenth.

13. The average life span of a beaver is 5 years. The average life span of a black bear is 260% more than a beaver. What is the average life span of a black bear? Source: World Almanac

14. In 1999, the average price of a bushel of oats in the United States was $1.12. The price in 2003 was 32% more. What was the average price of a bushel of oats in 2003? Source: U. S. Dept. of Agriculture

Maintain Your Skill

Simplify each expression. If no simpler form is possible, write "not possible." [4.4]

15. $\dfrac{3x+y}{3}$

16. $\dfrac{x+5}{y+5}$

17. $\dfrac{(2x+y)4}{4}$

18. $\dfrac{2+x-2}{x}$

19. $\dfrac{23}{x} - x$

20. $\dfrac{n-3}{3}$

Name each form and compute the basic numeral. [5.2]

21. $\dfrac{10-7}{3^2}$

22. $(4 \cdot 5)^2$

23. $7 + 3 \cdot 5$

24. $15 - 3 \cdot 4$

25. $3\left(5 - \dfrac{1}{3}\right)$

26. $5 \cdot 3^2$

Each equation in Exercises 27 – 30 can be viewed as consisting of exactly three terms. Identify the sum term (S) or the product term (P) as appropriate. Give all possible interpretations. [6.2 and 6.3]

27. $ab = c + d$

28. $\dfrac{a-b}{c} = m - n$

29. $\dfrac{m}{n} = a - b$

30. $x + y = a - b$

Extend Your Skill

31. Explain how to identify the base for a percent of change.

32. Suppose the original price of an item is $200. To make more money, the store raises the price by 10%. After a while the item goes on sale at 10% off. How does the final price compare with the original price. Explain your answer.

8.7 – A Linear Model for Percent Changes

OBJECTIVE

1. Draw a linear model to represent the percent of increase or decrease.

To draw a linear model for percent of increase or decrease, we label the amount of the change above the upper scale and the percent of change below the lower scale. In the last lesson we saw that 40 is 20% less than 50. Here is a linear model for this percent of decrease.

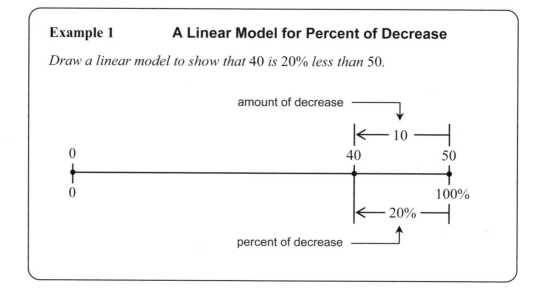

Example 1   **A Linear Model for Percent of Decrease**

Draw a linear model to show that 40 *is* 20% *less than* 50.

In Example 1, if the smaller amount of 40 is not known, then the question would be "What is 20% less than 50?" The model for this question looks like this, where x represents the unknown quantity:

We have a choice of two methods of solving for x. We can find the amount of the decrease (like we did in the last lesson) and subtract this from 50:

$(0.20)(50) = 10$ 20% is written as a decimal.

$50 - 10 = 40$ Subtract the decrease from 50.

Alternatively, we can find the percent that corresponds to x. Since x is 20% less than 100%, x must correspond to 80%. This gives the following model:

Remember:

Change percents into decimals when writing an equation or computing.

The model shows that x is 80% of 50. Now we can set up a percent equation and solve for x:

$$x = (0.80)(50)$$

$$x = 40$$

Or, we can set up a proportion as in Lesson 8.2, and solve for x:

$$\frac{x}{0.8} = \frac{50}{1} \quad \text{and} \quad x = 40.$$

Example 2   **A Linear Model for Percent of Increase**

Draw a linear model that represents the question:

        What is 70% more than 120?"

Then find the answer to the question.

Let x represent the number sought. The base is 120 and this is to be increased by 70% (of 120). Here is the model:

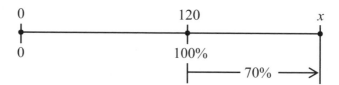

To find x, we may first find the amount of the increase: $(0.70)(120) = 84$. Then add this increase onto the base: $120 + 84 = 204$.

Or, we may find the percent rate that corresponds to x:

        $100\% + 70\% = 170\%$

Then compute 170% of the base 120: $(1.70)(120) = 204$.

Either way, we find that 204 is 70% more than 120.

Example 3   **Interpret a Linear Model for Percent of Change**

Consider the following model:

(a) *Write a verbal statement of the problem using percent.*

(b) *Solve the problem.*

(a) The base of the comparison is 75, since it corresponds to 100%. We want the percent of decrease from this base. That is,

        "45 is what percent less than 75?"

(b) Find the numerical amount of the decrease: $75 - 45 = 30$. Then write this decrease as a percent of the base:

$$\frac{30}{75} = \frac{2}{5} = 40\%$$

So 45 is 40% less than 75.

EXERCISE 8.7

DEVELOP YOUR SKILL

Exercises 1 – 6 give linear models for percent problems. Write a verbal statement of each problem. Then solve the problem.

1.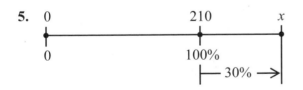

2.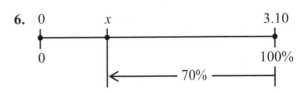

3. 0 x 120
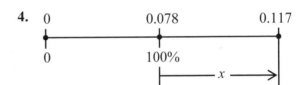

4.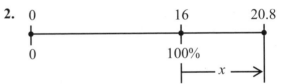

5. 0   210 x

6. 0 x 3.10

In Exercises 7 – 10, construct a linear scale to model each problem. Then solve the problem.

7. A suburban community has had a population growth of 15% since the last census. If the population then was 36,800, what is the population now?

8. The advertised price for a car at Fred's Barely Used Cars is his cost plus 30%. If his cost is $13,020, what is the advertised price?

9. If a sweater originally priced at $35 is offered for sale at $28, what is the percent of discount?

10. If a box of Sudsy costs 20% more than a box of Soapy, and the box of Soapy costs $1.40, what is the cost of a box of Sudsy?

MAINTAIN YOUR SKILL

Solve each equation by using an invariant principle. [3.6]

11. $28 \cdot 15 = 7 \cdot x$

12. $36 \cdot x = 39 \cdot 12$

13. $\dfrac{x}{35} = \dfrac{25}{7}$

14. $\dfrac{18}{30} = \dfrac{9}{x}$

Construct each expression in Exercises 15 – 18 by stating an operand and then listing a sequence of basic operators that can be joined one at a time to produce the given expression. [4.3, 5.2]

15. $4 \cdot 3^2 + 6$

16. $8 + (9 - 3)^2$

17. $5\left(\dfrac{12}{3} + 7\right)$

18. $\dfrac{(8-5)^2}{4}$

Write an equivalent expression in the form 3^n, where n is a counting number, when possible. Otherwise, write "not possible." [5.4]

19. $3^4 \cdot 3^5$

20. $3^4 - 3^2$

21. $\dfrac{3^4}{3^6}$

22. $(3^2)^3$

23. $3^4 + 3^4$

24. $\dfrac{3^5}{3^2 \cdot 3^3}$

25. $2\frac{1}{3}$ is what part of $8\frac{1}{3}$? [7.4]

26. $8\frac{1}{3}$ is how many times $2\frac{1}{3}$? [7.4]

Replace each common fraction by an equivalent decimal fraction. [7.7]

27. $\dfrac{9}{100}$

28. $\dfrac{2}{3}$

29. $\dfrac{12}{25}$

30. $\dfrac{23}{10}$

EXTEND YOUR SKILL

31. When drawing the arrow in a linear model for percent change, explain how to decide whether the arrow should point to the right or to the left.

32. Once you have drawn the arrow in a linear model for percent change, explain how to decide where the 100% goes.

8.8 – SIMPLE INTEREST

OBJECTIVE

1. Solve problems involving simple interest.

When you borrow money from a bank, you pay the bank **interest** for the use of their money. When you deposit money in a savings account, the bank pays you interest on the money you deposit. Here is the formula to use in solving problems with **simple interest**:

Annual Interest Rate (as a decimal)

$$\text{Interest} \longrightarrow I = prt \longleftarrow \text{Time (in years)}$$

Principal (amount of money borrowed or invested)

Example 1   **Find Simple Interest and Total Savings**

Katherine invests $400 *at* 3% *simple interest. Find the amount of interest she earns and the total amount she has at the end of* 5 *years.*

To find the interest, use the Simple Interest Formula.

$$I = prt$$ Write the formula.

$$I = (400)(0.03)(5)$$ Replace p with 400, r with 0.03, and t with 5.

$$I = 60$$ Compute.

The simple interest is $60. Add the interest to the initial amount to find the total amount.

$$A = p + I$$ Total amount = principal + interest

$$A = 400 + 60$$ Substitute.

$$A = 460$$ Compute.

Katherine will have a total of $460.

Study Tip:

The time t is always in years. 9 months is $\frac{9}{12}$ or $\frac{3}{4}$ of a year, so $t = \frac{3}{4}$.

Example 2   **Find Simple Interest**

Megan invests $400 *at* 6% *simple interest for* 9 *months. Find the amount of interest she earns.*

$$I = prt$$ Write the formula.

$$I = (400)(0.06)(\tfrac{3}{4})$$ Replace p with 400, r with 0.06, and t with $\frac{3}{4}$.

$$I = 18$$ Compute.

She earns $18 in interest.

Example 3   **Find the Rate of Interest**

Michael borrowed $3000 *at simple interest for* 5 *years. At the end of the* 5 *years he repaid* $4200. *Find the rate of interest.*

To find the amount of the interest, subtract the initial amount from the total amount repaid: $I = 4200 - 3000 = 1200$. Now use the formula.

$$I = prt \qquad \text{Write the formula.}$$

$$1200 = (3000)(r)(5) \qquad \text{Replace } I \text{ by 1200, } p \text{ by 3000, and } t \text{ by 5.}$$

$$1200 = 15000r \qquad \text{Simplify.}$$

$$r = \frac{1200}{15000} \qquad \text{Solve for } r.$$

$$r = 0.08 \qquad \text{Compute.}$$

The rate of interest rate was 8%.

EXERCISE 8.8

DEVELOP YOUR SKILL

Find the simple interest to the nearest cent.

1. $350 at 4% for 3 years

2. $684 at 6.3% for 2 years

3. $4,300 at 5.2% for 7 years

4. $238 at 4% for 18 months

Find the total amount to be repaid for each loan to the nearest cent.

5. $475 at $5\frac{1}{4}$% for 3 years

6. $3500 at 6.7% for 5 years

7. $1863 at 4.1% for 30 months

8. $1425 at 5.8% for 21 months

9. A savings account starts with $600. After 6 months, the amount is $613.50. Find the simple interest rate.

10. An investment of $1200 earned $438 in 5 years. Find the simple interest rate.

MAINTAIN YOUR SKILL

Replace each expression with an equivalent one in which the multipliers, dividers, and sign operators have been distributed. Do not compute. [4.7]

11. $5 + \dfrac{8-2}{4}$

12. $3 - \dfrac{5+7}{6}$

13. $15 - 2(6 - 8)$

14. $a - b(c + d)$

Use the GCF to factor each expression. [5.8]

15. $12x^2 + 21xy$

16. $25xy - 15y^2$

17. $14wx + 10x^2y$

18. $6xy^2 - 35x^2y$

19. In 2003, Honda built about 600,000 cars in the United States. Toyota built 36,000 more than two-thirds the number that Honda built the same year. How many cars did Toyota build in the United States in 2003? Define a variable, write an equation, and then solve the equation. Source: World Almanac, 2005. [6.10]

20. A 6 ounce carton of Youpay yogurt costs 39¢ and an 8 ounce carton of Fryers yogurt costs 50¢. Which is the better buy and what is its unit price? [7.8]

Solve each proportion. [8.1]

21. $\dfrac{17}{6} = \dfrac{x}{12}$

22. $\dfrac{3}{y} = \dfrac{12}{100}$

23. $\dfrac{m}{8} = \dfrac{7}{5}$

24. $\dfrac{4}{3} = \dfrac{20}{x-7}$

Estimate each percent. Do not use a calculator. [8.5]

25. 5 out of 21

26. 15 out of 44

Estimate the percent of each number. Do not use a calculator. [8.5]

27. 11% of 430

28. 48% of 27

In Exercises 29 and 30, construct a linear scale to model each problem. Then write a conditional equation with x as the variable and solve. [8.7]

29. It is estimated that a lack of rain this year will reduce the yield of the corn crop to 25% less than normal. If the present yield is figured to be 72 bushels per acre, what is the normal yield?

30. A salesman thinks his commission for the month might be as much as $2400. If so, this would be 20% more than his average the past 6 months. What was his average commission for the past 6 months?

EXTEND YOUR SKILL

31. Suppose you invested in an 8 month CD with simple interest. Explain how to determine the value of t to use in the simple interest formula.

32. Suppose you know the simple interest rate, the principal, and the time for a loan. Explain how to find the total amount repaid.

CHAPTER 8 REVIEW

1. Determine whether the ratios $\frac{5}{13}$ and $\frac{2}{5}$ form a proportion. [8.1]

Solve each proportion. [8.1]

2. $\frac{4}{5} = \frac{x}{35}$

3. $\frac{8}{x} = \frac{10}{3}$

4. $\frac{x+1}{8} = \frac{3}{4}$

Construct a linear scale to represent each problem. Then give an equation model for the problem and solve it. [8.2]

5. Andrew ate 8 pieces of candy from the candy jar. This was $\frac{2}{5}$ of the total number of pieces in the jar. How many pieces of candy were originally in the jar?

6. Jennifer walked 4 blocks in 5 minutes. At this rate, how long will it take for her to walk 10 blocks?

Write each percent as a decimal and as a fraction in lowest terms. [8.3]

7. 36%

8. 0.2%

9. 120%

Write each decimal or fraction as a percent. [8.3]

10. 0.6

11. $\frac{7}{5}$

12. $\frac{9}{20}$

13. 2.3

Exercises 14 and 15 give linear models for percent problems. Write a verbal statement of each problem. Then set up a conditional equation with x as the variable and solve. [8.4]

14.

15.

16. Draw a linear model to represent the following problem. Then construct a conditional equation with x as the variable and solve. [8.4]

"The quarterback completed 70% of his passes during the season. If he completed 56 passes, how many passes did he attempt?"

Estimate the percent of each number. [8.5]

17. 34% of 66

18. 20% of 131

Estimate each percent. [8.5]

19. 24 out of 49

20. 20 out of 59

Find the percent of change to the nearest percent. State whether the percent of change is an *increase* or a *decrease*. [8.6]

21. From 30 to 42

22. From 40 to 28

23. A lawn mower originally priced at $430 was on sale at 20% off. What was the sale price? [8.6]

Exercises 24 and 25 give linear models for percent. Write a verbal statement of each problem. Then solve the problem. [8.7]

24.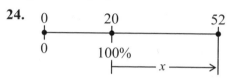

25.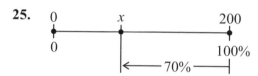

26. Construct a linear scale to model the following problem. Then solve the problem. [8.7]

> "The gross sales of the Heritage Fan Company this year were 12% more than last year. If their sales last year were $2,700,000, what were their sales this year?

Find the simple interest to the nearest cent. [8.8]

27. $500 at 7.4% for 3 years

28. $382 at 6.8% for 30 months

Find the total amount to be repaid for each loan to the nearest cent. [8.7]

29. $450 at $6\frac{3}{4}$% for 5 years

30. $1235 at $8\frac{1}{2}$% for 4 years

Chapter 9 – Signed Numbers

9.1 – ADDING SIGNED NUMBERS

The extension of the number system from the counting numbers $\mathbb{C}$ to the quotients $\mathbb{Q}^+$, as in Lesson 7.1, still leaves the difference $x - y$ without meaning when $x < y$. We will now extend the number system again to overcome this limitation. A method for doing this is suggested by the vector model that we developed in Lessons 2.2 and 2.3 for increases and decreases.

Example 1   **Vector Models for Increases and Decreases**

For each pair of operators, construct a vector model that shows the two given operators and their composite operator.

   (a) $+ 5, - 2$ (b) $+ 3, - 7$

(a)   The increase $+ 5$ and the decrease $- 2$ work against each other to give a composite change of $+ (5 - 2) = + 3$.

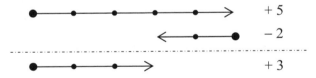

(b)   This time the increase $+ 3$ and the decrease $- 7$ give a composite change of $- 4$.

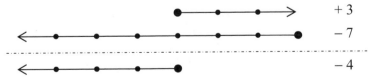

If we write the vector model from Example 1 part (a) underneath a linear scale and have the first operator, + 5, start at zero, then we find that the vector for the composite change, + 3 goes from zero to the number 3.

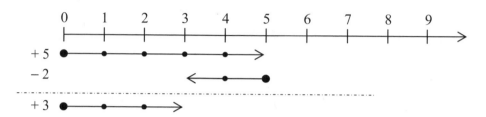

If, however, we try to follow this same pattern in part (b), we have a problem since the composite change is a decrease. We can eliminate this difficulty if we extend our scale to the left of zero and give each point a name that corresponds to the decrease operator that begins at zero and ends at the point:

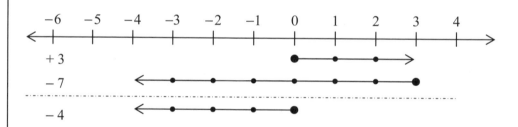

Using this extended number line, we have a system in which subtraction is always defined. The numbers to the right of zero are now called **positive numbers**. Those on the left of zero are called **negative numbers**. Zero is neither positive nor negative. Addition operators such as $+ n$ can be used as numerals for the positive numbers, but it is easier to continue using the familiar basic numeral. Hence, n and $+ n$ are considered to name the same number. From now on, $+ n$ and $- n$ will be used both as operators (addition and subtraction) and as numerals for **signed numbers**.

The extended rational number system that includes both positive and negative rational numbers and zero is denoted by $\mathbb{Q}$ (without the raised +), and we have new names for the members of $\mathbb{N}$ and $\mathbb{C}$.

- The natural numbers $\mathbb{N}$ are now called the **positive integers**.

Study Tip:

We may use "$+ n$" and "$+n$" interchangeably. Sometimes the "$+ n$" notation (with more space between the plus sign and the numeral) is used to emphasize the operator point of view and "$+n$" is used to emphasize its role as a signed number, but we may interpret them in either way that is helpful. Similar comments apply to "$- n$" and "$-n$."

- The counting numbers $\mathbb{C}$ are called the **nonnegative integers**.

- The opposites of $\mathbb{N}$ are called the **negative integers**.

- The **rational numbers** $\mathbb{Q}$ consist of the positive rationals and zero (this is $\mathbb{Q}^{+}$) and the negative rationals.

Addition with signed numbers follows the same pattern as the composition of addition and subtraction operators. We recall from Lesson 4.6 that the sign operator $+(\ )$ does not change an increase or a decrease. That is, $+(+n) = +n$ and $+(-n) = -n$. To add signed numbers,

Adding Signed Numbers

Think:	increases and decreases (using $+n$ for n)	
See:	vectors, as in Chapter 2	
Write:	numbers, guided by the rules for composition of addition and subtraction operators.	

Example 2   **Compute the Sum of Signed Numbers**

Compute the sum of -6 *and* $+4$.

   We want to think of this as the composition of a decrease of 6 and an increase of 4. Since 6 is larger than 4, the combined change is a decrease.

Think: a decrease of 6 and an increase of 4.

This is a negative number.

$$-6 + (+4) = -6 + 4 = -(6-4) = -2 = -2$$

This is a decrease of 2.

We can see this in our mind by visualizing the vectors:

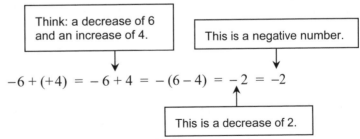

Example 3   **Compute the Sum of Signed Numbers**

Compute the sum of 6.7 *and* −3.5 .

We think of this as an increase of 6.7 and a decrease of 3.5. Since the increase is larger, the combined change is an increase.

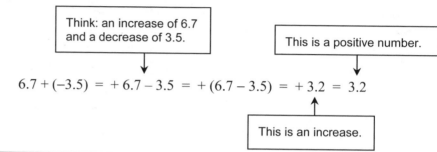

Think: an increase of 6.7 and a decrease of 3.5.

This is a positive number.

$$6.7 + (-3.5) \;=\; +\,6.7 - 3.5 \;=\; +\,(6.7 - 3.5) \;=\; +\,3.2 \;=\; 3.2$$

This is an increase.

Example 4   **Compute the Sum of Signed Numbers**

Compute the sum of $-\frac{1}{2}$ *and* $-\frac{2}{3}$.

The composition of two decreases is a larger decrease.

$$-\frac{1}{2} + \left(-\frac{2}{3}\right) = -\frac{1}{2} - \frac{2}{3} = -\left(\frac{1}{2} + \frac{2}{3}\right) \quad \longleftarrow \boxed{\text{The LCD is 6.}}$$

$$= -\left(\frac{3}{6} + \frac{4}{6}\right) = -\frac{7}{6} = -\frac{7}{6}$$

This is a decrease.   This is a negative number.

It is not so easy to draw exact vector models when the magnitudes are not integers, but even with fractions, the idea is the same. The two decreases will be represented by vectors pointing to the left, and their composition will be a longer vector pointing to the left. Without the scale markings we can visualize it like this:

$-\frac{1}{2}$

$-\frac{2}{3}$

$-\frac{7}{6}$

EXERCISE 9.1

DEVELOP YOUR SKILL

Compute the sum of each pair of numbers.

1. -4 and $+7$

2. 3 and -5

3. -2.1 and -4.8

4. $-\frac{1}{3}$ and $\frac{2}{5}$

5. $\frac{2}{3}$ and $-1\frac{1}{2}$

6. -4 and -9

MAINTAIN YOUR SKILL

Simplify each expression. [4.5]

7. $3\left(\dfrac{x}{21}\right)$

8. $\dfrac{\frac{21}{x}}{3}$

9. $\dfrac{21}{\frac{x}{3}}$

10. $\dfrac{\frac{21}{3}}{x}$

Solve each equation for x. [6.4, 6.5, 7.3]

11. $5x - 3 = 14$

12. $15 = 10 - 8x$

13. $12 - \dfrac{7}{x} = 8$

14. $7 - 8x = 4x$

15. $2x + 15 = 5x$

16. $ax + bx = c$

17. $\dfrac{3}{4}x = \dfrac{7}{8}$

18. $\dfrac{\frac{2}{3}}{x} = \dfrac{4}{5}$

19. $\dfrac{5}{4}x = 2\dfrac{1}{4}$

In Exercises 20 – 23, write each statement as an algebraic equation using x as the variable. Do not solve the equation. [6.9]

20. The product of 5 and 6 more than a number is 80.

21. The sum of 4 times a number and 7 is 51.

22. Three less than twice a number is 17.

23. Five times a number is 8 more than this number.

24. An 8 ounce jar of Golfer's instant coffee costs \$4.16 and a 12 ounce jar costs \$5.88. Which is the better buy and what is its unit price? [7.8]

25. Convert $3\frac{1}{2}$ feet to inches. [7.8]

26. Convert $2\frac{1}{2}$ yards to feet. [7.8]

Solve each proportion. [8.1]

27. $\dfrac{12}{x} = \dfrac{3}{12}$

28. $\dfrac{20}{35} = \dfrac{4}{y}$

29. $\dfrac{3}{4} = \dfrac{x-1}{12}$

30. $\dfrac{5}{2} = \dfrac{x+2}{3}$

Extend Your Skill

31. When adding signed numbers, what should we be thinking and seeing?

32. When adding a positive number and a negative number, does the sign of the sum always come from the larger of the two numbers? Explain your answer.

9.2 – Subtracting Signed Numbers

OBJECTIVES

1. Find the opposite of a number.

2. Subtract with signed numbers.

3. Find the difference comparison of two numbers.

In Lesson 4.6 we referred to the operator $-(\ )$ as the opposite operator because it changes increases into decreases and decreases into increases:

$$-(+n) = -n \quad \text{and} \quad -(-n) = +n.$$

The same principle applies when working with signed numbers. That is, the operator $-(\ )$ changes a positive number into a negative number and it changes a negative number into a positive number.

Example 1   **The Opposite of a Number**

The opposite of 5 is $-(5)$, or -5. The opposite of -5 is $-(-5)$, or $+5$. This must be written as $+5$ if -5 is an operator, but if -5 is a number, then its opposite may be written simply as 5.

Operators	Numbers
$-(+5) = -5$	$-(5) = -5$
$-(-5) = +5$	$-(-5) = 5$

The behavior of the opposite operator gives us a model to follow when defining subtraction of signed numbers. Since

$$-(+n) = -n = +(-n) \quad \text{and} \quad -(-n) = +n = +(+n)$$

we see that subtracting a signed number is the same as adding its opposite.

Definition of Subtraction

$$a - b = a + (-b).$$

Example 2   **Compute the Difference of Signed Numbers**

Compute the difference of -3.1 *and* -8.5.

We want to evaluate $(-3.1) - (-8.5)$. Think of increases and decreases. The minus sign operator changes the decrease of 8.5 into an increase:

$$(-3.1) - (-8.5) = -3.1 + 8.5$$

Since the increase is larger, the combined change is an increase. The magnitude of the change is the difference $8.5 - 3.1$:

$$+(8.5 - 3.1) = +5.4$$

This can be viewed as an increase of 5.4 or the (positive) number 5.4.

Example 3   **Compute the Difference of Signed Numbers**

Compute the difference of -5 *and* 2.

We want to evaluate $(-5) - (2)$. Again, we think of operators and see two decreases.

$$-5 - 2$$

We combine the two decreases as we did in Section 1.4.

$$-5 - 2 = -(5 + 2) = -7$$

This can be viewed as a decrease of 7 or the (negative) number -7.

When we compute an expression containing both addition and subtraction, it is often convenient to combine the increases and decreases separately, and then combine the results.

Example 4   **Combinations of Addition and Subtraction**

Compute $-2 + (-3) - (-1) + (+7) - (+6)$

First we apply the sign operators to obtain

$$-2 - 3 + 1 + 7 - 6.$$

Then we group the increases together and the decreases together and compute.

$$+(1 + 7) - (2 + 3 + 6) = +8 - 11 = -3$$

While we obtained this result thinking of it as a decrease of 3, we can now consider it the signed number -3.

In Lesson 7.4 we discussed the ratio comparison of two numbers. Now that we have extended our number system so that subtraction is always defined, we can also make a **difference comparison** between any two numbers. A first number is said to be so much more, equal to, or so much less than a second number. This difference comparison is found by taking the first number and subtracting the second number. For example, if this difference is a positive number, say $+d$, then the first number is d more than the second number. If this difference is a negative number, say $-d$, then the first number is d less than the second.

Study Tip:

Recall that the **ratio** comparison of *x* to *y* is

 x **divided by** *y*.

In a similar way, the **difference** comparison of *x* to *y* is computed as

 x **minus** *y*.

Example 5   **Find the Difference Comparison**

Write a sentence that states the difference comparison of the first number to the second.

 (a) 23, 15   (b) -4, -9 (c) $\dfrac{5}{6}$, $\dfrac{7}{8}$

(a) $23 - 15 = 8$. Since 8 is positive, we write "23 is 8 *more than* 15."

(b) $-4 - (-9) = -4 + 9 = 5$, so "-4 is 5 *more than* -9."

(c) $\dfrac{5}{6} - \dfrac{7}{8} = \dfrac{20}{24} - \dfrac{21}{24} = -\dfrac{1}{24}$. This time the difference is negative, so we write "$\dfrac{5}{6}$ is $\dfrac{1}{24}$ *less than* $\dfrac{7}{8}$."

EXERCISE 9.2

DEVELOP YOUR SKILL

Find the opposite of each number.

1. 24   **2.** -6 **3.** $\frac{1}{3}$ **4.** -0.43

Compute the basic numeral.

5. $6 - (+3) + (-11)$ **6.** $-6 + (-3) - (+11)$

7. $-6 + (+3) - (-11)$ **8.** $-6 - (-3) - (+11)$

In Exercises 9 – 12, a pair of numbers is given. Write a sentence that states the difference comparison of the first number to the second number.

9. $14, -3$ **10.** $-8, -2$

11. $-\frac{2}{3}, \frac{4}{5}$ **12.** $\frac{1}{6}, \frac{7}{8}$

MAINTAIN YOUR SKILL

Use the GCF to factor each expression. [5.8]

13. $25x - 20x^2 y$ **14.** $15x^2 - 16xy^2$

15. $21wx^2 + 14wxy$ **16.** $18x^2 y + 3x^2$

Solve each equation. [7.6]

17. $x + \frac{1}{4} = \frac{2}{3}$ **18.** $\frac{4}{5} = \frac{1}{3} - x$

19. $\frac{5}{6} + x = \frac{7}{8}$ **20.** $\frac{5}{8} = x - \frac{3}{4}$

Find the value of each expression when $x = -2$, $y = 4$, and $z = -1$. [8.5]

21. $xy - z^{-2}$ **22.** $yz - x^{-2}$ **23.** $xz - y^{-2}$

24. $xz^2 - y$ **25.** $x^2 z^{18} - y^{-1}$ **26.** $yz^{19} - x^{-1}$

Construct a linear scale to represent each problem in Exercises 27 and 28. Then give an equation model for the problem and solve. [8.2]

27. A test car used a measured $\frac{3}{5}$ of a gallon in traveling 27 miles. At this rate, how many miles per gallon can be expected?

28. A salesman has planned to spend $\frac{3}{20}$ of his income on travel expenses. How much a month must he earn in order to budget $450 a month for travel?

Find the sale price of each item to the nearest cent. [8.6]

29. riding lawn mower: $1295.84 at 10% off

30. recliner: $230 at 20% off

EXTEND YOUR SKILL

31. What does the minus operator do to a negative number?

32. Explain how the difference comparison of two numbers is similar to the ratio comparison of two numbers.

9.3 – ABSOLUTE VALUE

OBJECTIVE

1. Find the absolute value of a number.

The **absolute value** of a number is its distance from 0 on the number line. The absolute value of a number x is represented by $|x|$. Length is measured by unsigned numbers which correspond to the positive numbers. Thus $|5| = 5$ since 5 is 5 units away from 0. Likewise, $|-5| = 5$, since -5 is also 5 units away from 0.

In general, the absolute value of a positive number is equal to itself. And the absolute value of a negative number is equal to its opposite, since this is the positive number that corresponds to its distance from 0.

Definition of	The absolute value of a number x, written $|x|$, is the distance from x to 0 on the number line. Thus
Absolute Value	

$$|x| = x \text{ if } x \geq 0 \quad \text{and} \quad |x| = -x \text{ if } x < 0.$$

Example 1   **Expressions with Absolute Value**

Evaluate each expression.

    (a) $|23| + |-14|$ (b) $|5 - 12|$ (c) $|5| - |-8|$

(a) $|23| + |-14| = 23 + 14$ The absolute value of 23 is 23.
                     $= 37$ The absolute value of −14 is 14.

(b) $|5 - 12| = |-7| = 7$ The absolute value bars act like parentheses.
                                 Compute inside the absolute value sign first.

(c) $|5| - |-8| = 5 - 8$ The absolute value of 5 is 5.
               $= -3$ The absolute value of −8 is 8.

Example 2   **Algebraic Expression with Absolute Value**

Evaluate $|x| - y$ when $x = -2$ and $y = 5$.

         $|x| - y = |-2| - 5$ Replace x with −2 and y with 5.
               $= 2 - 5$ The absolute value of − 2 is 2.
               $= -3$ Compute 2 − 5.

EXERCISE 9.3

DEVELOP YOUR SKILL

Evaluate each expression.

1. $|12 - 7|$ **2.** $|7 - 12|$ **3.** $|7| - |12|$

4. $|-12| + |-7|$ **5.** $|12| - |-7|$ **6.** $|-7| - |-12|$

Evaluate each expression when $x = -5$ and $y = 6$.

7. $8 + |x|$ **8.** $8 - |x|$ **9.** $x - |y|$ **10.** $2|x + 3|$

MAINTAIN YOUR SKILL

Name each form and compute the basic numeral. [5.2]

11. $10 - 3 \cdot 4$ **12.** $5 \cdot 2^3$

13. $4\left(7 - \frac{1}{2}\right)$ **14.** $5 \cdot 6 + 2$

15. $(4 - 3^2)^2$ **16.** $\dfrac{2 \cdot 5}{2 \cdot 5^2}$

Indicate which operators are accessible for removal. [6.6]

17. $x - \dfrac{a}{b}$ **18.** $(x^2 + y)z$ **19.** $2x + 2y$

20. $\dfrac{5a}{b}$ **21.** $5(x + 3y)$ **22.** $\dfrac{a + 3b}{4x}$

In Exercises 23 – 28, one of three forms is given: common fraction, decimal fraction, or percent. In each case, the other two equivalent forms are to be written. [8.3]

23. $\dfrac{2}{5}$ **24.** 6%   **25.** 1.45

26. $\dfrac{6}{5}$ **27.** 0.3   **28.** 3.5%

29. Michelle invested $1500 at 4% simple interest for 3 years. Find the value of her investment at the end of the 3 years. [8.8]

30. An investment of $2500 earned $775 interest in 5 years. Find the simple interest rate. [8.8]

EXTEND YOUR SKILL

31. Complete the following sentence: "The absolute value of a number is the distance _____."

32. When is $|x| = -x$? Why doesn't this imply that the absolute value of some numbers is negative?

9.4 – MULTIPLYING AND DIVIDING SIGNED NUMBERS

OBJECTIVES

1. Multiply and divide signed numbers.

2. Solve equations with signed numbers.

As a guide in multiplying signed numbers, we recall the way that the double operators $+ a(\ )$ and $- a(\ )$ change the operands $+ b$ and $- b$. When we look at the vector models for the operands $+ b$ and $- b$, the multiplication operators $a(\ )$ and $- a(\ )$ change the length of the vector, and the sign operators $+(\ )$ and $-(\ )$ control the positive or negative sense of direction. The left column in the box below lists the changes made by these operators. (See Lesson 4.6.) In the right column we give the corresponding rules for products of signed numbers.

Rules

for

Multiplication

Operators and Operands	Products of Signed Numbers
$+ a(+ b) \ = \ + ab$	$(a)(b) \ = \ ab$
$+ a(- b) \ = \ - ab$	$(a)(-b) \ = \ -ab$
$- a(+ b) \ = \ - ab$	$(-a)(b) \ = \ -ab$
$- a(- b) \ = \ + ab$	$(-a)(-b) \ = \ ab$

Example 1   **Compute with Signed Numbers**

Compute the following:

   (a) $4 - 3(5) + 2(-7)$ (b) $-8 - 2(-3) + 5(- 4)$

(a) Since $-3(5) \ = \ -15$ and $+2(-7) \ = \ -14$, we have

$$4 - 3(5) + 2(-7) \ = \ 4 - 15 - 14 \ = \ 4 - 29 \ = \ -25$$

(b) Since $-2(-3) \ = \ +6$ and $+5(- 4) \ = \ - 20$, we have

$$-8 - 2(-3) + 5(4) \ = \ -8 + 6 - 20 \ = \ -2 - 20 \ = \ - 22$$

Division in $\mathbb{Q}$ is defined in terms of multiplication, just as in $\mathbb{C}$ and in $\mathbb{Q}^+$.

Rules

for

Division

$$a \div (-b) = -\frac{a}{b}, \quad \text{since} \quad (-b)\left(-\frac{a}{b}\right) = +b\left(\frac{a}{b}\right) = a. \text{ That is, } \frac{a}{-b} = -\frac{a}{b}.$$

$$(-a) \div b = -\frac{a}{b}, \quad \text{since} \quad b\left(-\frac{a}{b}\right) = -b\left(\frac{a}{b}\right) = -a. \text{ That is, } \frac{-a}{b} = -\frac{a}{b}.$$

$$(-a) \div (-b) = \frac{a}{b}, \quad \text{since} \quad (-b)\left(\frac{a}{b}\right) = -(b)\left(\frac{a}{b}\right) = -a. \text{ That is, } \frac{-a}{-b} = \frac{a}{b}.$$

The rule of signs (as used for operators) continues to hold for products and quotients: Count the number of minus signs to be considered in a product or a quotient.

If this number is odd (1, 3, 5, …) the sign should be minus.

If this number is even (2, 4, 6, …) the sign should be plus.

When writing or computing powers of signed numbers, it is important to pay careful attention to the use of parentheses. Recall that powers are computed *before* addition and subtraction (and before multiplication and division). This means that the exponent only applies to the numeral immediately to the left of it.

Study Tip:

Powers are computed before addition and subtraction. Thus -5^2 is the negative of 5^2 :

$$-5^2 = -25$$

To square the quantity –5, parentheses are needed:

$$(-5)^2 = 25$$

Example 2   **Powers of Negative Numbers**

Compute the following:

(a) -5^2 (b) $(-5)^2$ (c) $(-2)^7$

(a) The exponent only applies to the 5: $-5^2 = -(5)(5) = -25.$

(b) The parentheses make the exponent apply to –5:
$$(-5)^2 = (-5)(-5) = 25.$$

(c) The exponent is odd, so the final sign is minus.
$$(-2)^7 = -2^7 = -128.$$

The sign operator $-(\ )$ and the multiplication operator $(-1)(\ )$ are each useful in changing the form of an equation to a desired equivalent form. The operator

$-(\ )$ is its own inverse since $-(-(\ )) = +(\ )$, for no change in sign. So removing this operator makes the same change as joining it to an operand. Similarly, -1 is its own reciprocal, since $(-1)(-1) = 1$. Multiplying twice by -1 makes no change, and dividing by -1 is the same as multiplying by -1.

Example 3   **Multiplying and Dividing by -1**

The equation $-x = -5$ is equivalent to $x = 5$.

> Remove $-(\ )$ from each side or multiply each side by -1.

The equation $-x = 5$ is equivalent to $x = -5$.

> Remove $-(\ )$ from the left side and join $-(\ )$ to the right side. Or, multiply each side by -1.

Example 4   **Solve an Equation with Signed Numbers**

Solve the equation for x: $-4 - 6x = 11$

We will solve this by removing operators and joining inverse operators.

$-4 - 6x = 11$	Write the equation.
$-6x = 11 + 4$	Add 4 to both sides of the equation by removing -4 from the left side and joining $+4$ to the right side
$-6x = 15$	Compute 11 + 4.
$x = \dfrac{15}{-6}$	Divide both sides by -6 by removing $-6(\ )$ from the left side and joining $\dfrac{(\ )}{-6}$ to the right side.
$x = -\dfrac{15}{6} = -\dfrac{5}{2}$	Replace $\dfrac{15}{-6}$ by $-\dfrac{15}{6}$ and reduce.

Example 5   **Solve an Equation with Signed Numbers**

Solve the equation for x: $-4 - 6x = 11$

We will solve this by using the 3-number method of Lesson 6.4.

Study Tip:

Rewriting the equation as

$-6x - 4 = 11$

and grouping

$(-6x) - (4) = 11$

changes the roles of the terms, but it leads to the same answer. Solve for the sum $(-6x)$:

$-6x = 11 + 4$

etc.

$(-4) - (6x) = (11)$ Write the equation, grouping the terms as shown.

$6x = (-4) - 11$ The addend $(6x)$ is the sum (-4) minus the other addend (11).

$6x = -15$ Compute $-4 - 11 = -15$.

$x = \dfrac{-15}{6}$ The factor x is the product -15 divided by the other factor 6.

$x = -\dfrac{15}{6} = -\dfrac{5}{2}$ Replace $\dfrac{-15}{6}$ by $-\dfrac{15}{6}$ and reduce.

EXERCISE 9.4

DEVELOP YOUR SKILL

Compute the basic numeral.

1. $(4)(-5)$

2. $(-3)(-7)$

3. $6 - 3^2$

4. $(-3)(-2)^3$

5. $5 - (-4)^2$

6. $10 + (-2)^3$

7. $\left(-\dfrac{2}{3}\right)^2$

8. $\dfrac{-2^2}{3}$

9. $\dfrac{(-2)^2}{3}$

Solve each equation for x.

10. $5 - 4x = 21$

11. $-3x - 7 = 8$

12. $-9 - 2x = 6$

13. $3x + 4 = 5x - 10$

14. $0.2x - 4 = 1.4x + 0.8$

MAINTAIN YOUR SKILL

Simplify each expression. Compute as needed. [4.4]

15. $\dfrac{\frac{30}{x}}{6}$

16. $\dfrac{\frac{6}{x}}{30}$

17. $\dfrac{30}{\frac{x}{6}}$

18. $\dfrac{6}{\frac{30}{x}}$

Solve each equation for x. [6.4 – 6.7]

19. $rt = s - ux$

20. $r = \dfrac{t}{x - s}$

21. $\dfrac{s}{x} = t + r$

22. $x = t - rx$

Write each statement as an algebraic equation, using x as the variable. Then solve the equation. [6.9]

23. Three less than twice a number is 15.

24. The product of 6 more than a number and 3 is 2.

Write the opposite and reciprocal of each number. [7.2, 9.2]

25. 7   **26.** $-\dfrac{2}{3}$ **27.** 0.8   **28.** -1.5

29. If there are 3 teaspoons in a tablespoon, and 2 tablespoons in a fluid ounce, how many teaspoons are in 2 fluid ounces? [7.8]

30. If there are 25 sheets of paper in a quire and 500 sheets in a ream, how many quires are in a ream? [7.8]

EXTEND YOUR SKILL

31. Use operators to explain why the product of two negative numbers is a positive number.

32. What number is equal to its reciprocal? Is there more than one possible answer?

9.5 – NEGATIVE EXPONENTS

OBJECTIVE

1. Understand and use negative exponents.

If n is a counting number, then fractions and negative numbers can be used for the base a in the power a^n. But the use of rational numbers for the exponent n requires further study of the exponential operator $(\ )^n$, since to this point the exponent n has served only as a counter of multipliers.

In extending the use of n as an exponent we want to be sure that the properties of powers where n is a counting number will be retained as much as possible. If $a \neq 0$, then we know that

$$\frac{a^m}{a^n} = a^{m-n} \quad \text{when} \quad m \geq n.$$

Suppose we want this to be true for $m < n$ as well. Then, in particular, we must have

$$\frac{1}{a^n} = \frac{a^0}{a^n} = a^{0-n} = a^{-n}.$$

This suggests that if we define $a^{-n} = \dfrac{1}{a^n}$, then the rules for exponents as in Lesson 5.3 will still apply.

Definition of Negative Exponents

$$\text{If } a \neq 0, \text{ then } a^{-n} = \frac{1}{a^n}.$$

In particular, when $n = 1$ we have $a^{-1} = \dfrac{1}{a}$, so that $()^{-1}$ is the **reciprocal** operator.

Study Tip:

The answer to part (c) is negative *not* because of the −1 exponent, but because the base, −8, is negative.
  In general, the reciprocal of a positive number is positive, and the reciprocal of a negative number is negative.

> **Example 1**   **Use −1 as an Exponent**
>
> *Compute the following:*
>
>   (a) 7^{-1} (b) $\left(\dfrac{1}{3}\right)^{-1}$ (c) $(-8)^{-1}$
>
> (a) $7^{-1} = \dfrac{1}{7}$ The reciprocal of 7 is $\dfrac{1}{7}$.
>
> (b) $\left(\dfrac{1}{3}\right)^{-1} = 3$ The reciprocal of $\dfrac{1}{3}$ is 3.
>
> (c) $(-8)^{-1} = \dfrac{1}{-8} = -\dfrac{1}{8}$ The reciprocal of −8 is $-\dfrac{1}{8}$.

Recall from Lesson 5.4 that for $a \neq 0$ we have

$$\left(a^m\right)^n = a^{mn} = \left(a^n\right)^m.$$

Since $-n = (-1)(n)$, this suggests that $()^{-n}$ can be thought of as a double operator such that $()^n$ and $()^{-1}$ can be used separately and in either order. That is, when $-n$ is used as an exponent it indicates two operations: taking the reciprocal and taking the nth power. Either of these two operations may be performed first.

Example 2 **Use Negative Exponents**

Compute 4^{-2}.

$4^{-2} = \left(4^2\right)^{-1} = 16^{-1} = \frac{1}{16}$ The power operation is performed first.

$4^{-2} = \left(4^{-1}\right)^2 = \left(\frac{1}{4}\right)^2 = \frac{1}{16}$ The reciprocal operation is performed first.

Example 3 **Write a Number as a Power**

Write each number as a power of 5.

   (a) 25^3 (b) $\frac{1}{25}$ (c) $\frac{5^4}{25^2}$

(a) $25^3 = (5^2)^3 = 5^6$ (b) $\frac{1}{25} = 25^{-1} = (5^2)^{-1} = 5^{-2}$

(c) $\frac{5^4}{25^2} = \frac{5^4}{(5^2)^2} = \frac{5^4}{5^4} = 5^{(4-4)} = 5^0$

In Example 4 we show the pattern of using positive and negative exponents.

Example 4 **Pattern of Positive and Negative Exponents**

$$5^0 = 1$$

$5^1 = 1 \cdot 5$ $5^{-1} = \frac{1}{5}$

$5^2 = 1 \cdot 5 \cdot 5$ $5^{-2} = \frac{1}{5 \cdot 5}$

$5^3 = 1 \cdot 5 \cdot 5 \cdot 5$ $5^{-3} = \frac{1}{5 \cdot 5 \cdot 5}$

This is a helpful summary.

We see from Example 4 that all integer exponents (positive, zero, and negative) can be interpreted as counters. When the exponent is a positive integer, it counts the number of times that 1 is multiplied by the base. When the exponent is a negative integer, it counts the number of times that 1 is divided by the base. When the exponent is zero, then the 1 is left unchanged.

Example 5 **Change into Positive Exponents**

Simplify $\dfrac{x^{-2}y^3}{xy^{-2}}$ *using only positive exponents.*

We combine the x's and the y's separately.

$$\frac{x^{-2}}{x} = \frac{1}{x^2 \cdot x} = \frac{1}{x^3} \quad \text{since} \quad x^{-2} = \frac{1}{x^2}.$$

$$\frac{y^3}{y^{-2}} = y^3 \cdot y^2 = y^5 \quad \text{since} \quad \frac{1}{y^{-2}} = \left(\frac{1}{y^2}\right)^{-1} = y^2.$$

So, $\dfrac{x^{-2}y^3}{xy^{-2}} = \dfrac{y^5}{x^3}$.

Exercise 9.5

Develop Your Skill

Compute the basic numeral.

1. 4^{-1} **2.** $\left(\frac{3}{5}\right)^{-1}$ **3.** 3^{-2} **4.** $\left(\frac{1}{4}\right)^{-2}$

5. $(3^2)^{-1}$ **6.** $(2^{-1})^3$ **7.** $\left(-\frac{1}{3}\right)^{-1}$ **8.** $\left(2\frac{1}{2}\right)^{-1}$

Write each number as a power of 2.

9. 4^2 **10.** 8^{-1} **11.** $\left(\frac{1}{2}\right)^5$ **12.** $\frac{1}{2} \cdot \frac{1}{8}$

Write equivalent forms, using only positive exponents.

13. x^{-3} **14.** $\dfrac{1}{x^{-3}}$ **15.** $\dfrac{1}{3x^{-2}}$ **16.** $\dfrac{x^5}{x^{-2}}$

Simplify, using only positive exponents.

17. xy^{-2}

18. $\dfrac{x^2}{y^{-3}}$

19. $\dfrac{x^{-3}y}{y^{-1}}$

20. $(xy)^{-2}$

21. $\dfrac{x^2 y^{-3}}{xy}$

22. $\dfrac{x^{-3}y}{x^{-2}y^{-4}}$

MAINTAIN YOUR SKILL

Find the value of each expression when $x = -3$, $y = 4$ and $z = -1$. [5.2, 8.4]

23. $xy - z^2$

24. $x^2 y + z$

25. $x^2(y + z)$

26. $y(x - z)$

Each equation in Exercises 27 – 30 can be viewed as consisting of exactly three terms. Identify the sum term (S) or the product term (P) as appropriate. Give all possible interpretations. [6.2, 6.3]

27. $x^2 + y = wz + r$

28. $m\left(\dfrac{n}{p}\right) - r = \dfrac{e}{fg} + h$

29. $w + x^2 y = \dfrac{m}{n}$

30. $(x+2)(y-3) = \dfrac{z}{w-3}$

EXTEND YOUR SKILL

31. What does a positive integer exponent count?

32. What does a negative integer exponent count?

33. What does a zero exponent indicate?

34. Give an example to show that the reciprocal operator does not distribute over sums.

9.6 – SCIENTIFIC NOTATION

One important use of positive and negative exponents is in constructing the special decimal numeral form known as **scientific notation**. This notation provides a compact way of writing very large and very small decimal numbers. To write a number in scientific notation, we place a decimal point after the first nonzero digit (reading from the left) and then multiply by the power of 10 necessary to make the numbers equal. By doing this we obtain a number in the form

$$N \times 10^k \quad \text{where} \quad 1 \le N < 10 \quad \text{and} \quad k \text{ is an integer.}$$

Multiplying by 10^k, where k is positive, moves the decimal point to the right k places. Multiplying by 10^k, where k is negative, moves the decimal point to the left k places.

Example 1　　　　**Express Numbers in Standard Form**

Write each number in standard form.

　　(a) 5.71×10^4　　　　(b) 4.6×10^{-3}

(a) $5.71 \times 10^4 = 5.71 \times 10{,}000$

　　　　　　　$= 57{,}100$　　　　The decimal point moves 4 places to the right.

(b) $4.6 \times 10^{-3} = 4.6 \times \dfrac{1}{10^3} = 4.6 \times 0.001$

　　　　　　　$= 0.0046$　　　　The decimal point moves 3 places to the left.

Example 2　　　　**Express Numbers in Scientific Notation**

Write each number in scientific notation.

　　(a) 6,250,000　　　　(b) 0.00053

(a)   The number will start with 6.25. To make it as large as 6,250,000, the decimal point must move to the right 6 places. We have

$$6.25 \times 10^6$$

(b)   The number will start with 5.3. To make it as small as 0.00053, the decimal point must move to the left 4 places. We have

$$5.3 \times 10^{-4}$$

   If a number is almost in scientific notation, but the decimal point is in the wrong place, we can adjust the position of the decimal point and compensate by changing the power of 10. To do this we apply the invariant principle for products.

Example 3   Express Numbers in Scientific Notation

Write each number in scientific notation.

   (a) 583×10^6 (b) 0.035×10^7

(a) In order to write this in scientific notation, the 583 must be divided by 100. Using the invariant principle for products, the 10^6 must be multiplied by 100 or 10^2 to keep the product the same. Thus,

$$583 \times 10^6 = 5.83 \times 10^8$$

(b) This time we want to multiply 0.035 by 100, so 10^7 must be divided by 100. That is, we multiply 10^7 by 10^{-2}. Thus

$$0.035 \times 10^7 = 3.5 \times 10^5$$

   Writing numbers in scientific notation can be helpful in computations involving products, quotients, and powers.

Example 4   Use Scientific Notation in Problem Solving

The moon is about 240,000 miles from the earth. How many paper clips hooked end to end would it take to reach from the earth to the moon? Write the answer in scientific notation. There are 5,280 feet in a mile, and assume it takes about 11 paper clips per foot.

Using dimensional analysis we want

$$\text{miles}\left(\frac{\text{feet}}{\text{mile}}\right)\left(\frac{\text{clips}}{\text{foot}}\right) = \text{clips},$$

so we calculate $240,000 \times 5,280 \times 11$. Write all the numbers in scientific notation:

$$(2.4 \times 10^5) \times (5.28 \times 10^3) \times (1.1 \times 10^1).$$

Then combine the decimal parts and the powers of 10:

$$2.4 \times 5.28 \times 1.1 \approx 13.9 \quad \text{and} \quad 10^5 \times 10^3 \times 10^1 = 10^9$$

It takes about 13.9×10^9 clips to reach the moon. In scientific notation this is 1.39×10^{10}.

EXERCISE 9.6

DEVELOP YOUR SKILL

Write each number in decimal numeral form.

1. 5.6×10^{-4} 2. 6.04×10^{-1}

3. 2.9×10^5 4. 1.07×10^3

Write each number in scientific notation.

5. 35,000   6. 0.00000869   7. 2,600,000

8. 53.4×10^3 9. 0.91×10^{-2} 10. 618.3×10^{-6}

11. At the beginning of 2005, the national debt in the United States was about \$7,500,000,000,000 and the population was about 300,000,000. What was the average debt per person at that time?

12. Light travels 300,000,000 meters per second. If the distance from the sun to the earth is 1.5×10^{11} meters, about how many minutes does it take for light to travel from the sun to the earth?

Maintain Your Skill

In Exercises 13 and 14, state the key phrase and the operator equation that correspond to the situation described. [4.7]

<u>Key Phrase</u>	<u>Operator Equation</u>
"If you receive more, you will have more."	$+(+a) = +a$
"If you receive less, you will have less."	$+(-a) = -a$
"If you give more away, you will have less left."	$-(+a) = -a$
"If you give less away, you will have more left."	$-(-a) = +a$

13. George was running for the U. S. Senate from Illinois. He was hoping for a big turnout in Chicago where he was popular to offset his opponent's advantage in downstate Illinois. On election day, it rained in Chicago and the turnout was lower than expected. How did the rain in Chicago affect his total vote?

14. Harold was promoting the sales of Krispy Krackers by giving away free samples at the local supermarket. He would usually give away a whole box of crackers by noon on Saturday. But one Saturday it snowed hard and very few people came to the supermarket. How did the snow affect the number of crackers he had left at noon?

Determine which fraction is larger. [7.6]

15. $\frac{3}{7}$ or $\frac{4}{9}$

16. $\frac{2}{3}$ or $\frac{5}{8}$

Write a sentence that states the difference comparison of the first number to the second. [9.2]

17. $-5, 8$

18. $\frac{2}{3}, -\frac{1}{9}$

19. The average temperature T_a of the temperatures T_1, T_2, and T_3 is given by $T_a = \frac{T_1+T_2+T_3}{3}$. What is T_3, if $T_a = -3$, $T_1 = -7$, and $T_2 = 2$? [9.4]

20. The Fahrenheit temperature F is related to the Celsius temperature C by the formula $F = \frac{9C}{5} + 32$. What is C if $F = 23$? [9.4]

Compute the basic numeral. [9.1 – 9.5]

21. $(-3)(-4)$

22. $4 - |-7|$

23. $15 + (-4)^2$

24. $8 - 2^{-1}$

25. $|18| - |12|$

26. $\frac{-3^2}{6}$

27. $-3 - (-2)^{-2}$

28. $-3 - |-4|$

29. $(-5)(-3)^2$

30. $-10 + |13|$

EXTEND YOUR SKILL

31. Explain how to write 5,600 in scientific notation.

32. Explain how to write 235×10^7 in scientific notation.

9.7 – ARITHMETIC AND GEOMETRIC SEQUENCES

OBJECTIVE

1. Identify and extend arithmetic and geometric sequences.

For a long distance call, NeverTell Phone company charges 5¢ for the first minute and 4¢ for each additional minute. These charges are shown in the table below.

Schedule of Charges for NeverTell Phone Co.								
Length of call in minutes	1	2	3	4	5	6	7	8
Charge in cents	5	9	13	17	21	25	29	33

Study Tip:

The common difference can either be positive or negative.

An ordered list of numbers is called a **sequence**. Each number in the sequence is called a **term**. In an **arithmetic sequence**, the difference between one term and the preceding term is always the same. This difference is called the **common difference**. The common difference can be added to each term to get the next term. The list of phone charges from NeverTell is an example of an arithmetic sequence.

$$5, \quad 9, \quad 13, \quad 17, \quad 21, \quad \ldots$$

$$+4 \quad +4 \quad +4 \quad +4$$

Example 1 **Identify an Arithmetic Sequence**

Determine if each sequence is arithmetic. If it is, give the common difference and write the next three terms.

(a) 5, 8, 11, 14, 17, ...   (b) 1, 2, 4, 5, 7, 8, 10, ...

(a) Look at the difference between each term and the term before it:

$$5, \quad 8, \quad 11, \quad 14, \quad 17, \quad ... \qquad 8 - 5 = 3, \quad 11 - 8 = 3, \text{ etc.}$$
$$+3 \quad +3 \quad +3 \quad +3$$

This is an arithmetic sequence, and the common difference is 3. The next three terms are 20, 23, and 26.

(b) We have

$$1, \quad 2, \quad 4, \quad 5, \quad 7, \quad 8, \quad 10, \quad ... \qquad 2 - 1 = 1, \quad 4 - 2 = 2, \text{ etc.}$$
$$+1 \quad +2 \quad +1 \quad +2 \quad +1 \quad +2$$

There is a pattern to the differences, but they are not all the same. This is not an arithmetic sequence.

The counting number that identifies the position of a term in a sequence is called the **index** of the term. Sometimes we use a letter with subscripts to denote the index names for the terms. For the NeverTell sequence of charges, we can display the terms as follows, where we have shown the common difference added each time:

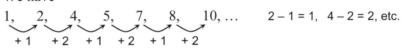

a_1	a_2	a_3	a_4	a_5	...
5	9	13	17	21	...
5	$5 + 4$	$(5 + 4) + 4$	$(5 + 4 + 4) + 4$	$(5 + 4 + 4 + 4) + 4$	...
5	$5 + (1 \cdot 4)$	$5 + (2 \cdot 4)$	$5 + (3 \cdot 4)$	$5 + (4 \cdot 4)$	...

Note that the number of additions of the common difference 4 is one less than the index number of the term. We can summarize this by the formula

$$a_n = 5 + (n - 1)4.$$

A similar analysis can be done for any arithmetic sequence.

nth Term of an Arithmetic Sequence

The nth term a_n of an arithmetic sequence with the first term a_1 and a common difference of d is given by

$$a_n = a_1 + (n - 1)d.$$

Example 2   Find a Given Term of an Arithmetic Sequence

Find the charge for a 60-minute call with NeverTell.

$$a_n = a_1 + (n - 1)d \qquad \text{Write the formula.}$$

$$a_{60} = 5 + (60 - 1)(4) \qquad \text{Substitute } a_1 = 5, n = 60, \text{ and } d = 4.$$

$$a_{60} = 5 + (59)(4) = 241 \qquad \text{Compute.}$$

The charge is 241¢ or $2.41.

If the terms in a sequence have a common quotient instead of a common difference, the sequence is called a **geometric sequence**. The quotient between a term and the preceding term is called the **common ratio**. Each term can be multiplied by the common ratio to get the next term.

Example 3   Identify a Geometric Sequence

Determine if the sequence is geometric. If it is, give the common ratio and write the next three terms.

$$3,\ -6,\ 12,\ -24,\ 48,\ \dots$$

Look at the ratio between each term the term before it.

$$3,\quad -6,\quad 12,\quad -24,\quad 48,\ \dots \qquad \frac{-6}{3} = -2,\ \frac{12}{-6} = -2, \text{ etc.}$$

$$\times(-2)\quad \times(-2)\quad \times(-2)\quad \times(-2)$$

This is a geometric sequence, and the common ratio is -2. The next three terms are -96, 192, and -384.

Study Tip:

The ratio of -6 to 3 is -2. This means we can multiply 3 by -2 to get -6.

Example 4   **Identify a Geometric Sequence**

Determine if the sequence is geometric. If it is, give the common ratio and write the next three terms.

$$54, \ 18, \ 6, \ 2, \ \frac{2}{3}, \ ...$$

We have

$$54, \quad 18, \quad 6, \quad 2, \quad \frac{2}{3}, \quad ... \qquad \frac{18}{54} = \frac{1}{3}, \ \frac{6}{18} = \frac{1}{3}, \ \text{etc.}$$
$$\times \tfrac{1}{3} \quad \times \tfrac{1}{3} \quad \times \tfrac{1}{3} \quad \times \tfrac{1}{3}$$

This is a geometric sequence, and the common ratio is $\frac{1}{3}$. The next three terms are $\frac{2}{9}$, $\frac{2}{27}$, and $\frac{2}{81}$.

To obtain any term in a geometric sequence after the first one, we multiply the preceding term by the common ratio r:

$$a_1$$
$$a_2 = a_1 r$$
$$a_3 = a_2 r = (a_1 r)r = a_1 r^2$$
$$a_4 = a_3 r = (a_1 r^2)r = a_1 r^3$$
$$a_5 = a_4 r = (a_1 r^3)r = a_1 r^4$$
$$\vdots$$

In general, we have the following formula:

nth Term of a Geometric Sequence

The nth term a_n of a geometric sequence with the first term a_1 and a common ratio of r is given by

$$a_n = a_1 r^{n-1}.$$

Example 5   **Find a Given Term of a Geometric Sequence**

Find the 8th term in the geometric sequence 5, 15, 45, 135, ...

$$r = \frac{15}{5} = 3$$ Divide 15 by 5 to get the common ratio.

$$a_8 = 5(3)^7$$ Substitute $a_1 = 5$, $n = 8$, and $r = 3$ in the formula.

$$a_8 = 10{,}935$$ Compute.

EXERCISE 9.7

DEVELOP YOUR SKILL

Determine whether each sequence is arithmetic, geometric, or neither. If it is arithmetic or geometric, state the common difference or common ratio and write the next three terms.

1. 14, 17, 20, 23, 26, ...

2. $\frac{3}{4}$, 3, 12, 48, 192, ...

3. 3, 7, 13, 17, 23, ...

4. 2, −2, 2, −2, 2, ...

5. 20, 11, 2, −7, −16, ...

6. $\frac{2}{3}$, $\frac{7}{3}$, 4, $\frac{17}{3}$, $\frac{22}{3}$, ...

7. 8, 2, 1, $\frac{1}{2}$, $\frac{1}{8}$, ...

8. 567, 189, 63, 21, 7, ...

Find the given term in each arithmetic or geometric sequence.

9. 12th term: 3, 5, 7, 9, ...

10. 32nd term: 20, 17, 14, 11, ...

11. 7th term: 2, −6, 18, −54, ...

12. 45th term: 5, −5, 5, −5, ...

MAINTAIN YOUR SKILL

Replace each expression with an equivalent one in which the multipliers, dividers, and sign operators have been distributed. Do not compute. [4.7]

13. $30 - 5(2 + 7)$

14. $26 + 3(4 - 7)$

15. $15 + \frac{8 - 5}{21}$

16. $37 - \frac{7 + 2}{12}$

Compute the basic numeral. [9.1 – 9.5]

17. 3^{-1}

18. $\left(\frac{2}{3}\right)^{-1}$

19. $\left(\frac{1}{5}\right)^{-1}$

20. $\left(\frac{2}{7}\right)^{0}$

21. $(4^{-1})^2$ **22.** $\left(3\frac{1}{2}\right)^{-1}$ **23.** $6 + (-3)^2$

24. $7 - 4^2$ **25.** $18 - |-3|$ **26.** $5 + 3^{-2}$

Write each number in scientific notation. [9.6]

27. 270,000   **28.** 0.00035

29. 210×10^6 **30.** 0.052×10^7

EXTEND YOUR SKILL

31. Can the terms in an arithmetic sequence decrease as we go farther in the sequence? Explain.

32. Can the terms in a geometric sequence decrease as we go farther in the sequence? Explain.

CHAPTER 9 REVIEW

Write a sentence that states the difference comparison of the first number to the second. [9.2]

1. −5, −8   **2.** 14, −3

Compute the basic numeral. [9.1, 9.2]

3. $9 + (-4) - (-3)$ **4.** $-2 - (+8) + (+3)$

5. $-3 + (-4) - (+5)$ **6.** $5 - (-7) + (-3)$

Compute the basic numeral. [9.3]

7. $|8 - 5|$ **8.** $|8 - (-5)|$

9. $|4 - 9| - |9 - 4|$ **10.** $|3| - |-7|$

Compute the basic numeral. [9.4]

11. $(-4)^2$ **12.** $3 - 5^2$ **13.** $(-4)(3^2 - 2^2)$

14. $\left(-\frac{3}{4}\right)^2$ **15.** $\frac{-3^2}{4}$ **16.** $2(-3)^3$

Solve each equation for x. [9.4]

17. $-5x - 3 = 17$ **18.** $4 - 3x = 15$ **19.** $5x - 3 = 7x - 8$

Compute the basic numeral. [9.5]

20. 5^{-1} **21.** 6^{-2} **22.** $\left(1\frac{1}{2}\right)^{-1}$

Simplify, using only positive exponents. [9.5]

23. xy^{-5} **24.** $\dfrac{x^{-1}y^2}{xy}$ **25.** $\dfrac{x^{-2}y^3}{(xy)^3}$

Write each number in scientific notation. [9.6]

26. 29,300   **27.** 0.0047   **28.** 250×10^6

29. Determine whether the sequence 2, 9, 16, 23, 30, … is arithmetic or geometric. State the common difference or ratio and write the next 3 terms. [9.7]

30. Find the 8th term of the geometric sequence $\frac{1}{9}$, $-\frac{1}{3}$, 1, -3, …. [9.7]

Chapter 10 – Real Numbers

10.1 – SQUARE ROOTS

OBJECTIVES

1. Find square roots.

2. Estimate square roots.

The number 9 is called a perfect square because 9 square tiles can be arranged in a pattern that makes a larger square. In this case, there are 3 tiles on each side.

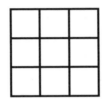

$$3^2 = 9$$

Other perfect squares can be found by squaring any counting number.

$$0^2 = 0, \ 1^2 = 1, \ 2^2 = 4, \ 3^2 = 9, \ 4^2 = 16, \ 5^2 = 25, \ 6^2 = 36, \ 7^2 = 49, \ldots$$

So 0, 1, 4, 9, 16, 25, 36, 49, … are all perfect squares.

Because $3^2 = 9$, we say that 9 is the square of 3, or that 3 is a **square root** of 9. Since $(-3)^2 = (-3)(-3) = 9$, we see that 9 is also the square of –3. Thus –3 is also a square root of 9. In fact, every positive number has a positive square root and a negative square root. The positive square root is called the **principal square root**. The symbol $\sqrt{\ }$ is used for the principle square root operator. If we want to indicate the negative square root of a number c, we write $-\sqrt{c}$.

Study Tip:

The symbol $\sqrt{\ }$ is called a radical sign.

Definition of

Square Root

If $x^2 = c$, then x is called a **square root** of c.

If $x^2 = c$ and $x \geq 0$, then x is called the **principle square root** of c and we write $x = \sqrt{c}$.

Example 1   **Find Square Roots**

Find each square root.

  (a) $\sqrt{49}$ (b) $-\sqrt{25}$

(a) Since $7^2 = 49$, $\sqrt{49} = 7$.

(b) $-\sqrt{25}$ indicates the *negative* square root of 25. We have $\sqrt{25} = 5$, so

$$-\sqrt{25} = -5.$$

While every counting number has a square root, not every square root is a counting number. Since $\sqrt{9} = 3$ and $\sqrt{16} = 4$, we see that $\sqrt{11}$ must be between 3 and 4.

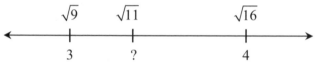

Since 11 is closer to 9 than 16, the best integer estimate for $\sqrt{11}$ is 3. Using a calculator we can find a better estimate for $\sqrt{11}$:

$$\sqrt{11} \approx 3.31662479$$

This value is still only an approximation for $\sqrt{11}$ because the decimal portion never ends.

Example 2   **Estimate Square Roots**

Estimate each square root to the nearest integer.

  (a) $\sqrt{27}$ (b) $-\sqrt{50}$

(a) We begin with the two perfect squares that are closest to 27:

$25 \; < \; 27 \; < \; 36$	27 is between 25 and 36.
$\sqrt{25} \; < \; \sqrt{27} \; < \; \sqrt{36}$	$\sqrt{27}$ is between $\sqrt{25}$ and $\sqrt{36}$.
$5 \; < \; \sqrt{27} \; < \; 6$	$\sqrt{25} = 5$ and $\sqrt{36} = 6$.

Since 27 is closer to 25 than 36, the best integer estimate for $\sqrt{27}$ is 5.

(b) Since $49 < 50 < 64$, we have $7 < \sqrt{50} < 8$. The best integer estimate for $\sqrt{50}$ is 7, since 50 is closer to 49 than 64. This means that the best integer estimate for $-\sqrt{50}$ is –7.

The square root symbol $\sqrt{}$ has the effect of grouping everything inside the radical symbol like parentheses. In computing an expression such as $\sqrt{9+16}$, the addition must be done first.

Example 3   **Compute Using Square Roots**

Simplify the expression $8-\sqrt{9+16}$.

$$8-\sqrt{9+16} = 8-\sqrt{25} \qquad \text{Add 9 + 16.}$$
$$= 8-5 \qquad \text{Evaluate the square root.}$$
$$= 3 \qquad \text{Subtract.}$$

Example 4   **Compute Using Square Roots**

Simplify the expression $3\sqrt{25}+4$.

$$3\sqrt{25}+4 = 3(5)+4 \qquad \text{Evaluate the square root.}$$
$$= 15+4 \qquad \text{Multiply.}$$
$$= 19 \qquad \text{Add.}$$

EXERCISE 10.1

DEVELOP YOUR SKILL

Find each square root.

1. $\sqrt{16}$ 　　　　　　**2.** $\sqrt{36}$ 　　　　　　**3.** $-\sqrt{49}$

4. $-\sqrt{4}$ 　　　　　　**5.** $-\sqrt{81}$ 　　　　　　**6.** $\sqrt{121}$

Estimate each square root to the nearest integer. Do not use a calculator.

7. $\sqrt{34}$ 　　　　**8.** $\sqrt{65}$ 　　　　**9.** $-\sqrt{85}$ 　　　　**10.** $-\sqrt{20}$

Simplify each expression.

11. $3+\sqrt{49}\times 2$ 　　　　　　　　**12.** $\sqrt{144}\div 3\times 2$

13. $7+\sqrt{40-4}$ 　　　　　　　　**14.** $5\sqrt{64}-9$

MAINTAIN YOUR SKILL

15. Show that $16 > 9$ by writing the equation required by its definition. [1.2]

Construct each expression in Exercises 16 – 20 by stating an operand and then listing a sequence of basic operators that can be joined one at a time to produce the given expression. [4.3, 5.2]

16. $[3(15-4)]^2$ **17.** $2 \cdot 5^3 + 8$ **18.** $\dfrac{(6-2)^2}{3}$

19. $4(10-3)^2$ **20.** $\dfrac{13-5}{2} + 7$

21. $5\frac{1}{2}$ is how many times $3\frac{1}{2}$? [7.4]   **22.** $5\frac{1}{3}$ is what part of $7\frac{1}{3}$? [7.4]

23. Sally wants to buy a box of Saddios toasted oat cereal. The 20 oz. box costs $2.97, but the 15 oz. box is on sale for $2.25. Which size is the better buy? [7.8]

24. If a lion can run 40 ft/sec, how long will it take for it to run 140 feet? [7.8]

Write the reciprocal and the opposite of each number. [7.2, 9.2]

25. 5   **26.** $\frac{1}{3}$ **27.** -7

Write each percent as a fraction in lowest terms. [8.3]

28. 60%   **29.** 45%   **30.** 22%

MAINTAIN YOUR SKILL

31. How many square roots does a positive number have?

32. How many square roots does a negative number have?

10.2 – THE REAL NUMBER SYSTEM

OBJECTIVES

1. Identify and classify real numbers.

2. Compare real numbers.

One helpful way to visualize rational numbers and their relative sizes is to picture them as points on a number line. For example,

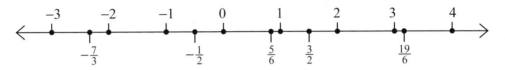

The ancient Greeks discovered that $\sqrt{2}$ is irrational about 500 B.C.

While it is true that each rational number can be represented by a point on the line, there are other points on the line which do not correspond to rational numbers. For example, there is no rational number x such that $x^2 = 2$. That is, $\sqrt{2}$ is not rational. Since

$$\left(1\tfrac{1}{3}\right)^2 = \left(\tfrac{4}{3}\right)^2 = \tfrac{16}{9} = 1\tfrac{7}{9} \quad \text{and} \quad \left(1\tfrac{1}{2}\right)^2 = \left(\tfrac{3}{2}\right)^2 = \tfrac{9}{4} = 2\tfrac{1}{4},$$

we must have $1\tfrac{1}{3} < \sqrt{2} < 1\tfrac{1}{2}$. But there is no fraction that is exactly equal to $\sqrt{2}$. In general, if a counting number is not a perfect square, then its square root is not rational.

The numbers that correspond to *all* points on the line are called **real numbers** and are denoted by $\mathbb{R}$. The real numbers that are not rational are called **irrational** (not rational). When expressed as a decimal, the rational numbers either terminate or repeat and the irrational numbers do not terminate or repeat.

Remember:
   The counting numbers include 0 and the natural numbers start with 1, 2, 3, 4, ...

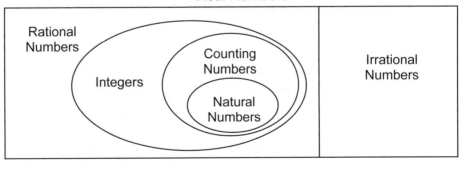

Example 1   **Classify Real Numbers**

Write all names (integer, rational, irrational) that apply to each real number.

$$8, \quad \frac{2}{3}, \quad -5, \quad \sqrt{7}, \quad 2.010010001..., \quad 14.\overline{6}, \quad 0, \quad \sqrt{16}, \quad 3.515151...$$

8 is an integer and a rational. $\frac{2}{3}$ is rational. -5 is an integer and a rational. $\sqrt{7}$ is irrational. $2.010010001...$ is irrational since the decimal does not repeat or terminate. $14.\overline{6}$ is rational since the decimal repeats. 0 is an integer and a rational. $\sqrt{16} = 4$ is an integer and a rational. $3.515151...$ is rational since the decimal repeats.

When we originally defined the relation "greater than" we were working only with the natural numbers. For example, we said that $5 > 2$ since there is a natural number 3 such that $5 = 2 + 3$. To extend this definition to the real numbers, we replace "natural number" by "positive number." Thus we say that $x > y$ if there is a positive number z such that $x = y + z$. But $x = y + z$ means that $z = x - y$. Thus, to require that z be positive is the same as requiring $x - y$ be positive. That is, $x - y > 0$. Here then is the new definition:

Definition of

Greater Than

If x and y are real numbers, then $x > y$ if there is a positive number z such that $x = y + z$. Equivalently, $x > y$ if $x - y > 0$.

Example 2   **Compare Real Numbers**

Replace ? *with <, >, or = to make a true sentence.*

(a) 3 ? -7 (b) -5.1 ? -7.3

(a) $3 > -7$ because $3 - (-7) = 3 + 7 = 10 > 0$. Furthermore, 10 is the positive number such that $3 = -7 + 10$. In general, any positive number is greater than any negative number.

(b) $-5.1 > -7.3$ because $-5.1 - (-7.3) = -5.1 + 7.3 = 2.2 > 0$

Example 3   **Compare Real Numbers**

Replace ? *with <, >, or = to make a true sentence.*

(a) 3.5 ? $\sqrt{12}$ (b) $-\sqrt{20}$? 4 (c) -5 ? $-\sqrt{25}$

(a) Since $(3.5)^2 = 12.25 > 12$, we see that $3.5 > \sqrt{12}$.

(b) If we square both numbers like we did in part (a), we have

$$\left(-\sqrt{20}\right)^2 = 20 \quad \text{and} \quad 4^2 = 16.$$

This might lead us to think that 4 is smaller than $-\sqrt{20}$. But $-\sqrt{20}$ is negative and 4 is positive, so $-\sqrt{20} < 4$.

(c) $\sqrt{25} = 5$, so $-\sqrt{25} = -5$, and the numbers are equal.

As an alternate approach to Example 3(a), we could use a calculator to find the approximate decimal value of the square root. We find

$$\sqrt{12} \approx 3.4641 < 3.5$$

Example 4   **Compare Real Numbers**

Match each number with its position on the number line.

$$-\sqrt{3}, \quad \sqrt{2}, \quad \sqrt{12}, \quad -\sqrt{10}, \quad \sqrt{0.25}$$

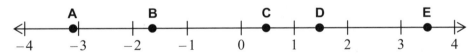

$1 < \sqrt{3} < 2$, so $-\sqrt{3}$ is between -2 and -1. $-\sqrt{3}$ is point **B**.

$1 < \sqrt{2} < 2$, so $\sqrt{2}$ is point **D**.

$3^2 = 9$ and $4^2 = 16$, so $\sqrt{12}$ is between 3 and 4. $\sqrt{12}$ is point **E**.

$3^2 = 9$, so $\sqrt{10}$ is a little to the right of 3. This means $-\sqrt{10}$ is a little to the left of -3, and $-\sqrt{10}$ is point **A**.

$\sqrt{0.25} = 0.5$, so $\sqrt{0.25}$ is point **C**.

EXERCISE 10.2

DEVELOP YOUR SKILL

Write all names (integer, rational, irrational) that apply to each real number.

1. $\dfrac{4}{5}$ **2.** $\sqrt{8}$ **3.** $-\sqrt{9}$ **4.** $5.\overline{2}$

5. $-\sqrt{11}$ **6.** 15 **7.** -5.78 **8.** $2.468101214\ldots$

Replace ? with $<$, $>$, or $=$ to make a true sentence. You may use a calculator.

9. $\sqrt{11}$? $3\dfrac{1}{3}$ **10.** $\sqrt{15}$? 3.8 **11.** $\sqrt{6.25}$? $2\dfrac{1}{2}$ **12.** $-\sqrt{3}$? 5

Write the letter that corresponds to the position of each square root on the number line below. Do not use a calculator.

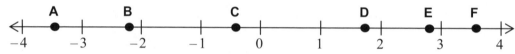

13. $-\sqrt{5}$ **14.** $\sqrt{8}$ **15.** $-\sqrt{0.16}$

16. $-\sqrt{12}$ **17.** $\sqrt{13}$ **18.** $\sqrt{3}$

MAINTAIN YOUR SKILL

Simplify each expression. [4.5]

19. $\dfrac{\frac{5}{x}}{15}$ **20.** $\dfrac{\frac{x}{15}}{5}$ **21.** $\dfrac{\frac{15}{x}}{5}$ **22.** $\dfrac{15}{\frac{x}{5}}$

Name each form and compute the basic numeral. [5.2, 9.1]

23. $12-5\cdot 6$ **24.** $\left(\dfrac{3+5}{16}\right)^2$ **25.** $\dfrac{7-9}{2^3}$ **26.** $4+\sqrt{9}$

Translate each statement into a mathematical equation. [6.9]

27. r is $\frac{2}{3}$ of s.   **28.** m is 5 less than n.

Determine whether each sequence is arithmetic, geometric, or neither. If it is arithmetic or geometric, state the common difference or common ratio and write the next three terms. [9.7]

29. $14,\ 7,\ \frac{7}{2},\ \frac{7}{4},\ \frac{7}{8},\ \ldots$ **30.** $11,\ 18,\ 25,\ 32,\ 39,\ \ldots$

EXTEND YOUR SKILL

31. Explain how to compare the size of 1.7 and $\sqrt{3}$ without using a calculator.

32. Use the definition to show why $\frac{1}{2} > \frac{1}{3}$.

10.3 – INEQUALITIES AND THEIR GRAPHS

OBJECTIVES

1. Graph an inequality.

2. Solve a simple inequality.

When an inequality involves a variable, there are usually many possible solutions. For example, the inequality $x > 3$ is satisfied by 5, $\frac{22}{3}$, $\sqrt{15}$, and many other real numbers. One way to display the solutions of an inequality is to graph them on a number line. If the endpoint of a line is to be included in the graph, it is indicated by a closed (solid) dot. If the endpoint is not included, an open (hollow) dot is used.

Example 1   **Graph an Inequality**

Graph each inequality on a number line.
   (a) $x > 3$ (b) $x \leq 5$

(a) The numbers that are greater than 3 are to the right of 3 on the number line. Since 3 is not included, an open dot is used at the left endpoint. The arrow pointing to the right indicates that any number to the right of 3 is a solution.

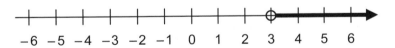

(b) The numbers that are less than or equal to 5 are to the left of 5 on the number line. Since 5 is included, a closed dot is used at the right endpoint.

There are several ways to describe an inequality in an English sentence. Some of the more common ways are given in the following table, together with their mathematical equivalents.

$<$	$>$	$\leq$	$\geq$
• is less than • is fewer than	• is greater than • is more than • exceeds	• is less than or equal to • is no more than • is at most	• is greater than or equal to • is no less than • is at least

Example 2   **Write an Inequality**

Define a variable and write an inequality for each sentence.

(a) Your speed is less than 65 miles per hour.

(b) A suitcase weighs no more than 40 pounds.

(a) Let s = your speed in mph. Then $s < 65$.

(b) Let w = weight of suitcase in pounds. Then $w \leq 40$.

An inequality like $1 < 5$ says that 1 is to the left of 5 on the number line. If the same number, say 2, is added to 1 and to 5, the resulting values maintain the same relationship. Both numbers have just been translated to the right by 2 units.

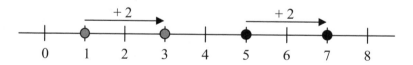

This illustrates that an inequality remains valid when both sides are increased (or decreased) by the same amount.

Example 3   **Solve an Inequality**

Solve $x + 6 \geq 4$ *and graph the solution..*

$x + 6 \geq 4$

$x \geq 4 - 6$ Subtract 6 from both sides. Or, remove the increase of 6 from the left side and join a decrease of 6 to the right side.

$x \geq -2$ Compute.

EXERCISE 10.3

DEVELOP YOUR SKILL

Define a variable and write an inequality for each sentence.

1. Aunt Helen is more than 30 years old.

2. Jacob's height is no more than 60 inches.

3. The tank holds no less than 74 gallons.

4. The rock's weight exceeds 210 pounds.

Solve each inequality and graph the solution.

5. $x + 7 < 4$

6. $m - 3 \leq 5$

7. $t - 5 \geq 7$

8. $y + 3 > -8$

MAINTAIN YOUR SKILL

Replace each expression with an equivalent one in which the multipliers, dividers, and sign operators have been distributed. Do not compute. [4.7]

9. $17 - 2(9 - 3)$

10. $6 + 5(8 - 1)$

11. $25 - \dfrac{3 + 5}{4}$

12. $14 - \dfrac{2 - 9}{5}$

Find the largest square factor of each expression. Write your answer in factored form. [5.6]

13. $3^4 \cdot 5^3$

14. $x^5 \cdot y^6$

Solve each equation for x. [6.4, 7.6, 8.4]

15. $\dfrac{7-x}{3} = 5$ **16.** $3 - 2x = 8$ **17.** $8x = 3x - 4$

18. $3 = \dfrac{6}{x} + 5$ **19.** $x + \dfrac{2}{3} = \dfrac{5}{6}$ **20.** $\dfrac{3}{4} = \dfrac{1}{6} - x$

21. $a + x = bx$ **22.** $m + \dfrac{n}{x} = r$

Estimate the percent of each number. Do not use a calculator. [8.5]

23. 26% of 80   **24.** 65% of 18   **25.** 5% of 139   **26.** 90% of 151

Find each square root or estimate to the nearest integer. Do not use a calculator. [10.1]

27. $\sqrt{25}$ **28.** $\sqrt{40}$ **29.** $-\sqrt{47}$ **30.** $-\sqrt{79}$

EXTEND YOUR SKILL

31. Explain how to determine whether to use a solid dot or a hollow dot when graphing an inequality.

32. In Example 2(b), could we have let s be the suitcase and have $s \leq 40$? Explain your answer.

10.4 – SOLVING INEQUALITIES

OBJECTIVE

1. Solve an inequality.

In the last lesson we saw that in solving an inequality, the same number may be added to or subtracted from each side. This is the same technique we used in solving an equation. When multiplying and dividing, however, inequalities do not always behave the same as equations. For example, $4 > 2$. If we multiply each side of this inequality by -3 we obtain -12 and -6. But -12 is *less than* -6. This illustrates that when an inequality is multiplied or divided by a negative number, the direction of the inequality must be reversed. When multiplying or dividing by a positive number, the direction of the inequality remains the same.

Here are the general rules for strict inequalities. Similar rules apply to weak ($\leq$ and $\geq$) inequalities.

Multiplying and Dividing an Inequality by a Negative Number

If $a < b$ and $c < 0$, then $ac > bc$ and $\dfrac{a}{c} > \dfrac{b}{c}$.

If $a > b$ and $c < 0$, then $ac < bc$ and $\dfrac{a}{c} < \dfrac{b}{c}$.

Example 1 **Solve an Inequality**

Solve each inequality for x.

(a) $1 - 2x < 7$ (b) $-3x + 5 \geq -7$

(a) $1 - 2x < 7$

$\qquad -2x < 6$ Subtract 1 from each side.

$\qquad \dfrac{-2x}{-2} > \dfrac{6}{-2}$ Divide each side by -2 and reverse the inequality.

$\qquad x > -3$ Simplify and compute.

(b) $-3x + 5 \geq -7$

$\qquad -3x \geq -12$ Subtract 5 from each side.

$\qquad \dfrac{-3x}{-3} \leq \dfrac{-12}{-3}$ Divide each side by -3 and reverse the inequality.

$\qquad x \leq 4$ Simplify and compute.

With practice you can omit writing this line, but don't forget to reverse the inequality.

When solving an inequality it is customary to write the answer with the variable on the left. If we need to interchange the sides of an inequality, then the direction of the inequality is reversed. For example, if 5 is greater than x, then x is less than 5. This illustrates that the inequality $5 > x$ is equivalent to the inequality $x < 5$.

Example 2   **Solve an Inequality**

Solve each inequality for x.

   (a) $22 \leq 2x$ (b) $2x - 15 > 5x$

(a) $22 \leq 2x$

   $11 \leq x$ Divide each side by 2.
   [Since 2 is positive, the inequality is <u>not</u> reversed.]

   $x \geq 11$ Interchange the two sides and reverse the inequality.

(b) One way to solve this is to begin by adding 15 to each side.

   $2x - 15 > 5x$

   $2x > 5x + 15$ Add 15 to each side.

   $-3x > 15$ Subtract 5x from each side. Recall, $2x - 5x = (2 - 5)x = -3x$.

   $\dfrac{-3x}{-3} < \dfrac{15}{-3}$ Divide each side by –3 and reverse the inequality.

   $x < -5$ Simplify and compute.

Or, we can begin by subtracting $2x$ from each side.

   $2x - 15 > 5x$

   $-15 > 3x$ Subtract 2x from each side.

   $-5 > x$ Divide each side by 3. Don't reverse the inequality.

   $x < -5$ Interchange the two sides and reverse the inequality.

Caution

In Chapter 6 we introduced the

   [sum] = [addend] + [addend]   and   [product] = [factor] × [factor]

methods of solving equations. Do <u>not</u> use these methods when solving inequalities. They don't always give the correct direction for the inequality.

This example shows why you should <u>not</u> use the 3-number method of Chapter 6 in solving an inequality.

Example 3   **Solve an Inequality**

Solve the inequality $3 - x < 5$.

$-x < 2$ Subtract 3 from each side.

$x > -2$ Multiply both sides by –1 and reverse the inequality.

In the original inequality, if we see 3 as the sum and x and 5 as the addends, we might be tempted to write $x < 3 - 5$ and $x < -2$, which is not correct.

EXERCISE 10.4

DEVELOP YOUR SKILL

Solve each inequality.

1. $4 - n < 7$
2. $3 \le m + 8$
3. $-2 \ge 3y + 10$
4. $15 > 4t - 3$
5. $2 - 3x < 11$
6. $5 - 2x \ge -19$
7. $-3 - 4x > 9$
8. $-6 - 5x < -1$
9. $-4(2x - 3) \ge 0$
10. $2x - 3(x - 1) \le 0$

MAINTAIN YOUR SKILL

Solve each equation by using an invariant principle. [1.6]

11. What is x, if $2734 + 7452 = 2730 + x$?

12. What is x, if $8362 - x = 8367 - 5844$?

Name each form and compute the basic numeral. [5.2, 7.5]

13. $2\left(\dfrac{5 + 3}{6}\right)$
14. $\left(\dfrac{7 - 5}{3}\right)^2$
15. $\left(\dfrac{8 + 1}{4}\right)^0$
16. $\dfrac{7 - 2^2}{6}$

In Exercises 17 and 18, define a variable and write an equation to model each situation. Then solve the equation. [6.10]

17. Benjamin Franklin invented the lightning rod in 1752. This was 32 years before he invented the bifocal lens. When did he invent the bifocal lens?

18. In 1996 the legislative and judicial branches of the federal government had a total of 63,392 employees. If there were 35,357 employed by the legislative branch, how many were employed by the judicial branch? Source: *Kids Almanac*

19. Which is larger, $\dfrac{3}{7}$ or $\dfrac{5}{12}$? [7.6]

20. Which is larger, $\dfrac{4}{9}$ or $\dfrac{5}{11}$? [7.6]

Write each number in scientific notation. [9.6]

21. 490,000

22. 0.00052

23. 3520×10^6

24. 0.0044×10^8

Write all names (integer, rational, irrational) that apply to each real number. [10.2]

25. $\sqrt{17}$

26. $-\sqrt{16}$

27. $31.2\overline{5}$

28. 14.3

29. 1.35791113...

30. $-\dfrac{3}{8}$

Extend Your Skill

31. Explain why you think it might be better to write $x > 5$ rather than $5 < x$ for the answer to an inequality.

32. Explain why we should be careful not to use the 3-number method when solving an inequality.

10.5 – The Pythagorean Theorem

OBJECTIVE

1. Use the Pythagorean Theorem.

A **right triangle** is a triangle that has a right angle (one whose measure is 90°). The sides that form the right angle are called the **legs** of the triangle, and the side that is opposite the right angle is called the **hypotenuse**. The hypotenuse is always the longest side in a right triangle.

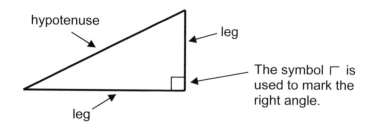

hypotenuse

leg

leg

The symbol ⌐ is used to mark the right angle.

The **Pythagorean Theorem** describes the relationship between the lengths of the legs and the hypotenuse for *any* right triangle. It is named after the Greek geometer Pythagoras (c.560 – c.480 B.C.) although the result was apparently known much earlier.

Pythagorean Theorem

> In a right triangle, the square of the length of the hypotenuse is equal to the sum of the squares of the lengths of the legs.

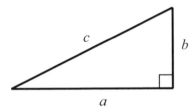

If we label the lengths of the legs as a and b, and the hypotenuse as c, then we have

$$c^2 = a^2 + b^2.$$

This formula is useful in finding the length of one side of a right triangle when the other two sides are known.

Example 1   **Find the Length of the Hypotenuse**

Find the length of the hypotenuse in a right triangle if the legs have lengths of 4 cm and 3 cm.

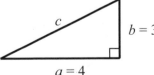

Substitute $a = 4$ and $b = 3$ in the formula $c^2 = a^2 + b^2$:

$c^2 = 4^2 + 3^2$ Substitute.

$c^2 = 16 + 9$ $4^2 = 16$ and $3^2 = 9$.

$c^2 = 25$ Add 16 and 9.

The equation $c^2 = 25$ is solved by taking the square root of each side. There are two solutions: $c = 5$ and $c = -5$. Since c represents a distance, it is not negative. We conclude that the hypotenuse is 5 cm long.

Example 2   Find the Length of a Leg

The hypotenuse of a right triangle is 10 *inches long and one of its legs is* 4 *inches. Find the length of the other leg. Round the answer to the nearest tenth of an inch.*

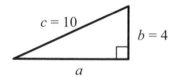

Study Tip:

To round off to the nearest tenth, look at the hundredth's digit. If it is 5 or more, add one to the tenths. If it is 4 or less, keep the tenths digit the same. In this case there are 6 hundredths. So 9.16 rounds up to 9.2.

Substitute $c = 10$ and $b = 4$ in the formula $c^2 = a^2 + b^2$:

$$10^2 = a^2 + 4^2 \qquad \text{Substitute.}$$
$$100 = a^2 + 16 \qquad 10^2 = 100 \text{ and } 4^2 = 16.$$
$$a^2 = 100 - 16 \qquad \text{Solve for } a^2.$$
$$a^2 = 84 \qquad \text{Compute.}$$
$$a = \sqrt{84} \qquad \text{Take the positive square root.}$$
$$a \approx 9.1652 \qquad \text{Use a calculator.}$$
$$a \approx 9.2 \qquad \text{Round off to the nearest tenth.}$$

The other leg is about 9.2 inches long.

Example 3   Use the Pythagorean Theorem

A 20 foot ladder is leaning against a wall so that the base of the ladder is 5 feet from the wall. About how high on the wall is the top of the ladder?

Let x be the distance from the ground to the top of the ladder. Then use the Pythagorean Theorem:

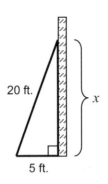

20 ft.

x

5 ft.

$$c^2 = a^2 + b^2 \qquad \text{Pythagorean Theorem}$$

$$20^2 = 5^2 + x^2 \qquad \text{Substitute } c = 20 \text{ and } a = 5.$$

$$x^2 = 20^2 - 5^2 \qquad \text{Solve for } x^2.$$

$$x^2 = 400 - 25 \qquad \text{Compute } 20^2 \text{ and } 5^2.$$

$$x^2 = 375 \qquad \text{Subtract.}$$

$$x = \sqrt{375} \approx 19.4 \qquad \text{Use a calculator and round off.}$$

The top of the ladder is about 19.4 ft above the ground.

EXERCISE 10.5

DEVELOP YOUR SKILL

In Exercises 1 – 6, find the length of the third side of each right triangle. First write your answer as an integer or a square root using the radical sign. Then use a calculator to round to the nearest tenth, if necessary.

1.
3
3

2.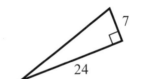
7
24

3.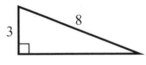
8
3

4.
15
9

5.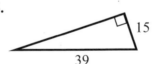
15
39

6.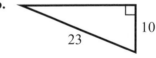
10
23

7. A surveyor is using a laser beam to sight a marker that is 21.2 meters north and 13.6 meters east of his present location. How far does the laser have to travel? Round your answer to the nearest tenth.

MAINTAIN YOUR SKILL

Do not compute, but write equivalent expressions without parentheses. Do not change the first term. Give a second alternate form for each answer. (Remember, we can now use negative numbers.) [2.5]

8. $10 - (3 + 8)$

9. $4 + (17 - 5)$

10. $3 + (5 + 11)$ **11.** $12 - (17 - 15)$

Each equation in Exercises 12 – 15 can be viewed as consisting of exactly three terms. Identify the sum term (S) or the product term (P) as appropriate. Give all possible interpretations. [6.2, 6.3]

12. $x + y = \dfrac{a}{b} - n$ **13.** $x - y = \dfrac{a^2 b}{m}$

14. $ax = m + 3n$ **15.** $\dfrac{m}{n} = x(y + b)$

Write the opposite and the reciprocal of each number. [7.2, 9.2]

16. $-\dfrac{1}{4}$ **17.** 2 **18.** $\dfrac{5}{3}$

19. Find the value of x that makes $\dfrac{2}{5}$ and $\dfrac{6}{x + 2}$ a proportion. [8.1]

20. A family budget allows 24% for housing. If they allow $600 for housing, what is the total budget? [8.4]

Find the simple interest. [8.8]

21. $700 at 3% for 2 years   **22.** $580 at 4.2% for 30 months

Compute the basic numeral. [9.5]

23. $7 - 3^{-1}$ **24.** $\dfrac{-4^2}{10}$

Write the letter that corresponds to the position of each real number on the number line below. Do not use a calculator. [10.2]

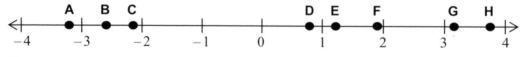

25. $\sqrt{0.7}$ **26.** $-\sqrt{7}$ **27.** -3.2

28. $\sqrt{14}$ **29.** $\sqrt{3.6}$ **30.** $\sqrt{1.5}$

EXTEND YOUR SKILL

31. Find two irrational numbers whose product is rational.

32. Find two irrational numbers whose sum is rational.

10.6 – THE DISTANCE AND MIDPOINT FORMULAS

OBJECTIVES

1. Graph ordered pairs on a coordinate plane.

2. Find the distance between two points in the plane.

3. Find the midpoint of a line segment.

A **coordinate plane** is formed by two number lines that cross at right angles and intersect at their zero points. The horizontal number line is called the **x-axis** and the vertical number line is called the **y-axis**. The point where they cross is called the **origin**. The axes are oriented so that the positive direction is to the right on the horizontal axis and upward on the vertical axis.

Each point in the coordinate plane can be identified by giving its horizontal and vertical position relative to the coordinate axes. We represent this as an ordered pair of numbers (x, y), where the first number (or **x-coordinate**) is the horizontal position of the point and the second number (or **y-coordinate**) is the vertical position. For example, to locate the point corresponding to $(3, 4)$, we start at the origin, move 3 units to the right and then move 4 units up. The point we end at is said to be the **graph** of the ordered pair $(3, 4)$.

Example 1   **Graph an Ordered Pair**

Graph the ordered pairs $(3, 4)$, $(2, -4)$, $(-5, 1)$, *and* $(-3, -2)$.

We have already described how to graph $(3, 4)$. To graph $(2, -4)$, begin at the origin, move 2 units to the right, and then move 4 units down. The last two points are graphed in a similar manner.

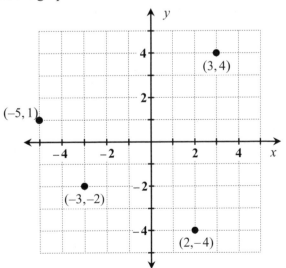

Example 2   **Find Distance in the Coordinate Plane**

Graph the ordered pairs $(1, 2)$ *and* $(4, -3)$. *Then find the distance between the points.*

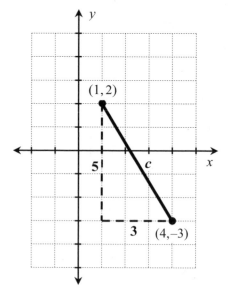

Make a right triangle by connecting the two points, drawing a horizontal line through $(4, -3)$, and a vertical line through $(1, 2)$. The length of the hypotenuse c is the distance between the two points. From the Pythagorean Theorem we have

$$c^2 = 5^2 + 3^2$$

$$c^2 = 25 + 9$$

$$c^2 = 34$$

$$c = \sqrt{34} \approx 5.8$$

By following the procedure in Example 2 with two general points (x_1, y_1) and (x_2, y_2), we obtain the **Distance Formula**.

The Distance Formula

The distance, d, between the points (x_1, y_1) and (x_2, y_2) is given by

$$d = \sqrt{(x_2 - x_1)^2 + (y_2 - y_1)^2}\,.$$

Example 3   **Use the Distance Formula**

Find the distance between the points $(2, -5)$ *and* $(-3, 1)$. *Round to the nearest tenth, if necessary.*

Study Tip:

It doesn't matter which point is called the first point and which point is called the second point.

Let $(x_1, y_1) = (2, -5)$ and $(x_2, y_2) = (-3, 1)$, then substitute into the distance formula:

$$d = \sqrt{(x_2 - x_1)^2 + (y_2 - y_1)^2}$$

$$= \sqrt{[(-3) - (2)]^2 + [1 - (-5)]^2} \qquad \text{Substitute } x_1 = 2, \ y_1 = -5,$$
$$x_2 = -3, \text{ and } y_2 = 1.$$

$$= \sqrt{(-5)^2 + (6)^2} \qquad \text{Simplify.}$$

$$= \sqrt{25 + 36} \qquad \text{Compute.}$$

$$= \sqrt{61} \approx 7.8 \qquad \text{Use a calculator and round off.}$$

The distance is about 7.8 units.

The **midpoint** of a line segment $\overline{AB}$ is the point on the segment that is halfway between A and B. We can find its coordinates by averaging the coordinates of A with the corresponding coordinates of B.

The Midpoint Formula

The midpoint of the line segment between (x_1, y_1) and (x_2, y_2) is the point whose coordinates are

$$\left(\frac{x_1 + x_2}{2}, \frac{y_1 + y_2}{2} \right).$$

Example 4   **Use the Midpoint Formula**

Find the midpoint of the line segment between the points $(-3, 0)$ and $(5, 2)$.

Let $(x_1, y_1) = (-3, 0)$ and $(x_2, y_2) = (5, 2)$, then substitute into the midpoint formula:

$$\left(\frac{x_1 + x_2}{2}, \frac{y_1 + y_2}{2} \right) = \left(\frac{(-3) + 5}{2}, \frac{0 + 2}{2} \right) = (1, 1)$$

Here is the graph:

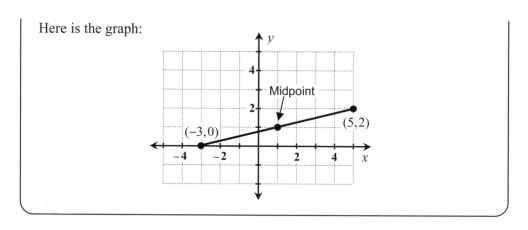

EXERCISE 10.6

DEVELOP YOUR SKILL

Exercises 1 – 6 use the coordinate plane at the right.
Write the ordered pair that corresponds to each point.

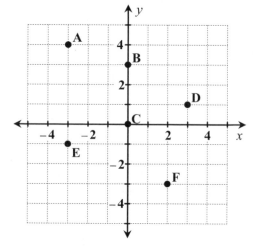

1. A
2. B
3. C
4. D
5. E
6. F

Find the distance between each pair of points. Write the answer as an integer or a square root using the radical sign. Then round to the nearest tenth, if necessary.

7. $(-1, 3)$ and $(2, -1)$ 8. $(-3, -4)$ and $(5, 2)$ 9. $(-1, 1)$ and $(3, 2)$ 10. $(1, 2)$ and $(2, 5)$

Find the midpoint of the line segment between the given pair of points.

11. $(2, 5)$ and $(4, -1)$ 12. $(-3, 1)$ and $(5, 7)$ 13. $(4, -1)$ and $(6, 2)$ 14. $(3, 2)$ and $(-5, 3)$

MAINTAIN YOUR SKILL

Solve each equation by using an invariant principle. [3.6]

15. $x \cdot 8 = 24 \cdot 25$

16. $36 \cdot 15 = x \cdot 60$

17. $\dfrac{21}{x} = \dfrac{3}{8}$

18. $\dfrac{21}{18} = \dfrac{x}{6}$

In Exercises 19 and 20, the entire expression is a numeral for a single number. Write this number in prime factored form. [5.6]

19. $11 \cdot 19 - 7 \cdot 19$

20. $15^3 + 15^4$

21. $7\frac{1}{3}$ is how many times $5\frac{1}{2}$? [7.4]

22. $2\frac{1}{4}$ is what part of $5\frac{1}{4}$? [7.4]

Determine whether each sequence is arithmetic, geometric, or neither. If it is arithmetic or geometric, state the common difference or common ratio and write the next three terms. [9.7]

23. 25, 19, 13, 7, 1, ...

24. 5, 0, 5, 0, 5, ...

Solve each inequality. [10.4]

25. $7 - x \geq 5$

26. $32 < 5y - 3$

27. $5 + 4x \leq 8$

28. $2 + 3x > 7x + 4$

29. $-5(4w + 3) < 0$

30. $3x - 4(x - 5) \leq 2$

EXTEND YOUR SKILL

31. When writing an ordered pair of numbers, does it matter which number is written first? Explain,

32. When using the distance formula, does it matter which point is labeled the first point and which one is labeled the second? Explain.

CHAPTER 10 REVIEW

Find each square root. [10.1]

1. $\sqrt{25}$

2. $-\sqrt{16}$

3. $\sqrt{49}$

Estimate each square root to the nearest integer. Do not use a calculator. [10.1]

4. $\sqrt{30}$

5. $-\sqrt{19}$

6. $\sqrt{75}$

Simplify each expression. [10.1]

7. $3 + 2\sqrt{25}$

7. $30 \div \sqrt{9} \times 2$

9. $2\sqrt{25 - 16}$

Write all names (integer, rational, irrational) that apply to each real number. [10.2]

10. $\sqrt{5}$

11. $\frac{14}{2}$

12. $7.2\overline{34}$

13. $\frac{3}{5}$

Write the letter that corresponds to the position of each square root on the number line below. Do not use a calculator. [10.2]

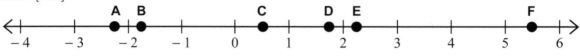

14. $-\sqrt{3}$ **15.** $\sqrt{5}$ **16.** $\sqrt{0.30}$

17. Define a variable and write an inequality for the sentence. "Uncle Bob is at least 70 years old." [10.3]

Solve each inequality and graph the solution. [10.3, 10.4]

18. $x + 5 > 8$ **19.** $5 - m \leq 7$ **20.** $4 < n - 5$

21. $15 - 2x \leq 10$ **22.** $2(x + 1) < -8$ **23.** $3(4 - x) \geq 5$

Find the length of the third side of each right triangle. First write the answer as an integer or a square root using the radical sign. Then use a calculator to round to the nearest tenth, if necessary. [10.5]

24.   **25.**   **26.**

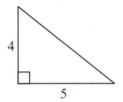

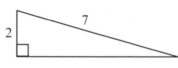

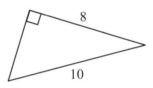

Find the distance between the given pair of points. Write the answer as an integer or a square root using the radical sign. Then round to the nearest tenth, if necessary. [10.6]

27. $(5, -2)$ and $(8, 3)$ **28.** $(-3, 0)$ and $(1, 3)$

Find the midpoint of the line segment between the given pair or points. [10.6]

29. $(7, -4)$ and $(5, -10)$ **30.** $(4, 8)$ and $(7, -2)$

Selected Answers

Exercise 1.1

1. True **3.** True **5.** $r + s$ **7.** $4 + 5$ **9.** 35 **11.** not possible **13.** 81

15. 59 **17.** 116 **19.** 61 **21.** not possible **23.** 182 **25.** $5 + 5 = 10$

27. $0 + 0 = 0$ **29.** $316 + 316 = 632$

Exercise 1.2

1. $7 + 3 = 10$ **3.** $12 = 5 + 7$ **5.** $11 = 9 + 2$ **7.** $0 + 3 = 3$ **9.** $15 + 8 = 23$

11. $40 = 21 + 19$ **13.** $5 + 5$ **15.** 60 **17.** not possible **19.** 92 **21.** 61 **23.** 191

25. not possible **27.** $6 + 6 = 12$ **29.** $19 + 19 = 38$

Exercise 1.3

1. 7 **3.** 9 **5.** 24 **7.** $12 - 8 = 4$ **9.** $5 + 6 = 11$ **11.** $43 - 27 = 16$

13. $56 + 24 = n$ **15.** $b + n = 43$ **17.** $m + x = h$ **19.** $17 + 17 = 34$ **21.** $5 + 7 = 12$

23. $30 = 22 + 8$ **25.** 61 **27.** 87 **29.** 429

Exercise 1.4

1. 11 **3.** 8 **5.** not defined **7.** 1 **9.** not defined **11.** 5 **13.** $21 + 21 = 42$

15. $25 + 6 = 31$ **17.** $64 = 33 + 31$ **19.** $23 + 29 = 52$ **21.** $43 = 16 + 27$ **23.** $7 + 25 = 32$

25. $67 - 45 = 22$ **27.** $15 + 37 = x$ **29.** $31 - 18 = y$

Exercise 1.5.

1. $(b + c) + a, (c + b) + a, a + (c + b)$ **3.** $(4 - n) + m$ **5.** $z + (x - y)$

7. (a) to (b) commutative, (b) to (c) associative, (c) to (d) commutative, (d) to (e) commutative, (e) to (f) associative

9. $25 + 27 = 52$ **11.** $m + 55 = 79$ **13.** $w - 83 = n$ **15.** 2 **17.** not defined **19.** 5

21. not defined **23.** not defined **25.** 16 **27.** 12 **29.** not defined

Exercise 1.6

[Note: in Exercises 1 – 6, other answers are possible.]

1. $233 + 100$ **3.** $200 + 304$ **5.** $239 - 100$ **7.** $x = 5962$ **9.** $x = 5962$

11. $613 + 749 = 625 + x, x = 737$ **13.** $17 + 6 = 23$ **15.** $m - 14 = x$ **17.** $r + a = h$

19. not defined   **21.** 5 **23.** 12 **25.** 21 **27.** $a - (c + b)$ **29.** $z + (x - y)$

Chapter 1 Review

1. $5 + 7$ **3.** $18 + 18 = 36$ **5.** $5 + 3 = 8$ **7.** $15 = 3 + 12$ **9.** $15 + 7 = 22$

11. $50 - 31 = m$ **13.** 18 **15.** 14 **17.** not defined   **19.** 12 **21.** 13 **23.** $(5 + x) - y$

25. $10 - (y + x)$ **27.** $x = 7782$ **29.** $x = 984$

Exercise 2.1

1. The operand is x and the operator is $+ 23$, or the operand is 23 and the operator is $x +$.

3. The operand is x and the operator is $- 8$.   **5.** The operand is 34 and the operator is $- x$.

7. The operand is $(a + 4)$ and the operator is $- x$.

9. The operand is $(k - 7)$ and the operator is $+ x$, or the operand is x and the operator is $(k - 7) +$.

11. The operand is $(m + 3)$ and the operator is $+ x$, or the operand is x and the operator is $(m + 3) +$.

13. $13 + d = 46$ **15.** $b - a = 5$ **17.** 9 **19.** 12 **21.** not defined   **23.** 2

25. $(s + t) + r, (t + s) + r, r + (t + s)$ **27.** $d - (f + e)$ **29.** $x = 5771$

Exercise 2.2

1. (a) $+ 6$ (b) $+ 4$ (c) $+ 10$ (d)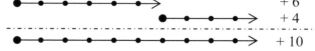
$+ 6$
$+ 4$
$+ 10$

3. (a) $- 5$ (b) $- 4$ (c) $- 9$ (d)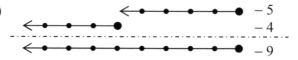
$- 5$
$- 4$
$- 9$

5.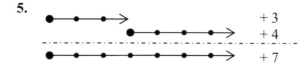
$+ 3$
$+ 4$
$+ 7$

7.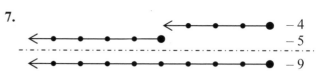
$- 4$
$- 5$
$- 9$

9.

+ 2
+ 5
+ 1
+ 8

11. + 16   **13.** – 15   **15.** + (x + y)

17. 27 + 27 = 54   **19.** 38 + 18 = 56

21. 56 + 23 = x   **23.** y + d = m

25. 31   **27.** not defined   **29.** 21

Exercise 2.3

1. (a) + 6   (b) – 4   (c) + 2   (d)

+ 6
– 4
+ 2

3. (a) – 8   (b) + 4   (c) – 4   (d)

– 8
+ 4
– 4

5.

+ 2
+ 3
+ 5

7.

– 2
+ 7
+ 5

9.

– 3
+ 2
+ 4
+ 3

11. + 2   **13.** + 18   **15.** – 19   **17.** – 4

19. + (y – x)   **21.** – 7   **23.** + 8

25. 16   **27.** not defined

29. The operand is x and the operator is – (n – 17).

Exercise 2.4

1. 15 – (8 + 2), 15 – (2 + 8)   **3.** 15 + (8 – 2)   **5.** 15 – (8 – 2)   **7.** 15 + (8 + 2), 15 + (2 + 8)

9. 24 – (m + n), 24 – (n + m)   **11.** 24 + (m – n)   **13.** 24 – (m – n)   **15.** 8   **17.** 10

19. 14   **21.** 9   **23.** x = 3249   **25.**

+ 7
– 3
+ 4

27. + 2   **29.** – 12

Exercise 2.5

1. 20 – 7 – 3, 20 – 3 – 7   **3.** 5 + 10 – 7   **5.** 5 + 9 + 3, 5 + 3 + 9   **7.** 5 + 8 – 10

9. 34 – a – b, 34 – b – a   **11.** 13 + r + t, 13 + t + r   **13.** 40 – 23 = 17   **15.** x + 15 = 87

17. x = 6823

19.

+ 7
− 3
+ 4

21.

− 5
+ 3
− 2

23. − 6   **25.** − 33   **27.** − 1   **29.** + 15

Exercise 2.6

Note: in 1 – 12, when the answer is a sum, it can be written in either order.

1. $x + 11$ **3.** $y - 5$ **5.** $8 + z$ **7.** $x - 14$ **9.** $7 - y$ **11.** $x + 9$ **13.** 6

15. 0   **17.** − 8   **19.** − 11   **21.** + 12   **23.** $48 + (5 - 3)$ **25.** $13 - (12 - 4)$

27. $55 + 23 - 17, 55 - 17 + 23$ **29.** $38 - 14 - 11, 38 - 11 - 14$

Chapter 2 Review

1. The operand is x and the operator is $+ 10$, or the operand is 10 and the operator is $x +$.

3. + 11   **5.** − 12   **7.** $-(n - m)$ **9.** − 14 degrees

13. + 12   **15.** $6 + (9 - 5)$ **17.** $25 - (10 + 7), 25 - (7 + 10)$

19. $12 + (7 + 3), 12 + (3 + 7)$ **21.** $23 + 14 - 5, 23 - 5 + 14$

23. $67 + 75 - 84$ **25.** $x - 3$ **27.** $20 - z$ **29.** $14 - y$

11.

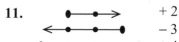

+ 2
− 3
+ 4
+ 3

Exercise 3.1

1. $6 \cdot 8$ **3.** 40   **5.** 36   **7.** 64   **9.** 49   **11.** 48   **13.** not possible

15. $0 + 2 + 2 + 2 + 2 + 2 + 2, 0 + 6 + 6$

17. 2( )   **19.** $19 + 19 = 38$ **21.** The operand is x and the operator is $-(4 + m)$.

23. $+ (r - s)$ **25.** $24 - 15 - 6, 24 - 6 - 15$ **27.** $43 - 21 + 14, 43 + 14 - 21$ **29.** $x - 7$

Exercise 3.2

1. $4 \cdot 13 = 52$ **3.** $\dfrac{6}{3} = y$ **5.** $b(c + d) = a$ **7.** none   **9.** 0, 1, 2, 3   **11.** 0, 2, 4, 6

13. 1, 3, 9   **15.** 0, 9, 18, 27   **17.** $\dfrac{(\ )}{4}$ **19.** $68 - 41 = 27$

21. $(b + a) - c$ **23.** $r + (q - p)$ **25.** $5 + x$ **27.** $6 - x$ **29.** $y - 7$

Exercise 3.3

1. 2   **3.** 2, 3   **5.** none   **7.** 1, 2, 5, 10, 25, 50   **9.** 1, 2, 3, 4, 6, 7, 12, 14, 21, 28, 42, 84

11. $x = 6109$ **13.** -5 **15.** -7 **17.** $+0$ **19.** $+5$ **21.** -23

23. $86 - 23 - 42$, $86 - 42 - 23$ **25.** $54 + 17 + 39$, $54 + 39 + 17$ **27.** $7 \cdot 14 = 98$

29. $\dfrac{x}{b-s} = d$

Exercise 3.4

1. sum, 17   **3.** difference, 10   **5.** quotient, 16   **7.** sum, 26   **9.** product, 30

11. -3 **13.** -28 **15.** $18 - (2 + 10)$, $18 - (10 + 2)$ **17.** $9 + (22 - 6)$

19. $+5$ **21.**   **23.** 0, 3, 6, 9   **25.** 1, 2, 3, 6

27. 1, 2, 3, 5, 6, 10, 15, 30   **29.** 1, 3, 5, 15, 25, 75

Exercise 3.5

1. (a) to (b) commutative, (b) to (c) associative, (c) to (d) commutative, (d) to (e) associative, (e) to (f) associative

3. $(6)(5) + (6)(3)$ **5.** $\dfrac{24}{4} - \dfrac{16}{4}$ **7.** $\dfrac{18}{3} + \dfrac{15}{3}$ **9.** $8(5 - 4)$ **11.** $(7 - 3)y$ **13.** $\dfrac{x-z}{y}$

15. $4(a - b)$ **17.** 6   **19.** 3   **21.** $x = 3929$ **23.**

25. $17 - (5 + 3)$, $17 - (3 + 5)$ **27.** $14 - (11 - 7)$

29. $35 + (17 - 13)$

Exercise 3.6

1. $x = 14$ **3.** $x = 12$ **5.** $x = 4800$ **7.** $-(n - m)$ **9.** $36 + 14 - 6$, $36 - 6 + 14$

11. $29 + 20 - 34$ **13.** 5, 10, 15, 30   **15.** 3, 5   **17.** difference, 3   **19.** product, 15

21. $(7)(12) + (7)(15)$ **23.** $\dfrac{45 - 20}{5}$ **25.** $2(x + y)$ **27.** $\dfrac{ab}{d} + \dfrac{c}{d}$ **29.** $(y + 3x)w$

Chapter 3 Review

1.   **3.** $7 \cdot 8 = 56$ **5.** $s \cdot 24 = m$ **7.** 1, 2, 5, 10

9. 1, 2, 3, 4   **11.** 0, 30, 60, 90   **13.** 3   **15.** product, 20   **17.** sum, 17   **19.** product, 9

21. difference, 3   **23.** $4(x + y)$ **25.** $max - mb$ **27.** $xy + 5y$ **29.** $x = 848$

Exercise 4.1

1.

$4(2(\ ))$

3. $30(\ )$ **5.** $\dfrac{(\ )}{12}$ **7.** $6(5(\ ))$ **9.** $\dfrac{\dfrac{(\ )}{4}}{3}$

11. $16 + 48 = 64$ **13.** $16 \cdot 4 = 64$

15. $42 - 14 - 15,\ 42 - 15 - 14$ **17.** $15 + 28 - 26$ **19.** $7 + x$ **21.** $x - 13$ **23.** $y - 6$

25. difference, 19   **27.** product, 25   **29.** product, 6

Exercise 4.2

1.

$4\left(\dfrac{(\ )}{2}\right)$

3. $2(\ )$ **5.** not defined   **7.** $\dfrac{(\ )}{21}$ **9.** $\dfrac{(\ )}{4}$

11. $3\left(\dfrac{(\ )}{15}\right)$ **13.** $\dfrac{6(\ )}{18}$ **15.** $\dfrac{r(\ )}{s}$ **17.** $\dfrac{(\ )}{2}$

19. $+14$ **21.** $+2 + 5 + 4 - 6 = +5$ **23.** $3, 5$ **25.** 3 **27.** $x = 50$ **29.** $x = 15$

Exercise 4.3

1. $\dfrac{5+3}{2} - 1,\ 3$ **3.** $\dfrac{2(6+3)}{3},\ 6$ **5.** $13; -5$ **7.** $3; (\ )5, 4 +$ or $5; 3(\ ), 4 +$ **9.** $32; \dfrac{(\ )}{8}$

11. $a; -b, w(\ )$ **13.** $b; \dfrac{(\ )}{c}, a +$ **15.** $426 - 400 = 26$

17. $\begin{array}{c} -4 \\ +7 \end{array}$ **19.** $-(y - x)$ **21.** $\dfrac{(\ )}{\dfrac{y}{x}}$ **23.** $18 + 31 - 27$

$+3$

25. $38 - 12 - 9,\ 38 - 9 - 12$ **27.** $\dfrac{15+27}{3}$ **29.**

$\dfrac{3(\ )}{6}$

Exercise 4.4

1. x **3.** $r - s$ **5.** not possible   **7.** $a + b$ **9.** not possible   **11.** $m - n$

13. sum, 11   **15.** product, 30   **17.** product, 60   **19.** sum, 50   **21.** $\dfrac{7(\ )}{20}$

23. $3\left(\dfrac{(\ )}{8}\right)$ **25.** $\dfrac{(\ )}{7}$ **27.** $5(\ )$ **29.** $5(\ )$

Exercise 4.5

1. $19 - x$ **3.** $4 + x$ or $x + 4$ **5.** $14x$ **7.** $\dfrac{10}{x}$ **9.** $\dfrac{x}{5}$ **11.** $\dfrac{8}{x}$ **13.** -3 **15.** -4

17. $18; -x$ **19.** $x; \dfrac{(\ )}{5}$ **21.** -7 **23.** $\dfrac{(\ )}{3}$ **25.** $27; -13, +2$ **27.** $7; -3, 2(\ )$

29. $x; 3(\ ), m +$ or $3; (\ )x, m +$

Exercise 4.6

1. $(3)(9) + (3)(2)$ **3.** $\dfrac{25}{5} + \dfrac{15}{5}$ **5.** $(10)(5) - (4)(5)$ **7.** $12 - x + 3$ **9.** $m + k = a$

11. $cy = d$ **13.** 1, 3, 5, 9, 15, 45   **15.** difference, 5   **17.** difference, 18   **19.** sum, 9

21. $\dfrac{(\ )}{4}$ **23.** $\dfrac{\frac{10}{2} + 5}{3}$, not defined   **25.** $5; (\ )6, 12 +$ or $6; 5(\ ), 12 +$ **27.** $21; \dfrac{(\ )}{3}, -5$

29. not possible

Exercise 4.7

1. "If you give more away, you will have less left." $-(+a) = -a$

3. "If you receive less, you will have less." $+(-a) = -a$

5. $40 - (2)(9) - (2)(8)$ **7.** $3 + \dfrac{20}{5} - \dfrac{5}{5}$ **9.** $37 - (3)(9) + (3)(4)$ **11.** $a + bc - bd$

13. $w - \dfrac{x}{z} + \dfrac{y}{z}$ **15.** $+3 - 5 + 1 = -1$ **17.** $47 - (12 + 8), 47 - (8 + 12)$ **19.** $54 + (32 - 27)$

21. 7   **23.** $x = 9$ **25.** $x = 2$ **27.** $24; -15, \dfrac{(\ )}{3}, 2(\ )$ **29.** $\dfrac{27}{x}$

Chapter 4 Review

1.
$$\frac{()}{\frac{3}{2}}\left(\frac{\frac{()}{3}}{\frac{()}{2}}\right.$$

3.
$$2\left(\frac{()}{6}\right)\left(\frac{\frac{()}{6}}{2()}\right.$$

5. $\dfrac{()}{6}$ **7.** $32(\ )$ **9.** $\dfrac{\frac{()}{y}}{x}$ **11.** $7(\ )$ **13.** $\dfrac{()}{5}$ **15.** $\dfrac{9+3}{2}-1,\ 5$

17. $24;\ \dfrac{()}{x},\ 3+$ **19.** $29-x$ **21.** not possible   **23.** not possible   **25.** $\dfrac{36}{x}$

27. $\dfrac{4}{m}$ **29.** $a-bc-bd$

Exercise 5.1

1. $1\cdot2\cdot2\cdot2=8$ **3.** $1\cdot2\cdot2\cdot2\cdot2\cdot2=32$ **5.** 49 **7.** 64 **9.** 81 **11.** 1 **13.** 5^3

15. d^4 **17.** $+3$ **19.** $7(\ )$ **21.** r **23.** not possible   **25.** $2m$ **27.** $(5)(7)-(5)(4)$

29. $\dfrac{24}{3}+\dfrac{45}{3}$

Exercise 5.2

1. sum, 34   **3.** power, 9   **5.** product, 24   **7.** power, 216   **9.** difference, 2   **11.** 32

13. -14 **15.** $\dfrac{()}{7}$ **17.** $+(s-r)$ **19.** $\dfrac{()}{\frac{s}{r}}$ **21.** not possible   **23.** 7   **25.** $b-1$

27. $52-(3)(21)-(3)(5)$ **29.** $47+\dfrac{35}{7}-\dfrac{21}{7}$

Exercise 5.3

1. 5^5 **3.** 3^6 **5.** $(x+1)^7$ **7.** 2, 6, 14, 42   **9.** $\dfrac{24}{x}$ **11.** $\dfrac{x}{4}$ **13.** $\dfrac{7}{x}$ **15.** $\dfrac{20}{x}$

17. $2\left(\dfrac{17-5}{3}\right),\ 8$ **19.** $4;\ (\ )5,-2,\dfrac{()}{3}$ or $5;\ 4(\ ),-2,\dfrac{()}{3}$ **21.** sum, 13   **23.** power, 343

25. power, 49   **27.** difference, 1   **29.** power, 64

Exercise 5.4

1. $3^2 \cdot 5^2$ **3.** $(4st)^3$ **5.** $\left(\dfrac{12}{2}\right)^2$ **7.** $\dfrac{a^3}{b^6}$ **9.** not possible   **11.** 3^0 **13.** 3^6

15. $a + b = m$ **17.** $xm = c$ **19.** $41 - (30 - 16)$ **21.** $21 + (37 - 15)$

23. 1, 2, 3, 6, 7, 14, 21, 42   **25.** quotient, 162   **27.** power, 81   **29.** quotient, 54

Exercise 5.5

1. $2 \cdot 13$ **3.** $2^2 \cdot 7$ **5.** 2^5 **7.** $3 \cdot 5^2$ **9.** x^4 **11.** xy^2z **13.** x^2y^2z

15. $26 + 26 = 52$ **17.** $+3$ **19.** $18(\ )$
                                                                                      -7
                                                                                      -4

21. not defined   **23.** $\dfrac{(\ )}{18}$ **25.** $11 - 8 - 3$ **27.** $20 - \dfrac{16}{4} - \dfrac{12}{4}$ **29.** $12 + (5)(10) - (5)(4)$

Exercise 5.6

1. $2^4 \cdot 3^2$ **3.** $2^4 \cdot 5^2$ **5.** $2^2 \cdot 3^7$ **7.** $2 \cdot 3 \cdot 31$ **9.** 5^2 **11.** x^4 **13.** -12

15. $\dfrac{(\ )}{8}$ **17.** $\dfrac{(\ )}{15}$ **19.** $8(\ )$ **21.** -23 **23.** $\dfrac{(\ )}{6}$ **25.** 6   **27.** $x = 30$ **29.** $x = 70$

Exercise 5.7

1. $5, 2 \cdot 3 \cdot 5^2$ **3.** $3, 2 \cdot 3^3 \cdot 5$ **5.** $rs^2, r^2s^4t^2u$ **7.** relatively prime   **9.** relatively prime

11. 360 seconds or 6 minutes   **13.** $b - c = m$ **15.** $3R = k$ **17.** $-(r - s)$ **19.** $\dfrac{(\ )}{\dfrac{r}{s}}$

21. "If you give less away, you will have more left." $-(-a) = +a$ **23.** sum, 19   **25.** product, 18

27. difference, 31   **29.** x^2y^6

Exercise 5.8

1. $4(2x + 7y)$ **3.** $4y^2(5x - 4y)$ **5.** $4xy^2(4x^2 - 1)$ **7.** $3xy(3x + y + 2)$ **9.** $y(2x + 8w^2 - 5wx)$

11. $5x$ **13.** $\dfrac{2}{x}$ **15.** $56 - 2x - 2y$ **17.** $15 + \dfrac{m}{3} + \dfrac{n}{3}$ **19.** 7^8 **21.** not possible

23. 2^8 **25.** $2^9 \cdot 3^4$ **27.** 43   **29.** $2 \cdot 5 \cdot 11^3$

Chapter 5 Review

1. 7^5 **3.** 11   **5.** sum, 28   **7.** product, 12   **9.** sum, 17   **11.** power, 27

13. $(w + x)^5$ **15.** not possible   **17.** 5^{12} **19.** $x^4 y^8$ **21.** $2^3 \cdot 3 \cdot 5$ **23.** $2^{10} \cdot 5^5$

25. 3^{16} **27.** GCF $= 2 \cdot 7$, LCM $= 2^2 \cdot 3 \cdot 5^2 \cdot 7^2$ **29.** $3y(2x + 5)$

Exercise 6.1

1. $4 = 12 - 8,\ 8 = 12 - 4$ **3.** $13 = 6 + 7,\ 7 = 13 - 6$ **5.** $25 = 62 - 37,\ 37 = 62 - 25$

7. $314 = 189 + 125,\ 125 = 314 - 189$

9.

11.

13. not possible   **15.** not possible   **17.** not possible   **19.** $\dfrac{22 + 3}{5} - 2,\ 3$

21. $3;\ (\ )4, 9 +,\ (\ )^2$ or $4;\ 3(\ ), 9 +,\ (\ )^2$ **23.** $20;\ -5,\ \dfrac{(\ )}{3},\ +4$ **25.** 5^6 **27.** not possible

29. 5^2

Exercise 6.2

1. 23   **3.** x **5.** $\dfrac{a}{b}$ **7.** $x = 23 - a$ **9.** $x = 30 + 4m$ **11.** $x = \dfrac{a}{b} - 2$ **13.** $x = 8$

15. $x = 17$ **17.** $x = 18$ **19.** $y + m = x$ **21.** $\dfrac{t}{c} = x$ **23.** $2^2 \cdot 3^4$ **25.** $2^7 \cdot 3^2$

27. $3y^2(6x - 5y)$ **29.** $2x(2x^2 + 5x + 6)$

Exercise 6.3

1. x **3.** y **5.** $m + n$ **7.** $y = \dfrac{x}{3}$ **9.** $y = 12(b - c)$ **11.** $y = \dfrac{m + n}{t}$

13. $x = 3$ **15.** $x = 50$ **17.** $x = 8$ **19.** $-s - r$ **21.** $\dfrac{a(\ )}{b}$ **23.** 3^4 **25.** $5^2 \cdot 7^2$

27. $3x(6 + 7)$ **29.** $2y(3y + 4x)$

Exercise 6.4

1. $880 = 23 \cdot 37 + 29, \quad 29 = 880 - 23 \cdot 37, \quad 23 = \dfrac{880 - 29}{37}, \quad 37 = \dfrac{880 - 29}{23}$

3. $899 = 31(17 + 12), \quad 17 = \dfrac{899}{31} - 12, \quad 12 = \dfrac{899}{31} - 17, \quad 31 = \dfrac{899}{17 + 12}$

5. $x = 6$ **7.** $x = 3$ **9.** $x = 13$ **11.** $x = 2$ **13.** $x = 7$ **15.** -24 **17.** $\dfrac{(\ )}{15}$

19. $17 + (3)(12) - (3)(5)$ **21.** $50 - \dfrac{48}{4} - \dfrac{8}{4}$ **23.** sum, 29   **25.** product, 32

27. difference, 5   **29.** 21

Exercise 6.5

1. $x = 3$ **3.** $x = 8$ **5.** $d = 2$ **7.** $a = 7$ **9.** $n = 5$ **11.** $46 - (35 - 24)$

13. $25 + (29 - 13)$ **15.** $\dfrac{x}{3}$ **17.** $\dfrac{x}{75}$ **19.** $\dfrac{75}{x}$ **21.** $5; (\ )^3, (\ )7, 3 +$

23. $3; (\ )^4, + 1, \dfrac{(\ )}{2}$ **25.** $7x(2w + 3)$ **27.** $5x(3x + 4y^2)$ **29.** $10xy(3y - 4)$

Mid-Chapter 6 Review

1. $15 = 27 - 12$ **3.** $15 = 33 + 18$ **5.** $15 = 3 + \dfrac{48}{4}$ **7.** $\dfrac{m}{n}$ **9.** am **11.** $\dfrac{m}{n} - x$

13. $bk + \dfrac{x}{y}$ **15.** $x = 7$ **17.** $x = 60$ **19.** $x = 4$ **21.** $x = 7$ **23.** $x = 36$

25. $x = 4$ **27.** $x = 6$ **29.** $x = 3$

Exercise 6.6

1. sum; $\dfrac{12}{3} +$ and $+ 7$ **3.** difference; $- 13$ **5.** product; $3(\ )$ and $(\ )\left(\dfrac{5 + 7}{4}\right)$

7. sum; $8 +$ and $+ 5^2$ **9.** quotient; $\dfrac{(\ )}{m}$ **11.** $x = 13$ **13.** $x = 15$ **15.** $x = 7 + a$

17. $x = 13$ **19.** $b - c$ **21.** not possible   **23.** $rs - rt + t$ **25.** 56   **27.** 8   **29.** 22

Exercise 6.7

1. $15 = \dfrac{66}{3} - 7$, $7 = \dfrac{66}{3} - 15$, $66 = 3(15 + 7)$, $3 = \dfrac{66}{15 + 7}$

3. $5 = \dfrac{23 + 17}{8}$, $8 = \dfrac{23 + 17}{5}$, $23 = (5)(8) - 17$, $17 = (5)(8) - 23$

5. $y = \dfrac{x - 13}{2}$ **7.** $y = \dfrac{x}{3} - 5$ **9.** $y = \dfrac{5x + 3}{2}$ **11.** $P = \dfrac{I}{R}$, $R = \dfrac{I}{P}$

13. $T = C - PN$, $P = \dfrac{C - T}{N}$, $N = \dfrac{C - T}{P}$

15.
-8
$+4$
-4

17.
$4\left(\dfrac{(\;)}{8}\right)$ $\dfrac{(\;)}{8}$ $4(\;)$

19. $2^6 \cdot 3^2$ **21.** $2 \cdot 3^2$ **23.** $2^2 \cdot 3^4$ **25.** $2 \cdot 3^2 \cdot 17^2$ **27.** $x = 9$ **29.** $x = 7$

Exercise 6.8

1. "the sum of x and 10" or "10 more than x"   **3.** "the product of 3 and x" or "3 times x"

5. "the quotient of x and one more than y" or "the quotient of x and the sum of y and 1"

7. "the difference of x and 3 times n" or "the difference of x and the product of 3 and n"

9. "the square of the sum of x and y"   **11.** "the difference of x squared and y"

13. 1, 2, 3, 4, 6, 9, 12, 18, 36   **15.** $3xy(5x + 6)$ **17.** $xy(3x - 1)$ **19.** $4x(3x^2 - x + 2)$

21. $x = 8$ **23.** $x = 9$ **25.** $x = \dfrac{12 - y}{3}$ **27.** $x = \dfrac{5y + 11}{6}$ **29.** $x = 2y - 5$

Exercise 6.9

1. $x + 5$ **3.** $(m - n)^2$ **5.** $3y - 5$ **7.** $(x - 5)(y)$ **9.** $3x + 5 = 26$ **11.** $4(x + 2) = 20$

13. $3x = x + 16$ **15.** quotient, 200   **17.** sum, 29   **19.** power, 100   **21.** $3^4 \cdot 5^2$

23. $x^2 y^2$ **25.** $w^2 z^2$ **27.** $h = Ab$, $b = \dfrac{h}{A}$ **29.** $v_0 = v - 32t$, $t = \dfrac{v - v_0}{32}$

Exercise 6.10

1. M = Maria's Weight, $152 = M + 28$ **3.** A = Season Average, $15 = A - 7$

5. N = Amount of Nicole's Savings, $165 = 2N - 3$ **7.** -13 **9.** $\dfrac{(\ )}{2}$ **11.** $\dfrac{(\ )}{3}$ **13.** $x = 8$

15. $x = 4$ **17.** relatively prime   **19.** $3x(5x - 7y)$ **21.** $12wx(2y - x)$ **23.** $x = 4$

25. product; $(a - b)(\ )$ and $(\ )c$ **27.** power; $(\ )^r$ **29.** quotient; $\dfrac{(\ )}{c}$

Chapter 6 Review

1. $23 = 68 - 45$ **3.** xy **5.** $ab + \dfrac{c}{d}$ **7.** difference; $-\dfrac{14}{7}$,   **9.** product; $5(\ )$ or $(\ )(3 + 7)$

11. $x = 7$ **13.** $x = 22$ **15.** $x = 5$ **17.** $x = 3$ **19.** $x = \dfrac{20 - y}{3}$ **21.** $x = \dfrac{y}{5} + 3$

23. $x = \dfrac{24}{y + 3}$ **25.** "the sum of 2 times x and 3 times y"   **27.** $(3 + 5)^2 = x$ **29.** $3y = 2x + 12$

Exercise 7.1

1.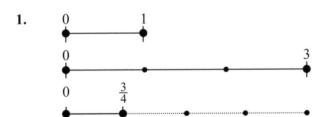

3. $\dfrac{3}{4}$ **5.** $\dfrac{5}{3}$ **7.** $\dfrac{1}{2}$

9. $9 + 8 - 3, 9 - 3 + 8$

11. $15 - 5 - 6, 15 - 6 - 5$

13. $8 + 10 - 12$ **15.** $2^3 \cdot 3^2 \cdot 5$ **17.** $2^4 \cdot 3^2 \cdot 7^2$ **19.** $2 \cdot 5 \cdot 19$ **21.** x

23. (S) is x or $x - y$ **25.** (S) is $\dfrac{s}{t}$ and (P) is s **27.** (S) is g and (P) is $g - h$ **29.** (P) is u or $\dfrac{u}{v}$

Exercise 7.2

1. $\dfrac{15}{49}$ **3.** $\dfrac{21}{20}$ **5.** $\dfrac{3}{8}$ **7.** $\dfrac{1}{13}$ **9.** $\dfrac{2}{7}$ **11.** $\dfrac{1}{8}$ **13.** $16\dfrac{1}{2}$ **15.** not possible

17. t **19.** $y - x$ **21.** $13; -7, \dfrac{(\ )}{3}, (\ )^2$ **23.** $3; (\ )^2, 5 +, \dfrac{(\ )}{2}$ **25.** 60 **27.** $x = \dfrac{2}{3}y$

29. $y = x + 3$

Exercise 7.3

1. $\dfrac{22}{35}$ **3.** $\dfrac{24}{5}$ **5.** $\dfrac{8}{15}$ **7.** $\dfrac{s}{r}$ **9.** $x = \dfrac{15}{16}$ **11.** $x = \dfrac{5}{12}$ **13.** $x = \dfrac{12}{25}$

15. $-(m-n)$ **17.** $+(m-n)$ **19.** $36x$ **21.** $\dfrac{4}{x}$ **23.** $\dfrac{4}{x}$ **25.** $14 - \dfrac{30}{6} - \dfrac{12}{6}$

27. $15 + \dfrac{12}{4} - \dfrac{8}{4}$ **29.** $27 - (3)(8) + (3)(2)$

Exercise 7.4

1. $\dfrac{2}{5}$ is $\dfrac{2}{3}$ of $\dfrac{3}{5}$ **3.** $\dfrac{3}{4}$ is $1\dfrac{3}{4}$ times $\dfrac{3}{7}$ **5.** $1\dfrac{2}{5}$ **7.** $\dfrac{9}{10}$ **9.** product, 36   **11.** sum, 16

13. power, 121   **15.** product, 18   **17.** $2^2 \cdot 3^2 \cdot 5$ **19.** $2^4 \cdot 11$ **21.** $2 \cdot 3^2 \cdot 7^2 \cdot 11$

23. (S) is rs or wx **25.** (S) is $\dfrac{a-b}{c}$ and (P) is $a-b$ **27.** (P) is x or $\dfrac{x}{y-z}$

29.

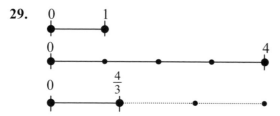

Exercise 7.5

1. $\dfrac{43}{35}$ **3.** $\dfrac{7}{8}$ **5.** $\dfrac{17}{30}$ **7.** $\dfrac{49}{120}$ **9.** $5\dfrac{5}{6}$ **11.** $10 + 24 - 15$ **13.** $13 + 19 - 22$

15. y **17.** $6 - m$ **19.** $x = \dfrac{18}{5}$ **21.** $x = \dfrac{25}{7}$ **23.** $x = 12$ **25.** $1\dfrac{9}{13}$ **27.** $2\dfrac{4}{5}$

29. $1\dfrac{4}{7}$

Exercise 7.6

1. $\dfrac{4}{9}$ **3.** $x + \dfrac{2}{15}$ **5.** $x + \dfrac{5}{12}$ **7.** $x = \dfrac{7}{24}$ **9.** $x = \dfrac{11}{30}$ **11.** $x = 6$ **13.** $x = 45$

15. $x = 240$ **17.** product, 48   **19.** sum, 14   **21.** quotient, $\dfrac{11}{9}$ **23.** not possible

25. 3^{10} **27.** not possible   **29.** $J =$ number of fish Jason caught, $8 = J - 5$

Exercise 7.7

1. 0.17   **3.** 0.4   **5.** 0.44   **7.** $\dfrac{3}{4}$ **9.** $\dfrac{1}{8}$ **11.** $x = 5.8$ **13.** $x = 0.7$ **15.** $5 + x$

17. $11 + x$ **19.** $x - 3$ **21.** (S) is ab and (P) is $ab - c$ **23.** $\dfrac{7}{4}$ **25.** $\dfrac{1}{28}$ **27.** $\dfrac{2}{3}$

29. $x - \dfrac{3}{20}$

Exercise 7.8

1. $8\dfrac{1}{6}$ miles   **3.** 60 km/hr   **5.** $1\dfrac{1}{2}$ yards   **7.** 0.46¢ per ml

9. $\begin{array}{l}+4\\-7\end{array}$ -3 **11.** 0   **13.** not possible   **15.** $\dfrac{(\ \ )}{x - y}$

17. $\dfrac{a - b}{x} +$ or $+ y$ **19.** $\dfrac{2}{5}, \dfrac{3}{5}$ **21.** $\dfrac{22}{75}$ **23.** $\dfrac{13}{60}$ **25.** 1.4   **27.** 2.3   **29.** $\dfrac{11}{25}$

Chapter 7 Review

1. $\dfrac{3}{7}$ **3.** $\dfrac{2}{3}$ **5.** $\dfrac{4}{13}$ **7.** $\dfrac{14}{15}$ **9.** $\dfrac{3}{8}$ **11.** 0   **13.** $x = \dfrac{11}{6}$ **15.** $x = \dfrac{3}{2}$

17. $\dfrac{7}{6}$ **19.** $\dfrac{23}{3}$ **21.** $\dfrac{7}{11}$ **23.** 0.057   **25.** $\dfrac{3}{5}$ **27.** $x = 1.5$ **29.** 31.1 miles per day

Exercise 8.1

1. yes   **3.** no   **5.** $y = 30$ **7.** $m = 13$ **9.** $k = \dfrac{24}{5}$ **11.** $x = 14$ **13.** $2^5 \cdot 3$

15. $2^3 \cdot 3^{10}$ **17.** $x = \dfrac{5}{8}$ **19.** $x = \dfrac{3}{4}$ **21.** $x = \dfrac{s}{r - t}$ **23.** $x = \dfrac{m}{p - 1}$ **25.** $x = y + 3$

27. 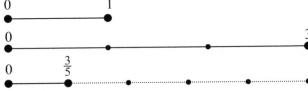   **29.** $\dfrac{7}{9}$

Exercise 8.2

1. $\frac{4}{10} = \frac{6}{15}$, $\frac{10}{4} = \frac{15}{6}$, $\frac{6}{4} = \frac{15}{10}$, $\frac{4}{6} = \frac{10}{15}$

3.

```
0          8                    22
•----------•--------------------•
0          1                     x
```

$\frac{x}{1} = \frac{22}{8}$, $x = \frac{11}{4} = 2\frac{3}{4}$

5.

```
0                  6        x
•------------------•--------•
0                  2         1
                   ─
                   3
```

$\frac{x}{1} = \frac{6}{\frac{2}{3}}$, $x = 9$

7.

```
0              $4200          $9450
•--------------•--------------•
0              1               x
```

$\frac{x}{1} = \frac{9450}{4200}$, $x = 2.25$

9. $12 + 10 - 18$ **11.** $16 + 27 - 21$ **13.** quotient, $\frac{3}{2}$ **15.** product, $\frac{9}{2}$ **17.** power, $\frac{144}{25}$

19. product, 100   **21.** difference, 8   **23.** $x = \frac{6}{5}$ **25.** $x = \frac{15}{32}$ **27.** $x = \frac{96}{5}$

29. 36.19 seconds

Exercise 8.3

1. $0.42, \frac{21}{50}$ **3.** $1.4, \frac{7}{5}$ **5.** 95%   **7.** 15%   **9.** 38.5%   **11.** 125%   **13.** 34%

15. $\frac{x}{4}$ **17.** $\frac{1}{4x}$ **19.** $\frac{100}{x}$ **21.** sum; $+ 17$ and $35 +$ **23.** quotient; $\frac{(\ )}{3}$

25. $\frac{1}{6}$ **27.** 66 inches   **29.**

```
0                    $1.20   x
•--------------------•-------•
0                    3        1
                     ─
                     4
```

$\frac{x}{1} = \frac{1.20}{\frac{3}{4}}$, $x = \$1.60$

Exercise 8.4

1. What is 40% of 65? $x = (.4)(65)$, $x = 26$

3. 56 is what percent of 32? $56 = (x)(32)$, $x = 1.75 = 175\%$

5. 84 is 80% of what number? $84 = (.80)(x)$, $x = 105$

7.

```
0      x                    $22,000
•------•--------------------•
0      15%                  100%
```

$\frac{x}{15} = \frac{22,000}{100}$, $x = \$3300$

9.

```
0   14,400                        180,000
•---•----------------------------•
0   x                            100%
```

$\frac{x}{1} = \frac{14,400}{180,000}$, $x = 8\%$

11. $435 + 100$ **13.** 5^{10} **15.** 5^{21} **17.** 5^3 **19.** $4xy(3 + 5y)$ **21.** $2(5x^2 - 6y^2)$

23. C = days Conrad spent in space; $69.66 = C + 20.53$, $C = 49.13$ days

25. $\dfrac{3}{5}$ **27.** 70%   **29.** 16%

Exercise 8.5

1. 200   **3.** 22   **5.** 16   **7.** 10%   **9.** 66%   **10.** Collie   **11.** Great Dane

13. $+7$ **15.** $\dfrac{(\ )}{5}$ **17.** $3^2 \cdot 7^2$ **19.** $x^2 y^4$ **21.** (S) a, (P) $a - b$

23. (P) a, (P) $\frac{a}{b}$ **25.** Let x = MW of largest U.S. hydroelectric plant. $18{,}200 = 7x$

27. Let F = Fred's age. $75 = 4F + 3$ **29.**

$$\dfrac{x}{\frac{3}{2}} = \dfrac{2280}{6}$$

$x = 570$ calories

Exercise 8.6

1. 50% increase   **3.** 33% decrease   **5.** 10% decrease   **7.** \$26.14   **9.** \$58.60

11. 38.7%   **13.** 18 years   **15.** not possible   **17.** $2x + y$ **19.** not possible

21. quotient, $\frac{1}{3}$ **23.** sum, 22   **25.** product, 14   **27.** (S) ab, (P) $c + d$ **29.** (S) a, (P) m

Exercise 8.7

1. 39 is what percent less than 65? $x = 40\%$ **3.** What is 80% less than 120? $x = 24$

5. What is 30% more than 210? $x = 273$

7.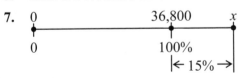

$x = 36{,}800 + (0.15)(36{,}800)$

$x = 42{,}320$

9.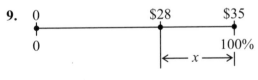

$x = 20\%$

11. $x = 60$ **13.** $x = 125$ **15.** $3;\ (\ )^2, 4(\ ), +6$ **17.** $12;\ \dfrac{(\ )}{3}, +7, 5(\ )$ **19.** 3^9

21. 3^{-2} **23.** not possible   **25.** $\frac{7}{25}$ **27.** 0.09   **29.** 0.48

Exercise 8.8

1. $42.00   **3.** $1565.20   **5.** $549.81   **7.** $2053.96   **9.** 4.5%   **11.** $5 + \frac{8}{4} - \frac{2}{4}$

13. $15 - (2)(6) + (2)(8)$ **15.** $3x(4x + 7y)$ **17.** $2x(7w + 5xy)$

19. Let T = number of cars built by Toyota. $T = \frac{2}{3}(600,000) + 36,000$. $T = 436,000$

21. $x = 34$ **23.** $m = \frac{56}{5}$ or $11\frac{1}{5}$ **25.** 25%   **27.** 47

29.

$72 = 0.75x,$

$x = 96$ bushels per acre

Chapter 8 Review

1. No   **3.** $x = 2.4$ **5.**

$\frac{x}{1} = \frac{8}{\frac{2}{5}}$, $x = 20$ pieces

7. 0.36, $\frac{9}{25}$ **9.** 1.2, $\frac{6}{5}$ **11.** 140%   **13.** 230%

15. 42 is what percent of 30? $\frac{x}{1} = \frac{42}{30}$, $x = 140\%$ **17.** 22   **19.** 50%   **21.** 40% increase

23. $344

25.

What is 70% less than 200?

$x = 60$ **27.** $111.00   **29.** $601.88

Exercise 9.1

1. 3   **3.** -6.9 **5.** $-\frac{5}{6}$ **7.** $\frac{x}{7}$ **9.** $\frac{63}{x}$ **11.** $x = \frac{17}{5}$ **13.** $x = \frac{7}{4}$ **15.** $x = 5$

17. $x = \frac{7}{6}$ **19.** $x = \frac{9}{5}$ **21.** $4x + 7 = 51$ **23.** $5x = x + 8$ **25.** 42 inches   **27.** $x = 48$

29. $x = 10$

Exercise 9.2

1. -24 **3.** $-\frac{1}{3}$ **5.** -8 **7.** 8 **9.** 14 is 17 more than -3

11. $-\frac{2}{3}$ is $1\frac{7}{15}$ less than $\frac{4}{5}$.   **13.** $5x(5-4xy)$ **15.** $7wx(3x+2y)$ **17.** $x=\frac{5}{12}$

19. $x=\frac{1}{24}$ **21.** -9 **23.** $\frac{31}{16}$ **25.** $\frac{15}{4}$

27.

$\frac{27}{\frac{3}{5}}=\frac{x}{1}$, $x=45$

29. $1166.26   **30.** $184

Exercise 9.3

1. 5   **3.** -5 **5.** 5   **7.** 13   **9.** -11 **11.** difference, -2 **13.** product, 26

15. power, 25   **17.** $-\frac{a}{b}$ **19.** $2x+,+2y$ **21.** $5(\ )$, $(\ )(x+3y)$ **23.** $0.4, 40\%$

25. $\frac{29}{20}, 145\%$ **27.** $\frac{3}{10}, 30\%$ **29.** $1680

Exercise 9.4

1. -20 **3.** -3 **5.** -11 **7.** $\frac{4}{9}$ **9.** $\frac{4}{3}$ **11.** $x=-5$ **13.** $x=7$

15. $\frac{5}{x}$ **17.** $\frac{180}{x}$ **19.** $x=\frac{s-rt}{u}$ **21.** $x=\frac{s}{t+r}$ **23.** $2x-3=15$, $x=9$

25. $-7, \frac{1}{7}$ **27.** $-0.8, \frac{5}{4}$ **29.** 12

Exercise 9.5

1. $\frac{1}{4}$ **3.** $\frac{1}{9}$ **5.** $\frac{1}{9}$ **7.** -3 **9.** 2^4 **11.** 2^{-5} **13.** $\frac{1}{x^3}$ **15.** $\frac{x^2}{3}$

17. $\frac{x}{y^2}$ **19.** $\frac{y^2}{x^3}$ **21.** $\frac{x}{y^4}$ **23.** -13 **25.** 27   **27.** (S) x^2+y, (S) $wz+r$

29. (S) $\frac{m}{n}$, (P) m

Exercise 9.6

1. 0.00056   **3.** 290,000   **5.** 3.5×10^4 **7.** 2.6×10^6 **9.** 9.1×10^{-3}

11. 2.5×10^4 or $25,000   **13.** "If you receive less, you will have less." $+(-a) = -a$

15. $\dfrac{4}{9}$ **17.** -5 is 13 less than 8.   **19.** $T_3 = -4$ **21.** 12   **23.** 31   **25.** 6

27. $-\dfrac{13}{4}$ **29.** -45

Exercise 9.7

1. arithmetic, $d = 3$; terms are 29, 32, 35   **3.** neither

5. arithmetic, $d = -9$; terms are -25, -34, -43 **7.** neither   **9.** 25   **11.** 1458

13. $30 - (5)(2) - (5)(7)$ **15.** $15 + \dfrac{8}{21} - \dfrac{5}{21}$ **17.** $\dfrac{1}{3}$ **19.** 5   **21.** $\dfrac{1}{16}$ **23.** 15

25. 15   **27.** 2.7×10^5 **29.** 2.1×10^8

Chapter 9 Review

1. -5 is 3 more than -8.   **3.** 8   **5.** -12 **7.** 3   **9.** 0   **11.** 16   **13.** -20

15. $-\dfrac{9}{4}$ **17.** $x = -4$ **19.** $x = \dfrac{5}{2}$ **21.** $\dfrac{1}{36}$ **23.** $\dfrac{x}{y^5}$ **25.** $\dfrac{1}{x^5}$ **27.** 4.7×10^{-3}

29. arithmetic with $d = 7$; 37, 44, 51

Exercise 10.1

1. 4   **3.** -7 **5.** -9 **7.** 6   **9.** -9 **11.** 17   **13.** 13   **15.** $16 = 9 + 7$

17. 5; $(\ )^3, 2(\ ), +8$ **19.** 10; $-3, (\ )^2, 4(\ )$ **21.** $1\frac{4}{7}$ **23.** 20 oz. size (The unit price of the

15 oz. size is 15¢ per oz., and the unit price of the 20 oz. size is less than 15¢. 14.85¢ to be exact.)

25. $\frac{1}{5}, -5$ **27.** $-\frac{1}{7}, 7$ **28.** $\dfrac{9}{20}$

Exercise 10.2

1. rational   **3.** integer, rational   **5.** irrational   **7.** rational   **9.** <   **11.** =   **13.** B

15. C   **17.** F   **19.** $\dfrac{1}{3x}$ **21.** $\dfrac{3}{x}$ **23.** difference, -18 **25.** quotient, $-\frac{1}{4}$

27. $r = \frac{2}{3}s$ **29.** geometric, $r = \frac{1}{2}$; terms are $\frac{7}{16}, \frac{7}{32}, \frac{7}{64}$

Exercise 10.3

1. Let H = Helen's age in years. $H > 30$ **3.** Let x = capacity of the tank in gallons. $x \geq 74$

5. $x < -3$ **7.** $t \geq 12$ **9.** $17 - (2)(9) + (2)(3)$ **11.** $25 - \frac{3}{4} - \frac{5}{4}$

13. $3^4 \cdot 5^2$ **15.** $x = -8$ **17.** $x = -\frac{4}{5}$ **19.** $x = \frac{1}{6}$ **21.** $x = \frac{a}{b-1}$ **23.** 20

25. 7   **27.** 5   **29.** −7

Exercise 10.4

1. $n > -3$ **3.** $y \leq -4$ **5.** $x > -3$ **7.** $x < -3$ **9.** $x \leq \frac{3}{2}$ **11.** $x = 7456$

13. product, $\frac{8}{3}$ **15.** power, 1

17. x = year Franklin invented the bifocal lens. $1752 = x - 32$, $x = 1784$

19. $\frac{3}{7}$ **21.** 4.9×10^5 **23.** 3.52×10^9 **25.** irrational   **27.** rational   **29.** irrational

Exercise 10.5

1. $\sqrt{18} \approx 4.2$ **3.** $\sqrt{55} \approx 7.4$ **5.** 36   **7.** 25.2 m   **9.** $4 + 17 - 5$, $4 - 5 + 17$

11. $12 - 17 + 15$, $12 + 15 - 17$ **13.** (S) x, (P) a^2b **15.** (P) m, (P) $\frac{m}{n}$ **17.** $-2, \frac{1}{2}$

19. $x = 13$ **21.** \$42   **23.** $\frac{20}{3}$ **25.** D   **27.** A   **29.** F

Exercise 10.6

1. $(-3, 4)$ **3.** $(0, 0)$ **5.** $(-3, -1)$ **7.** 5   **9.** $\sqrt{17} \approx 4.1$ **11.** $(3, 2)$ **13.** $(5, \frac{1}{2})$

15. $x = 75$ **17.** $x = 56$ **19.** $2^2 \cdot 19$ **21.** $1\frac{1}{3}$

23. arithmetic, $d = -6$; terms are −5, −11, −17

25. $x \leq 2$ **27.** $x \leq \frac{3}{4}$ **29.** $w > -\frac{3}{4}$

Chapter 10 Review

1. 5   **3.** 7   **5.** – 4   **7.** 13   **9.** 6   **11.** integer, rational   **13.** rational

15. E   **17.** Let B = Bob's age in years. $B \geq 70$

19. $m \geq -2$

21. $x \geq \dfrac{5}{2}$

23. $x \leq \dfrac{7}{3}$

25. $\sqrt{45} \approx 6.7$ **27.** $\sqrt{34} \approx 5.8$ **29.** $(6, -7)$

Index